Endorsements for *Being White Today*

In the myriad of recent books centered on Whiteness and antiracism, *Being White Today: A Roadmap for a Positive Antiracist Life* by Tochluk and Saxman stands at the top of the must-read list. Through humanized narrative, real life examples, and multiple resources, White readers will engage in a life changing journey to becoming, and supporting, an antiracist society.

—Eddie Moore Jr., PhD, founder, The White Privilege Conference

"Whiteness" is an acute field of battle in the political and cultural wars of this country. It continues to govern how we think, act, and interact. Can we move forward? Can we be un-trapped? Tochluk and Saxman say yes! Any further clarity on how we got here and where we need to go must consider the exhaustive and complex work they've contributed in this important book.

—Luis J. Rodriguez, author of *Always Running, La Vida Loca, Gang Days in L.A.* and *From Our Land to Our Land: Essays, Journeys & Imaginings of a Native Xicanx Writer.*

Based on their years of working with white people, Saxman and Tochluk's *Being White Today* offers keen insight and a wealth of suggestions for creating a positive, antiracist white identity and provides extensive practical tools for deepening our understanding and increasing our effectiveness in inviting other white people to join us in antiracism activism. Read this book to develop a white identity that will make you a more effective ally to people of color in the urgent multiracial struggle for racial justice.

—Paul Kivel, educator, activist and author of *Uprooting Racism: How White People Can Work for Racial Justice* and a founding member of SURJ—Showing Up for Racial Justice www.paulkivel.com

Magnificent! Challenging and affirming, *Being White Today* is a brilliant, must-have guide for people who care about ending racism. Capturing the feeling of a kitchen table conversation, it combines a theoretical framework with relatable scenarios and realistic responses that add to our toolbox for "doing the work." Practicing what they preach, Tochluk and Saxman remind us that all people, regardless of racial background, deserve compassion as we heal from the effects of race and learn to do better. In fact, the authors make a strong case that we are more likely to achieve our vision of a racially just society if we center dignity, humanity, and compassion in our work. This includes supporting white people to develop healthy racial identities.

—Aisha Blanchard-Young, lead coordinator of human rights education, California Teachers Association

Throughout my career, white friends and colleagues have asked me for a "next level" resource to help them be better allies. Even after reading the most popular books on antiracism, they felt confused about a range of issues. I always struggled with how to respond, until now. *Being White Today* is filled with practical and insightful applications for white people who struggle with race and whiteness and want guidance on what to do. I highly recommend it!

—Vincent C. Flewellen, AVP diversity, equity and inclusion and chief diversity officer, Webster University, St. Louis, Missouri

Being White Today is a breakthrough contribution to the antiracism field. It brilliantly connects longstanding scholarship on racial identity and contemporary developments on the far-right with practical guidance for effective messaging in the one-to-one conversations that are the foundation for social change. The book uses a throughline of compelling characters that will keep any reader's attention so that experienced as well as novice antiracists will deepen their understanding of how to apply this comprehensive, unflinching, analytical, and compassionate way of understanding how white folks should call each other in to antiracism. A great book for antiracists of any racial background!

—David Campt, founder of The Dialogue Company and author of *The White Ally Toolkit*

What does it mean to develop a positive, anti-racist white identity? One where we actively and effectively partner with colleagues of color to create true racial equity and liberation? Authors Tochluk and Saxman offer pragmatic, strategy focused processes to help educators, trainers and change agents more effectively meet white people at varying places on their racialized journey, build enough connection to support white colleagues to question their racist socialization, and then shed white supremacist beliefs they still hold. Their practical strategies can help all of us to find new ways of being productive, anti-racist white change agents and take responsibility for doing our part to dismantle racist systems and co-create true racial justice for all.

—Kathy Obear, trainer for The Center for Transformation and Change and author of ...But I'm Not Racist!: Tools for Well-Meaning Whites to Dismantle Racism

Being White Today: A Roadmap for a Positive Antiracist Life is a much-needed book for White people at all stages of engagement with anti-racism. Tochluk and Saxman take a creative and insightful approach to this work by introducing us to White characters with different mindsets related to race. Through scenarios that reveal the characters' White racial identity development, reader reflect on their own journey. *Being White Today* will prompt reflection, introspection, discussion, and action and should be included in community book discussions, teacher preparation programs, social work education, church groups, and more.

—Karen Gaffney, professor of English at Raritan Valley Community College and author of *Dismantling the Racism Machine: A Manual and Toolbox*

BEING WHITE TODAY

BEING WHITE TODAY

A Roadmap for a Positive Antiracist Life

SHELLY TOCHLUK

AND CHRISTINE SAXMAN

ROWMAN & LITTLEFIELD

Lanham • Boulder • New York • London

Published by Rowman & Littlefield
An imprint of The Rowman & Littlefield Publishing Group, Inc.
4501 Forbes Boulevard, Suite 200, Lanham, Maryland 20706
www.rowman.com

86-90 Paul Street, London EC2A 4NE, United Kingdom

British Library Cataloguing in Publication Information Available

Library of Congress Cataloging-in-Publication Data

Names: Tochluk, Shelly, 1971– author. | Saxman, Christine, 1970– author.
Title: Being white today : a roadmap for a positive antiracist life / Shelly Tochluk and Christine
    Saxman.
Description: Lanham : Rowman & Littlefield, [2023] | Includes bibliographical references and
    index. | Summary: "Being White Today's suggested approaches guide readers to make strategic
    choices for themselves and others that resist white nationalist recruitment and reveal the benefits
    of antiracist appeals"—Provided by publisher.
Identifiers: LCCN 2022060950 (print) | LCCN 2022060951 (ebook) | ISBN 9781475870558
    (cloth) | ISBN 9781475870572 (epub)
Subjects: LCSH: White people—Race identity. | Anti-racism.
Classification: LCC HT1575 .T63 2023 (print) | LCC HT1575 (ebook) | DDC 305.809—dc23/
    eng/20230123
LC record available at https://lccn.loc.gov/2022060950
LC ebook record available at https://lccn.loc.gov/2022060951

This book is dedicated to the antiracist community that we love.

CONTENTS

ACKNOWLEDGMENTS

Shelly Tochluk:

This book is a product of community support, and my appreciation runs deep. A heartfelt thanks goes to Dr. Beverly Daniel Tatum for initially setting me on this journey and responding favorably to an admitted "fan girl." And to Christine, my co-author, with whom I spent the last decade exploring and wrestling over ideas, our collaboration is fundamental to who I have become, and I love you.

Most of the insights I contributed to the book's pages derive from two decades of transformative experiences made possible by the AWARE-LA community. Thank you especially to Jason David, Michele Dumont, David Gardinier, Dahlia Ferlito, Clare Fox, Sarah Glasband, Stephanie Goodman, Cameron Levin, Hillary Stephenson, Vitaly, Ariane White, and Liz Wiltsie for the conversations that have shaped me.

The White Privilege Conference community has also been instrumental in my development. A special shout out to Eddie Moore Jr. for creating the container and Beth Applegate, Pam Chambers, and Robin Parker for the years spent engaging me with critical care. Thank you to those who regularly uplift me and keep me striving: Jackie Battalora, Jenna Chandler-Ward, Elizabeth Denevi, Robin DiAngelo, Debby Irving, Ali Michael, and Kathy Obear.

The guidance of key individuals to whom I feel deeply accountable is what propelled this project forward. Thank you to Diane Burbie, Lecia Brooks, Beverly Daniel Tatum, David Campt, Vincent Flewellen, and Jorge Zeballos. Your mentorship gave me the courage to share my truth.

Thank you to those who offered feedback along the journey, adding comments to shared notes pages and reflecting on each another's insights. Some of you remained engaged as the pages transformed under your watchful eyes: Jackie Battalora, Aisha Blanchard-Young, Joan Braune, Kelly Court, Salina Gray, Debby Irving, Paul Kivel, Ali Michael, Aiden

O'Leary, Ryan O'Leary, Dina Polichar, Chandra Russo, Sheri Schmidt, Ayres Stiles-Hall, Jacqueline B. Swezey, Ariane White, Carrie Ungerman, and Jorge Zeballos.

Thank you to those who sat for interviews related to key topics, the material from which I pledge will someday find publication: Jason Biehl, Ben Beachy, Tyler Benjamin, Will Brummett, Chris Crass, Patrisse Cullors, Jason David, Eric Gatson-Michalak, Justic Haas, Noah Hughes-Dunn, Matt Harper, Justin Leroux, Gus May, Chuck Modiano, Arthur Smith, and Ryan Virden. Your insights contributed greatly to my thinking and this work.

A special thank you to Robin DiAngelo and Paul Kivel, who provided essential support and critical insight as Christine and I moved the work forward.

Through it all my foundation remains my parents, Cathy and Larry Tochluk, who allowed me to camp out in their living room for weeks on end, providing writing retreat space for myself and Christine. And finally, there is Ally, my four-legged companion. I am forever grateful for her unconditional love, kisses, tail wags, and daily walks that rejuvenated me when sorely needed.

A final word of gratitude to Mount Saint Mary's University–Los Angeles, for the semester-long sabbatical that allowed the time and space necessary for this project. The months spent writing this book were the most productive of my life.

———

Christine Saxman:

I know I did not co-author this book on my own. I need to thank Dr. Janet Helms for her White racial identity model, which grounds me and sustains me in my antiracist work with my White community. This book doesn't exist without her scholarship. Thank you to Andrea Johnson for starting me on my antiracist path and for your mentorship and friendship. Thank you to Robin DiAngelo for her guidance to embrace my writer self. And thank you to my coauthor, Shelly. From the moment I met you at WPC White caucus, you have been a friend, a support, and a motivation. I love you.

Thank you to my former Deerfield High School community as a whole, with special gratitude for Buffy Sallee, Eri Tanimoto, Kristan Jiggetts, Mirah Anti, Niki Antonakos, Suzanne Nice, Dan Cohen, Marisa Fiorito, Audris Griffith, and, most especially, my former students.

I am who I am because of my entire extended SEED family and these teachers: Gail Cruise Roberson, Donald Burroughs, Jondou Chase Chen, Ruth Condori Aragón, Loren Moye, Brenda Flyswithhawks, Toni Graves Williamson, Pat Badger, Becca Chase Chen, Emmy Howe, emily warren, Emily Styles, and Peggy McIntosh.

Pat Savage-Williams, Ismalis Nuñez, Corrie Wallace, Neelamjit Dhaliwal, Motoko Maegawa, Kirk LaRue, and Brian Corley—you are part of my SEED family *and* my Chicago family. I'm holding you so, so close in gratitude.

I must thank my White Privilege Conference family: that means you especially, Dr. Eddie Moore Jr., and Beth Applegate, Isla Govan, and Tilman Smith.

To my former Courageous Conversations family, I appreciate you all. Protocol changed my life, and you did too: Leidene King, Ismalis Nuñez, Krischanna Roberson, Nicole Shimizu-Nguyen, Fadzi Whande, Shaundra Brown, Lori Watson, Glenn Singleton, Courtlandt Butts, Tony Hudson, Marcus Moore, and Devon Alexander.

I appreciate my White community, which holds me in loving accountability: Maureen Benson, Jenna Chandler-Ward, Debby Irving, Ali Michael, Jackie Battalora, Elizabeth Denevi, Kathy Obear, Robin DiAngelo, and Ryan Virden.

To those who spent time and energy providing feedback on this book in its many iterations, thank you: Ismalis Nuñez, Robin DiAngelo, Carol Saxman, Dianna Saxman, Pat Savage-Williams, Corrie Wallace, and Amelia Erdman.

To my Saxman family, thank you for the love and support and pushes to grow: my mom Carol, my dad Peter, my brothers, Peter and Eric, my sister-in-law Dianna, my brother-in-law Mel, my nieces, Zowie, Kiah, and Riley, and my nephew, Dylan.

Finally, to my partner Matthew and our sweet four-legged Flannery, thank you for the shoulder to cry on, the kisses, the distractions, the refocusing, and the love.

INTRODUCTION

In 2017, flyers began appearing on college campuses across the United States and Canada. On plain white paper with big, black letters, the flyers stated, "It's Okay To Be White." That was it. No website address. No group name. Just the phrase, "It's Okay To Be White." The simplicity was astounding.

Many immediately recognized the negative intent underlying the flyers' message. After all, this was at a time when white nationalist groups felt empowered by then President Donald Trump, and mainstream conservatives were adopting far-right ideology at an alarming rate. Nationwide, college campus tours by alt-right provocateurs had come with claims that protests against hate speech were attacks on free speech, and a smattering of white nationalist groups called for schools to create White student unions. A lot of people recognized the connection between the flyers and white nationalists.

Reactions varied, though. Many on social media responded with what amounted to a viscerally negative message of "No, it's *not* okay to be White!" They associated anything having to do with being White as related to racism. Others offered a question: "Of course, it's okay to be White. Whoever said it wasn't?" Some articles and online posts asked, "When has it ever *not* been okay to be White?" and then described a long history of white dominance, white privilege, and systemic white supremacy within the United States. Still other articles appeared to explain the historical context that makes it necessary to say, "Black is beautiful," while there is no comparable need to validate the existence of White people.

As the months went by and the flyer campaign continued, we—your authors—reacted with a very nervous, "Oh, no." We understood the various reactions and explanations listed above. What made us nervous is that we also understood that the "It's okay to be White" tactic promoted by white nationalists could be extremely effective. It exploits a weakness within the antiracist community—the lack of positive messaging about White identity. In that vacuum, the far right recognizes an opportunity.

The white nationalists who posted the flyers did so not only to rile up people. They also took advantage of the fact that the majority of White people would not understand negative reactions from "social justice warriors"/antiracists. They knew the language of *structural racism* and *privilege* would not resonate with most White people. They understood the ensuing controversy would provoke White people to react negatively, seeking evidence that antiracists do not believe it is okay to be White.

The messaging and effectiveness of this white nationalist campaign and others remain an active concern. The "It's okay to be White" phrase appeared on flyers, stickers, and graffiti throughout the United States and in Canada, Australia, and the United Kingdom from 2018 through 2022. In 2021, related provocative messages included claims that "antiracism is anti-White," connecting any exploration of historical racism to the shaming of White students.[1]

In 2022, we learned about a group organizing under the name "White Lives Matter Official." A review of their activist manual revealed it to be a white nationalist effort. While the language and focus of these messages continues to evolve, the problem remains the same. White nationalists and white supremacists take advantage of the lack of a widespread antiracist vision for healthy White identity development.

THE VISION

This book addresses this problem by providing a vision for how a positive, antiracist White identity develops. It offers various strategies that can help us guide ourselves and others through the identity journey so we can create a larger, healthier, antiracist White community that works together to navigate the complexities and seeming contradictions we face while pursuing racial justice.

This vision is rooted in a desire to live in a society where people are kinder and gentler with one another, where we can be both inspired and capable of reaching across divisions within our families and communities. This book exists because we want to live in a society where our institutions and cultural ways of being lead to a more inclusive, multiracial democracy. This drives us to speak directly to our White community.

A directive offered by Malcolm X inspires this approach. In a 1965 interview with Jack Barnes and Barry Sheppard, Malcolm X asserted that "Whites who are sincere should organize themselves and figure out some strategies to break down the prejudice that exists in White communities. This is where they can function more intelligently and more effectively, in the White community itself."[2] We take this message as a mandate and focus on our White community. Often heard among antiracists is the phrase, "White people need to first do their own work." This book reflects our commitment to support as many White people as possible in that effort.

To that end, throughout this book the pronouns *we* and *us* speak specifically about the White community. This is an intentional choice meant to interrupt the way so many White people are socialized to focus on ourselves as individuals and not part of a larger collective of White people. We acknowledge the impact this language choice will have on many readers of color, making it feel distanced and less inclusive. To learn about decisions related to the capitalization of White, please see end notes.[3]

In hopes of pulling as many White people into antiracism as possible, we invite readers on a journey that begins with several key messages that we believe unequivocally:

- It's not our fault that we were born into a racist system.
- Racism is not good for any of us; it hurts everyone, including White people.
- We can all be part of ending racism; in fact, White people have an important role to play in influencing our family, friends, colleagues, and the wider White community.

This book is for White people who want to make a difference, be part of ending racism, and help bring healing to our fractured communities. We hope you will join us because too many have succumbed to an aggressive far-right movement that manipulates White people into identifying more with avowed racists than with people fighting for justice.

Message to Readers of Color

Given the focus on White people, readers may wonder if People of Color would benefit from reading this book. The answer is that it depends. People of Color invested in supporting White people's development are likely to benefit. Several colleagues of color who were early reviewers reported breakthrough moments while facilitating conversations with White people using insights gleaned from the book's contents.

We offer a caution, however, that some People of Color will find this book painful to read for a number of reasons, not least of which is that it focuses on White people's emotional and psychological experiences. Some will view the concern over White people and their psychological experience as either "centering whiteness" or "coddling White people." This critique is inevitable and understandable. Our commitment is that the book intentionally works to meet White people where they are in order to support the cultivation of an effective, healthy, and sustainable antiracism practice. This is part of our contribution for there to be less harm in the world.

Recognizing that this focus may not align with their interests and/or needs, People of Color can decide to read or not read this book based on what best suits them. We consulted with many People of Color about the book's approach (including the use of the term People of Color instead of BIPOC) as part of our accountability practice. This book would not be what it is without the encouragement, mentoring, and feedback of our solidarity partners of color.

Organization of the Book

The journey in this book begins with two orienting chapters that explore White identity development. Chapter 1 explains what underlies white nationalists' successful recruitment efforts, how many are confused by antiracist messaging, and how this leads to a failure to effectively push back against the organized bigotry of the far right. Chapter 2 defines terms such as White people, White culture, and whiteness and describes various approaches taken to White identity over time. It also introduces Janet Helms's White identity development model and how the analogy of a roundabout illustrates its dynamics.

Chapters 3 through 12 each explore points on the White identity journey. These chapters use character-driven scenarios to explain the various identity positions, how far-right and antiracist messaging affect people at each position, and what can support people to move toward antiracism.

Chapter 3 explores experiences typical of the Contact position, which is characterized by a White person's belief in colorblindness. Chapter 4 then introduces the *Disintegration* position as one filled with internal conflict that begins when White people encounter moral dilemmas related to race and justice. Because the moral dilemmas create inflexible either/or binaries, chapters 5 and 6 illustrate what happens when people operating from *Disintegration* feel pushed to choose a side and either defend whiteness or turn toward antiracism. Chapters 7 and 8 build on this critical juncture and highlight what happens in *Reintegration* as people either anchor solidly into whiteness or choose to follow an antiracist path.

Chapter 9 illustrates *Pseudo-Independence*, the first position where White people fully integrate an antiracist sense of self and worldview. The "pseudo" in the title, however, signals that the confidence is largely unfounded. Therefore, this chapter explores how an unhealed sense of self results in ineffective action and what we can do to support people to act more usefully.

Chapter 10 focuses on *Immersion/Emersion*, where people stand on firmer ground while engaging in an intertwined and cyclical process of *immersing* in learning and then *emerging* into action. This position is when White people engage in deep reflection about what it means to be White and to live an antiracist life.

Chapters 11 and 12 are the culmination. They explore *Autonomy*, the apex of the racial identity model, where an antiracist foundation solidifies, and White people feel more positive about themselves and their place in the world. These chapters assert that it is okay to be White and illustrate what is possible, providing a hopeful vision of what we can achieve together in pursuit of an inclusive, multiracial democracy.

We invite you to journey with us.

1

Deciding on a Direction

Which Way Do We Go?

"I'm so sick of this school making me feel guilty for being White. I'm ready to join the alt-right, and I'm Jewish!" His voice rings across the classroom as the students work in small groups. All eyes of the predominantly White students turn to me, the White teacher, as they collectively gasp a little. How will I respond?

I take a deep breath, prompted by the gasp. I move closer. "Tell me more about the school making you feel guilty."

At that moment in 2016, something shifted for me, Christine Saxman. The anguish of my student permeated the room as he, a high school senior, wrestled with a college essay activity that asked him to think about race.

In our conversation, to which the class listened while feigning *not* listening, he named the anti-Semitism of the alt-right. While troublesome to him, he still felt drawn in by their arguments that defended White people and their right not to feel guilty. It shook me.

As a teacher focused on social and racial justice, I felt responsible for how I had contributed to his distressed feeling in my class. As a member of my school's equity team, I felt responsible for how I had contributed to a school system that reinforced this idea of white guilt.

I had to reexamine my understanding of the alt-right and the far right. I had to reconsider my definition of antiracism. This examination eventually led to this book. But I'm getting ahead of myself.

In 2016, white nationalists came together under the term *alt-right* (an abbreviation meaning *alternative right*) as part of an effort to push against traditional conservatism and embrace more white-centric and white supremacist ideologies. They promoted their white nationalist ideas while claiming they were not racist, not white supremacist, and asserting that they only wanted to protect White identity and preserve White heritage. In doing so, they co-opted language focused on identity used within racial justice movements, terms like *racial consciousness* and *racial identity*.

The term alt-right, fell out of favor after the 2017 Unite the Right rally in Charlottesville, Virginia. This book uses the term *far right* to refer to all the various and differently motivated groups and individuals who continue to push a form of white supremacy and/or white nationalism, whether they admit to holding racist ideology or not. Serving as an umbrella term, far right also encompasses the many people who, in the ebb and flow of the times, were once considered mainstream conservatives, yet now embrace a number of white nationalist and white supremacist ideas. These individuals may have no affiliation with a hate group, and yet they are more ideologically aligned with white supremacists than with those pushing for racial justice.[4]

The far right includes people who espouse vehemently anti-feminist, anti-LGBTQIA+,[5] anti-immigrant, anti-Muslim, anti-Jewish, and racist views. In this way, the term far right casts a wide net, under which fits what people who study organized bigotry and white power groups might traditionally consider a less overtly violent, more political, right wing.

White nationalism is a political movement that advocates for a separate White nation. *White supremacy* is a larger concept, an overarching ideology that suggests White people and cultures are superior to People of Color and Jewish people and their cultures. This book puts white nationalists and white supremacists in the same category of the far right, as they both hold deeply racist views and advocate for policies that work to disproportionately harm People of Color.

All of this means that the far right is a varied and complex bunch, and includes some people who identify as Jewish and some People of Color as well. For example, Stephen Miller, a one-time senior advisor to Donald Trump, is a Jewish man with ties to white nationalism. Henry

"Enrique" Tarrio is an Afro-Cuban man who has served as a leader of the Proud Boys.

Casting this wide net does not imply that all conservatives are part of the far right and/or espouse white nationalist or white supremacist views. In fact, many people with traditionally conservative values are dismayed by the overt racism displayed by some of today's Republican Party leadership and its followers. It is important, however, to challenge conservatives who equivocate and fail to reject racist ideas and policies that result in racialized harm.

Thinking back to that day in 2016, as my student's outburst pushed me to learn more about the far right and its messages, it also prompted me to examine my understanding of my role as an antiracist. Hearing my student's deep emotion and conflict, I had to ask myself: is my approach to antiracism working? How could a White, Jewish student think joining the alt-right was a viable option after four years at a high school that prides itself on its antiracist reputation?

I am an *antiracist*. By that I mean that I am someone who is committed to taking action to end racism. Bringing more White people into antiracism is an important part of that. So, if White people find it easy to reject what I offer, I have to question my approach. Therefore, while my commitment remained the same, I opened myself to recognizing how I used guilt and shame in my attempt to influence others and realizing how damaging that was. I had to reconcile the fact that my intent (how I wanted to influence others) and my impact (how my actions actually affected others) were vastly different.

In that moment, with a room full of observers, I explored my student's desire to feel positively about being White. I offered ways that we could do so, based on my life-changing learning from Dr. Helms's work on racial identity development.[6] How could we work collaboratively to feel more liberation rather than frustration in the face of racism? This experience was an essential step in my personal antiracist journey.

Shelly Tochluk and I have spent years reflecting on important lessons we have learned from the collective of organizers, activists, academics, educators, policy makers, politicians, and others who take antiracist action and embody an antiracist identity. Shelly and I are part of a wider community dedicated to *antiracism*. Antiracism is a movement that seeks to end racism and promote racial justice and healing. This work cannot occur in isolation, though, and so antiracism necessarily appreciates *intersectionality*, examining how racism intersects systemically with feminism, LGBTQIA+ activism, disability rights, immigrant rights, anticolonialism, Indigenous rights, and so on.

In the antiracist community, there is a tendency to assume that all people who lean toward the Democratic Party are antiracist. However, many people on the political left are not necessarily antiracist and, in fact, some reject the rhetoric of antiracism. Similarly, there is a tendency on the political left to assume that people who favor the Republican Party politically cannot possibly be antiracist. This is also untrue. Because of the nuance and complexity of human life and belief systems, it is possible for people of all political persuasions to be antiracist.

Over the years, as we continue to hone our antiracist practice, an ongoing concern is how to more effectively influence White people to join the antiracism movement. A particular concern is reaching people who are skeptical about the value of paying attention to race and racial identity.

THE NEED FOR A POSITIVE WHITE RACIAL IDENTITY

A White, middle-aged woman in the back of the room looks up. She has just realized how the essay we are discussing manipulatively uses a quote by Martin Luther King, Jr., to tout colorblindness while simultaneously arguing a claim of white racial superiority. It is a shrewd piece of white nationalist propaganda.

"How are we supposed to counter this? How do we make sure the public at large understands what white nationalists are doing?" She stares, along with 50 other people, waiting for Christine or I to answer.

I feel my entire body flush with embarrassment. I have no good answer. None of us in the room does. An emerging sense of alarm and powerlessness envelopes us as we struggle to come up with sure-fire, ready responses to the propaganda.

My name is Shelly Tochluk. Although Christine and I had spent the prior eight months discussing the rise of far-right groups, exploring their messaging, and talking about their manipulation of antiracist ideas, I had yet to fully comprehend their expanding reach. How to effectively counter their myriad, false claims also eluded us.

In the year that followed this moment, a year that included an intensive review of documentaries, articles, and books, my concerns heightened. This resulted in me speaking as though the sky was falling. While wrestling with uncertainty about what to do about the far right's sophisticated tactics, technological savvy, and effective messaging, I also struggled with the inattention of my antiracist community.

For example, in the summer of 2018 a Black keynote speaker told an audience of over 2,000 mostly White conference-goers to stop worrying about the far right and instead look at themselves. She told the group that liberal White people are the ones who keep racism in place and harm People of Color the most. Witnessing this made me want to yell, "Why can't we pay attention to both? We need to pay attention to both!"

At that point, my long history with a White, antiracist community called AWARE-LA had helped me understand antiracism's expectations and the philosophical backstory to its messages. It also prompted me to value both/and thinking, where two seemingly contradictory things can be true at the same time. This is in contrast to either/or thinking, which creates a binary as if there are only two choices when, in fact, there are more options. This both/and orientation helped me stay engaged in antiracism when encountering people whose approach felt one-sided or off-putting.

Also key to staying involved was one of AWARE-LA's core principles. The organization prioritizes the need to develop a *positive, antiracist White identity*, which involves co-creating a new way of being White.[7] Although the organization has its own model of what goes into creating such an identity, educational leader Dr. Beverly Daniel Tatum was a huge influence, particularly as she advised that we need more public modeling of how to be healthy, antiracist White people who feel good about ourselves.[8] That idea struck a deep chord in me and has propelled my work ever since.

An essential insight is that the path to becoming an antiracist is long and not always clear. There is a lot to learn, and the pressure to act can be scary. It is also easy to feel demoralized. White people need a way to hold ourselves as decent people while on the road to becoming competent antiracist people. Helms's model of White identity development, as described by Tatum, helped me do that. It charted a path toward a healthy White identity rooted in the ability and dedication to work effectively with people of all racial backgrounds in service of racial justice. (Chapter 2 explains the White identity model.)

The journey to construct this positive, antiracist White identity is more life-giving and inspiring than many imagine. This is because the road necessarily involves becoming part of an antiracist community. Yes, antiracist communities are challenging. Yes, the terrain is always shifting, and there is constantly new information to absorb. Yes, it can be uncomfortable when ever-evolving expectations require change. All of this is true.

Also true is that being part of an antiracist community breeds a sense of liberation and the ability to relate more effectively across race. Within the wider antiracist community, I have found belonging, support, and an uncompromising dedication to helping one another become more generous, humane people. We are dedicated to becoming healthy while co-creating a society that achieves racial justice.

Underlying all of this is the belief that racial justice benefits everyone, White people as well as People of Color. We strive to build a society that values everyone. This orientation aligns with the abolitionist idea that "no one is disposable" and that everyone should be able to experience health and wellness.[9] Working toward this vision of a society where no one is left out is worth the struggle and inspires significant joy.

THE ROAD AHEAD

Maintaining the civil rights gains made since the 1960s (such as voting rights, immigrant rights, etc.) and continuing to advance racial justice depends on the country functioning as close to its democratic ideals as possible. Many in the United States understand that the institutional and social structures providing for the protection of civil rights are fragile and under extreme threat due to, among other things, a coordinated and widespread effort to suppress access to the ballot box.[10]

Amidst these larger issues, the role that White identity plays in nationwide trends and how it will help determine the country's future is a concern. People need to understand how white nationalists and extremists weaponize White identity and are attempting to use it to shape the country into their racist ideal via policies and legislation.

White supremacists are not uneducated buffoons, they are not concentrated in the rural south, and they are not as small in number as many believe. They are doctors, members of the military, school resource officers, and store managers.[11] They are your neighbors and maybe even your relatives. One of their greatest strengths is their ability to rebrand themselves to fit the cultural atmosphere of the time. They consistently repackage their messaging to activate White people's fears and mobilize mainstream people to adopt their beliefs and take action.[12]

For example, during Trump's presidency, white supremacists seized on the convergence of conspiracy theories related to the pandemic, racial uprisings in the wake of George Floyd's murder, and false claims about the 2020 presidential election. They infused their messaging throughout large swaths of the mainstream, conservative right. The call to "protect" White people now comes from many who otherwise disavow racism, not realizing how far-right manipulation fuels their fears.

That the United States is undergoing rapid social change is beyond dispute. How people view the change differs, however. The 2020 Census Report provides fodder ripe for the exploitation of some White people's fears; it notes that the only racial group population decline is among White people at 8.5 percent. This has particular meaning for White people worried about the United States becoming "minority white" by 2045.[13]

Another example of the far right using fear-based propaganda to mobilize supporters is the anti–critical race theory movement that began targeting schools in 2021. While the focus on critical race theory is new, the narrative about schools being sites of liberal indoctrination is not.[14] For decades, educators have worked to include themes of diversity, inclusion, and equity in their school's policies, practices, and curricula. As successes mount, resistance grows.

The amplification of the anti–critical race theory narrative is also due to the takeover of mainstream conservatism by the far right. The term *critical race theory* has become a stand-in for all curriculum and school programming activities related to diversity, inclusion, equity, race, socio-emotional learning, and related topics. This allows many more people to become mobilized and reactive. The *Washington Post* reported the following in May 2021:

> *Christopher Rufo, a prominent opponent of critical race theory, in March acknowledged intentionally using the term to describe a range of race-related topics and conjure a negative association.*
>
> *"We have successfully frozen their brand—'critical race theory'—into the public conversation and are steadily driving up negative perceptions," wrote Rufo, a senior fellow at the Manhattan Institute, a conservative think tank. "We will eventually turn it toxic, as we put all of the various cultural insanities under that brand category. The goal is to have the public read something crazy in the newspaper and immediately think 'critical race theory.'"*[15]

What sets this anti–critical race theory effort apart from the decades-long push and pull over social justice in schools is the new focus on White identity as the crux of the argument. The veiled language of the post–civil rights era has given way to explicit calls to protect White people's interests, feelings, and rights. White TV pundits and parents increasingly argue that a focus on critical thinking, a complex understanding of US history, and empathy are abusively shaming White children.

This more explicit focus means both parents and their children experience their race as an important feature of who they are and fear their identity that is under attack. How widespread is this concern? In 2021, the Pew Research Center reported that "14% of White Americans believe they face a lot of discrimination and 40% believe they face at least some discrimination."[16] Watching how these numbers shift will be important.

Research analyst Ben Lorber of Political Research Associates, a social justice think tank, explains that white nationalists like Nick Fuentes, the leader of America First, believe White identity will grow even more important for those who make up Generation Z. They will be the first US generation "to be nearly 50 percent People of Color, in a cultural milieu where the salience of race relations and identity politics looms large."[17] The way Fuentes sees it, White people in Generation Z will "more readily see themselves as a marginalized group and utilize the language of White identity to articulate perceived group interests and grievances." In other words, Fuentes predicts that today's White teens will be more likely to see themselves as the targets of racial discrimination. Even though much of Generation Z leans liberal, Fuentes believes all the ingredients are in place to generate a movement focused on defending White identity.

Although some readers may take comfort in a majority of Generation Z leaning toward liberalism, this falsely assumes that young people will be resistant to far-right messaging. This is problematic for several reasons:

1. The far-right groups are agile, organized, and well resourced. Their ability to pull young people toward them using popular culture, provocative messaging, manipulative content, and media platforms is well documented.[18]
2. The Black Lives Matter movement and racial justice uprisings, like those that occurred between 2013 and 2020 following the killings of Trayvon Martin, Michael Brown, Breonna Taylor, Ahmaud Arbery, and George Floyd, may have brought more White people into antiracist organizations and made conversations about systemic racism more commonplace. However, every year a new set of adolescents begins to pay attention to social issues. These teens will search for answers to complicated questions about race in the media landscape that surrounds them.
3. Most White people who care about antiracism, regardless of political affiliation, do not generally convey well-developed, positive messaging around what it means to be a White person. Although there is an argument to be made for a positive, antiracist White identity, too few people make it, leaving many with the sense that being White is shameful. This leaves White people susceptible to far-right recruitment tactics and messaging.

Assuming the next generation and the ones that follow will remain inclined toward an inclusive, multiracial democracy is naive. It ignores the white supremacists' influence, as they work to weaponize White identity to gain power and seek to shape policies for decades to come. Given population trends and the way that US electoral systems allow for minority rule, where those in power represent a small proportion of the overall population, the next generation of White voters will likely continue to wield outsized influence.

Our concern is not solely for young people and the next generation. We also need to engage today's adults. As racial justice efforts recently have gained more traction, there has been more backlash against these efforts. In these discussions, the mainstream political rhetoric increasingly names White people's fears, making their own racial identity more of a concern than it was in the past. Unfortunately, these more frequent conversations about race are not always helpful, as White people are often confused or turned off by the competing messages coming from the far right and antiracists.

It is essential that White people realize that a positive, antiracist White identity is not only possible, it is life-affirming and valuable. We believe this will support more White people, in the face of a distinct choice, to push back against hate and instead build new antiracist social, economic, and political systems that realize the dream of a vibrant, thriving, multiracial democracy that benefits everyone.

JOIN THE RACIAL JUSTICE FREEWAY

The analogy of a racial justice freeway describes how White people can find their lane and contribute meaningfully.[19] The freeway has many lanes. It heads toward a future where racial justice is realized. Drivers on this freeway share this goal even as their tactics and strategies for getting there differ. Organizers and activists typically travel in the lanes farthest to the left or the carpool lane. People from many walks of life occupy the middle lanes, advancing racial justice in their homes, workplaces, schools, and faith communities.

The slow lane is an oft-dismissed lane on the racial justice freeway. This is the lane where people new to issues of race enter the conversation.

Entering this lane is often scary, particularly if we do not yet have the skills to navigate well. We may fear the speed of people in other lanes who use signals we do not understand. This can make the slow lane very intense and psychologically fraught.

As authors, we position ourselves in this lane as driver's ed instructors. We coach people onto the onramps and support them to gain speed and change lanes with skill and confidence. We support them so they do not head for the exit ramp.

Both of us have traveled in various lanes on this freeway over the last two decades, educating liberal audiences a lot of the time, and more recently looking in the rear-view mirror to focus on the disruptive movements of the far right. This bidirectional attention allowed us to gain important insight into dynamics currently at play between the far right, antiracists, and those who feel caught in between, and how they undermine justice movements.

It is important that White people are not pushed away from racial justice or pulled toward a racist far-right movement. Too many feel ambivalent, viewing both sides as problematic and/or radical. People feeling apathetic about racial justice is a disaster. We need many more White people to join the freeway and head toward a future that holds the promise of collective liberation and justice.

White people travel in various lanes; therefore, you may experience more clarity at particular points than at others.

- *The slow lane:* If you have just gotten onto the onramp, merged in the slow lane, or are still building courage to try freeway driving at all, allow the material to wash over you. Gather insights as they arise. Do not worry when an idea is confusing. You do not need to understand everything at first. Trust that ideas can clarify as you move forward. We know that the material can be overwhelming. It's okay to take your time so that your experience merging onto the freeway is as constructive as possible.
- *The middle lanes:* If you already feel invested in racial justice and are traveling in a middle lane, we anticipate that you want other people to join you on the freeway. Use this material to learn how to

support and encourage others. You may also find answers to some long-simmering, confusing questions that you've experienced while navigating the freeway.

- *The fast lane and carpool (high occupancy vehicle) lanes:* If you are an organizer, activist, or educator traveling in the fast and carpool lanes, the information can help you consider the strategies and tactics to use when engaging White people.

Regardless of the lane you occupy, it is essential to understand the dynamics that arise when White people engage with questions of race and racism. Because the dynamics are layered, people navigating the various lanes will likely find value in different aspects of the book. That is okay. Take what works for you now. Consider returning later to gain additional insight.

> *Dear Reader:* You'll notice *Dear Reader* moments throughout the chapters. We offer them at particular points because, in our experience, these are places where many of us struggle and where ideas are often confusing. We hope these occasional notes of advice and encouragement keep you steady and striving with as few bumps in the road as possible. We wish you much joy on the journey.

2

Mapping the Road Ahead

Toward a Positive, Antiracist White Identity

"How do you define White culture?" I feel my anxiety creep up as I look at the other White people at the table around me.

"Boring?" someone tentatively offers. As the list grows ("bland," "bad dancer," "can't jump . . . "), each addition seems to mock White culture. Our Black facilitator visits our table and asks, "Is there a pattern you notice in your answers?"

Sitting in the Beyond Diversity training offered by the Pacific Educational Group in the early 2000s, I, Christine, learned to make a distinction between White people, White culture, and whiteness.[20] That distinction informs my antiracist practice to this day. Although my road to the racial justice freeway came in fits and starts, this distinction is what made my learning clearer and my path more direct. The fog slowly lifted.

At that moment, these questions arose. What did I like about White culture? What didn't I like? How does White culture vary among White people? How does ethnicity and religion make a difference in how we experience White culture? What do people mean when they talk about whiteness? What does it even mean to be White? Is it an identity I should care about?

PAVING THE WAY
In order to have as smooth a path forward as possible, we need a shared understanding of core ideas. A fundamental one is that race is a social construction, meaning that it is not biologically real.[21] Yet, for centuries,

the idea of race has shaped laws and policies and resulted in racial inequities. Therefore, although race is a social construction, it has real consequences for people's lives. Building from this foundation, we want to help tease apart three commonly conflated concepts: White people, White culture, and whiteness. For our journey, here is what we mean.

White People

When we say *White people*, we are referring to people whose skin color, hair texture, and facial features align with historical and cultural definitions of the White racial category. This includes people who recognize themselves as being White as well as people whom society treats as White. If this seems a loose definition, it is because the groups society deems as White are ever-evolving, and legal and social understandings have not always aligned.

Early in my journey, for instance, I thought all White people were of European heritage. Later, I learned that some Hispanic/Latinx people not from Europe also identify as White. In the United States, this is related to the fact that federal laws conferred "White" status on Mexican people at the close of the Mexican American war, even though state law did not necessarily extend the privileges that came with being White. So, socially Hispanic/Latinx people have not generally been treated as White by White society.[22]

This "conditionally White" status has made racial identity complicated for many Hispanic/Latinx people. A similar issue of federal status not matching social experience affects many people of Middle-Eastern heritage.[23] I have also met Native and Indigenous people who identify racially as White and culturally with their tribal affiliation.

Without delving into a long, detailed explanation of various ethnic groups and how they became White (entire books do this), we simply offer that trying to nail down exactly who is White will always be confusing.[24] And so we do the best we can. For Shelly and me, the important point is that when we say, "It's okay to be White," we mean that it's okay to be a White person. We haven't done anything wrong by being born into the White category.

White Culture

When we say *White culture*, we mean the norms, values, patterns, behaviors, attitudes, and expressions typical of White people in the United States. Yet, many White people don't believe there is a White culture. Some even think it's racist to say that White culture exists. However, as I learned from scholars of color, from W. E. B. Du Bois and Langston Hughes to Toni Morrison and Claudia Rankine, White culture is real and can be examined.

One White educator and strategist who helped me identify aspects of White culture is Judith Katz.[25] From her, I learned how to name and recognize White US culture. Her analysis set me on a path to understanding how European immigrants distanced themselves from their European cultural heritages to assimilate. I recall a moment when this knowledge helped me navigate a conversation with several White people, some of whom were recent immigrants from Eastern Europe.

The new immigrants shared the pressure they felt to reject the collectivism of their home culture and adopt a competitive approach to fit in with US society. Other White people hearing their experience, whose families had been in the United States for generations, struggled to understand how competition could be viewed negatively. The conversation gave us a chance to wrestle over the high value that White US culture places on competition and how we relate to it. Competition is just one aspect of White culture we can identify.

Saying that a White culture exists does not necessarily imply that White culture looks and feels exactly the same to all White people. In fact, much variety and richness exists among White people in the United States. For example, White culture is expressed differently depending on our geographical region. (Have you ever heard two White people talking about the differences between a Midwesterner and New Yorker?)

In addition, if we identify strongly with our ethnic or religious cultural histories and heritages, the degree to which we express White culture may also vary. This is why an Italian American, a Jewish person, someone from the deep South, and someone with roots in Latin America, all who identify as White, might relate to and express White culture differently, even while their values and patterns reflect an overarching, White US culture.

For those of us who do not easily recognize the features of White culture, an often-asked question that helps is: "Are fish aware of the water in which they swim?" In other words, do White people notice the White culture in which we exist? This question helped me understand how White culture could influence me without my awareness. More fog lifted once I learned how to identify and describe White people's practices, ways of being, and values.

We offer this overview because Shelly and I notice a difference between White people in the United States who have strong ethnic and religious identities (which provide a sense of cultural grounding) versus those of us who do not. Those of us without a clear sense of culture beyond being a White US citizen often struggle to name anything positive about our cultural background. This can create a problem when we want to cultivate a positive, antiracist White identity.

Over the years, People of Color have asked me to identify aspects of White culture I like so that my contribution to equity work can model a White identity not centered in shame and guilt. So, when I facilitate groups and raise the issue of White culture, I ask people, "What is White music?" The answers ring out without hesitation, "Classical! Country!" We recognize these styles as White music. We can enjoy them, appreciate them, perform them, and value them. People of Color can enjoy them, appreciate them, perform them, and value them too. The point is that White culture is identifiable and includes features we can enjoy and value.

This is essential because Shelly and I believe White culture is neither all bad, nor is it the best and only valid culture. White culture has positive and negative features just like every other culture, and as White people, we should be able to say what we like about it and what we don't.

Trouble arises when a single cultural group in a multicultural society dominates and exerts power in a way that dictates what the society's norms and cultural values should be. This is what occurred as White US culture developed.

Consider that classical music is often presented as the highest or most elevated form of music. Who decided that is true? What message does that deliver about other musical forms or the cultural groups that created them? What are the impacts socially, psychologically, and economically for people from other cultures? We explore what happens when power comes into play as we next discuss what we mean by *whiteness*.

Whiteness

Whiteness is defined as indicating a "quality or state of being White" or "the state of belonging to the racial category White."[26] However, this neutral-sounding definition does not capture what we mean when we use the term. When we talk about whiteness, we mean something more complex. To us, whiteness refers to two interwoven patterns that shape the life experience of everyone in the United States, which includes: 1) systemic/structural racism, and 2) a dominant White culture that prioritizes White norms and values.

The systemic/structural racism aspect of whiteness includes all the ways laws created throughout colonial and US history explicitly advantaged White people for centuries. Core to this understanding is that White people as a legal category did not exist until the late 1600s when the rich and powerful created it. The purpose was to stop dissatisfied laborers (free, indentured, and enslaved) from working together to overthrow an exploitative form of capitalism flourishing in the colonies.[27] The gambit worked.

In fact, it has worked for about 80 percent of the nation's history, through colonization and slavery (1776–1865) and the Jim Crow era (1877–1964). Centuries of legally sanctioned racial discrimination resulted in the solidifying of a White identity that sees itself as superior and a culture that prioritizes White people. Thus, whiteness is another word for white supremacy.

Whiteness is ongoing, as it continues to deny power and rights to People of Color and keep White people in a superior position. Carol Anderson's book, *White Rage*, details how any time laws and policies have shifted to support People of Color, White backlash strikes and involves significant White terrorism against People of Color.[28] Although White people are not the targets of this racial terror, that does not mean that whiteness leads to healthy outcomes for all White people.

Jonathan Metzl's *Dying of Whiteness*, and Heather McGhee's *The Sum of Us*, detail how White people buying into this system of inequity is part of what stops them from turning against an economic system that continues to chew them up and spit them out. Instead, White working-class and poor people are often socialized to be fearful and resentful of People of Color.[29] In this way, whiteness generally treats people as disposable and leads to significant, widespread harm that damages everyone.[30]

I, Christine, can remember the first time the systemic nature of whiteness came into focus for me. Attending SEED (Seeking Educational Equity and Diversity), I watched *Race: The Power of an Illusion*. I was shocked to learn about Supreme Court cases defining who was White, the internment of Japanese Americans during World War II, and the implementation of redlining that prevented returning Black soldiers from benefiting from the GI Bill.[31] It was a gut punch. First, I'd never learned any of this in my "excellent" education. Second, because as a woman in my 30s, that was the moment I finally began to understand systemic racism and how it continues today.

Although race-based discrimination is no longer legally allowed, the patterns, practices, and attitudes associated with whiteness continue and result in widespread racialized harm. Some examples include: 1) laws purporting to be race neutral that disproportionately exclude voters of color, 2) the overpolicing of communities of color, 3) predatory lending that targets People of Color, and 4) insurance carriers who charge higher premiums for those living in certain areas which, due to historic housing discrimination, disproportionately affects People of Color.[32]

The second aspect of whiteness is dominant White culture. This refers to what happens when those in power within a culture deem White culture to be the best. Assuming classical music to be the pinnacle of music is one example. The dominance goes further, however, as whiteness punishes people who express themselves outside of White norms. One example, relevant to employees and school children all over the United States, is the definition of professionalism and how dress codes often demand people to conform to White expressions of style and hair. This centering of White culture has necessitated laws like the CROWN Act, which seeks to protect Black people against race-based hair discrimination.[33]

People of Color regularly and purposefully push back against whiteness as the dominant, valued culture. For example, when Representative

Ocasio-Cortez of New York became a congresswoman, she wore braids one day to represent Afro-Latina culture so her nieces could see themselves represented in a place of power.[34] Important to note is that the push against whiteness in this form has nothing to do with devaluing White culture. Instead, it is designed to provide space for other cultural expressions and disrupt the idea that White culture is normal, the best, and the only respectable way to be or to act.

Very popular today is an essay that describes many features of dominant White culture, titled "White Supremacy Culture: Still Here" by educator and author Tema Okun.[35] The key to understanding the article's title is that when Okun uses the term white supremacy, she is not referring to the Ku Klux Klan or neo-Nazis. Instead, she is referring to the systemic racism that has historically prioritized dominant White culture and the entire range of behaviors, attitudes, and peoples associated with it. In other words, she is talking about whiteness. Whiteness has allowed White standards to be the most valued, to dominate, to reign supreme. And so, again, we find that whiteness is another word for white supremacy.

When we work with schools, corporations, not-for-profits, and government agencies, we hear over and over again how adherence to White culture is expected to such a degree that it feels oppressive to people whose cultures fall outside of White norms. For example, white supremacy culture tends to value hierarchical decision-making, conflict avoidance, and individual work over collaboration. When people challenge these norms and offer other cultural ways of thriving, they are often criticized as causing trouble or not being a good fit.

Like the fish in water analogy, White people and organizations steeped in whiteness typically do not recognize that what we experience as normal is actually racialized and advantages White people. When people talk about dismantling whiteness, they mean they want to dismantle this system that prioritizes one way of being over any other. It is not a statement against White people or White culture; it is a statement against the dominance of one group or way of being over all others.

The insidious part of whiteness and white supremacy culture is that you don't have to be a White person to take part in it and maintain it. In fact, becoming successful in US society typically demands that People of

Color assimilate into White norms and adopt White culture as their own. In this way, people of any racial background can participate in maintaining whiteness.

> *Dear Reader*: We recognize that this breakdown of concepts can feel discouraging and be confusing, especially if this is your first time engaging with these ideas. Feel free to pause and breathe. These concepts will become clearer as we introduce characters and scenarios in the chapters ahead.

WHEN WHITE CULTURE, WHITENESS, AND RELIGION CONVERGE

"Which Jesus do you follow, the modern Jesus or the historical Jesus?" The presenter advances his slide to reveal a side-by-side comparison. "The modern Jesus is weak. He turns the other cheek. They've emasculated him."

The presenter continues, "The historical Jesus is a warrior. He'll take up arms to fight for God. Are you going to abandon Jesus?"

I sit, stunned.

In spring 2019, I, Shelly, sat in the church where I had spent Sunday mornings as a child and teen. My attendance at this far-right Christian conference was prompted by my mother after she returned home from church with a flyer that concerned her. I was there to find out if this group renting space at the church had ties to white nationalism.

The experience opened my eyes to how a particular far-right brand of Christianity, Christian nationalism, with its anti-LGBTQIA+, anti-Muslim, and anti-Jewish rhetoric overlaps substantially with dominating whiteness (white supremacy) and white nationalism and is primarily focused on power.[36] Sitting in the pew, my body tensed as speakers sowed seeds of fear, claiming that a far-left agenda was dead-set on undermining traditional gender roles by recruiting children to become gay and supporting a communist takeover of the United States by importing immigrants.[37] I did not anticipate how widely versions of this message would spread over the next few years.

In the United States, Christianity is the dominant religion and elements of its beliefs and value system are infused throughout White US culture. Just as with White culture, we may like and dislike certain elements of Christian culture. Some Christian ideas are so prevalent in our cultural waters that even people who do not identify as Christian can absorb and express them. For example, when we hear people talking about "saving" people through a conversion experience and pulling people toward "our Truth," the one right way of seeing things, these ideas have roots in Christianity.

We highlight this because as we discuss race with people, we need to be aware of 1) the role Christian nationalism may play in some people's belief systems, 2) how traditional Christian beliefs and/or values might inform how people receive what we have to say, 3) how we might lean on Christian ideas without our awareness, and 4) why our efforts to influence people might be more challenging than we predict. Christian nationalism and/or traditional religious ideals, when forming the base of a person's worldview, can override many other considerations. We need to keep this in mind, and we will address it at various points throughout the book.

A Question of Identity

"Look, you can say my skin is olive or maybe tan, but not White." The professor offers me his outstretched arm. "We would all be better off if we stopped thinking of ourselves as White," he continues.

I cross him off my list of potential dissertation committee members.

In the early 2000s, I, Shelly, embarked on a research project to better understand what it meant to be White. At the time, I did not yet have an internalized map of the racial terrain, which left me feeling unsteady every time a conversation veered toward race. My face would flush and my heart would race. Not only did I not understand the distinctions among White people, White culture, and whiteness, I was unclear about people's varied reactions to what it meant to identify as White. Was there value in it? Was it only making things worse? With this lack of clarity, every conversation was like a potential pothole that could send me careening.

Once I realized that there are four distinct approaches, or orientations, that speak to the value of White identity, navigating race became smoother.

Whether encountering a lecture, a person, or a book, identifying the attitude toward racial identity allowed me to interpret the message without going into a tailspin. Understanding the four orientations will help you as well.

Orientation #1: Colorblindness (or Race-Blindness)

The colorblindness orientation represents the approach of the majority of White people in the United States since the 1960s. It reduces the work of Dr. Martin Luther King Jr. to the dream for people to be judged by "the content of their character rather than the color of their skin." The driving belief is that one's race does not matter, and, therefore, we should pay it no mind. With this logic, developing a White identity holds no value.

Media personalities aligned with the far right often manipulatively promote colorblindness to argue against race-conscious justice efforts.[38] Regardless of political affiliation, as race becomes more salient to White people, those who advocate for colorblindness are increasingly perceived as defensive, willfully ignoring the prevalence of ongoing racism.

Orientation #2: White Supremacy

White supremacists believe there is something inherently good about being White and that it is better than being part of any other group. They commonly expand the idea of White identity to include all of White culture, arguing that White, Western, Christian, American culture is superior to all other cultures. It is a feel-good position for White people.

A subgroup of white nationalists who call themselves "identitarians" exist within this orientation. They spread their message online about the need to protect and preserve White identity, calling for the separation of the races, all while insisting that they don't see Whites as better. They may argue that their position is different from white supremacy; however, the hate-filled commentary about People of Color that flows beneath their online posts readily reveals their followers' white supremacist attitudes.[39]

Beyond being built on a foundation of lies, the problem with aligning with a white supremacist orientation is obvious. It has been used for centuries as an excuse to enact violence against people who are not White and, therefore, cannot coexist with a vision for an inclusive, multiracial democracy.

Orientations #3 and #4: Antiracist Options

Antiracism includes two differing approaches to White identity: one that believes developing a White identity is a bad idea, and one that believes developing a positive, antiracist White identity is a good idea. While the philosophical roots of both positions provide important insights, and some people incorporate ideas from both into their personal philosophy, most antiracists tend to adopt one or the other perspective.

Orientation #3: White Abolition

People who believe that developing a White identity is a bad idea typically align with a philosophy popularized in the 1970s that advocated for abolishing the concept of the White race. (Please note that White abolition is not the same as the police/prison abolition movement.)

This orientation advocates for rejecting White identity as a step toward prioritizing humanity as a whole, rather than distinct and unequal groups. Some use the phrase, "treason to whiteness is loyalty to humanity," popularized by antiracist activist Noel Ignatiev.[40]

This orientation suggests that because race is a social construction that has led only to division and damage, we should not reinforce the identifier "White" as if it is a legitimate human category. People with this orientation sometimes preface a comment with the qualifier "so-called" White people. Some use quotations around the word "White" to indicate that people aren't *really* White. Many sociologists and racial justice activists speak from this perspective.

Part of what underlies this approach is the view that White racial identity is fruit from a poisoned tree, impossible to disentangle from white supremacy. This leaves no room for a redeemed White identity. In other words, from this perspective, identifying as White reinforces a concept that hurts people. White supremacists often respond to this orientation by arguing that "anti-racism is anti-White." However, it is important to remember that White abolition does *not* promote hating White people. It simply questions the value of the concept of White identity in the first place as it seeks to dismantle whiteness and white supremacy.

Orientation #4: Positive White Identity Development

People who believe developing a positive, antiracist White identity is a good thing often work in K–12 schools or fields related to psychology.

From this perspective, race may be a made-up idea, but as society categorizes us, whether we like it or not, White people will be viewed as White regardless of how we personally want to identify.

From this perspective, being White today shapes the way we think about and experience the world. It follows that figuring out what being White means for us is part of becoming fully aware of who we are. That process involves learning about ourselves and admitting that we might be unaware of how race affects us. People with this orientation believe that thoroughly examining history and how society continues to mislead people helps us become strong, confident, self-aware people who can join in the effort to create an inclusive, multiracial society.

The language of white supremacy (#2) and white abolition (#3) each play a major role on social media. Each offers provocative ideas, and many people who are concerned about moving beyond racial division experience them as extreme. Positive White identity development (#4) offers a way forward for White people who want to be antiracist, yet struggle to connect with the ideas related to white abolition (#3). Positive identity development condemns the hatred of the far right while not dismissing the value of the racial identity process. It takes seriously the need for White people to construct a supportive White identity that allows for positive self-regard.

Important to note is that many antiracist people incorporate ideas from both antiracist approaches within their personal philosophy. In this way, although the two perspectives differ, they are not mutually exclusive and their ultimate goal is shared—a place of convergence where race and racism is overcome. The roadmap we offer is rooted in positive White identity development (#4) because we believe that as we work toward the long-term vision, White people need a racial identity that we can feel good about and that supports sustainable racial justice action.

HELMS'S WHITE RACIAL IDENTITY DEVELOPMENT

"I really appreciate the scholarship of this. This is something I can work with." I feel a warm glow inside, knowing this is coming from a White colleague who previously dismissed and resisted the racial equity work within our district.

In my first attempt to share the work of Dr. Janet Helms with other White people, I see some of the same sparks in them that I felt in myself. I'm not alone in this struggle to figure out what it means to be White. We have a way forward.

Dr. Helms's work impacted me, Christine, more than words can express. Reading the slim book, *A Race Is a Nice Thing to Have: A Guide to Being a White Person or Understanding the White Persons in Your Life*, shifted my whole paradigm.[41] It provided me with a new way to live as a White person pursuing racial equity and justice, and a new way to work with my White community. Helms's work became the foundation for the collaborations Shelly and I would pursue together.

Helm's model identifies six stages within White identity development. We offer a brief overview here as a preview, while chapters 3 through 12 provide a deep dive into what can happen while we navigate each of the stages and how we can support ourselves and others.

1. *Contact*: This is where most White people begin their journey, where we focus on colorblindness with no recognition of systemic racism. When the denial of racism in *Contact* cannot be sustained, we move on.
2. *Disintegration*: This is when we begin to recognize moral dilemmas associated with racism. The stress of wrestling with these dilemmas creates cognitive dissonance that must be resolved. We either begin to alleviate our inner tension by defending whiteness or we move toward antiracism. Our tendency lands us more solidly in one of two positions in *Reintegration*.
3. *Reintegration*: If we retreat into whiteness, we often blame racism on People of Color. Alternatively, if we emerge into antiracism and take the side of People of Color, we tend to tell ourselves we can't be racist because we support People of Color. Although both positions resolve the moral dilemmas of *Disintegration*, neither provides an emotionally healthy outlook.
4. *Pseudo-Independence*: If we land here, we typically have a false confidence in ourselves. This is where we tend to focus on helping or "saving" People of Color. If we delve into a deeper learning process

that includes self-reflection and begin to challenge our internalized racism, we shift.

5. *Immersion/Emersion*: Here, we seek out knowledge and experience to understand how racism functions individually and systemically. We *emerge* from this learning with a steadier belief in the possibility of a positive, antiracist White identity.

6. *Autonomy*: From here, we can skillfully take action to disrupt racism and build larger multiracial collectives working together to end racism.

The Dynamics of Racial Identity

Dr. Beverly Daniel Tatum's best-selling book, *Why Are All the Black Kids Sitting Together in the Cafeteria: And Other Conversations about Race*, introduced me, Shelly, to Helms's White identity model.[42] Like Christine, learning about this model changed my life. It helped me feel excited about the journey ahead and envision how I could feel good about myself while becoming increasingly antiracist. However, the language describing the process confused me.

Talking about the process as a six-part series of "stages" gives the impression that we follow a linear journey that ends when we arrive at *autonomy*, as though we are climbing a ladder. In reality, the experience is far more dynamic. At one time, Tatum described the process as a "spiral," explaining how people can revisit points on the journey from different perspectives over time.[43] Still, the spiral image does not reflect the way we shift in and out of the positions without necessarily following a clean line.

Both Tatum and Helms more recently used language suggesting that each position is like a "frame of mind" or a "lens."[44] In a *Teaching While White* podcast episode, Helms suggests these "lenses" are like a set of glasses we put on to view the world.[45] As we shift from position to position, we wear different lenses. Christine and I find this language helpful. And, we continued wondering how to illustrate the interplay between these "lenses" or positions.

The Roundabout

> *"Do any of these flowcharts capture it?" My colleague asks.*
>
> *"No. It's more dynamic than any of these." I try to explain why the images she offers to illustrate the identity process do not work. "We can*

*go in and out of the various positions. It's not so direct, and we never
stop at an end point." I sigh with frustration.*
"Two dimensions are failing us," she says.

Liz, an AWARE-LA colleague, and I met for lunch. We had already
struggled for months to come up with an image that could capture what
Christine and I have experienced over the years. This day, we reflected on
other analogies we find useful. For example, we both love the racial justice
freeway described in chapter 1 for the way it highlights the value of all
people working toward justice who use various strategies and tactics. This
includes the drivers in the slow lane who host and attend book clubs,
those in the middle lanes who join committees to press for change, and
organizers traveling in the carpool lane who coordinate campaigns.

Knowing the freeway analogy expresses our *external* actions—what
we do in the world to end racism—we searched for something to express
our *internal* experience and the dynamics related to the identity process.
Circular scribbles on a napkin finally took shape. The White identity process emerged as a complex, somewhat messy, roundabout.

A complex and messy roundabout illustrates what we experience on the
road to a positive, antiracist White identity. It describes the different positions or "frames of mind" we may use as we learn about race and racism.
Looking at this roundabout in totality, it has a center position and multiple
circular offshoots. Each of us exists somewhere along this crowded roundabout. We navigate around one another as we try to make our way, operating
with differing levels of awareness. Some of us are more erratic, while some
are more cautious. Each of us is our vehicle, and we are in constant motion.

At the center is *Autonomy*. The closer we get to this center position,
the more often we experience a positive, antiracist White identity and
operate from that frame of mind. This is where we want to be. A sense
of liberation exists here, a feeling of calm and a relatively smooth flow
of traffic. However, getting to this position is a challenge. There are no
consistent lanes in the area surrounding *Autonomy*, so it is something of
a free-for-all. People zigzag from one position to the next, with most of
us unable to merge quickly and safely because it takes a lot of knowledge
and skill to navigate the traffic. In light of this, we often spend most of our

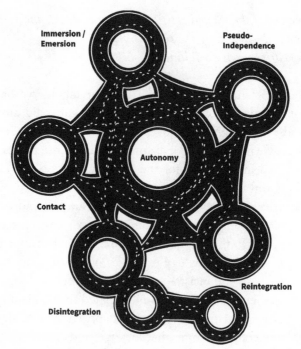

Figure 2.1 Identity Roundabout. ARTIST: LIZ WILTSIE

time sticking close to the outside edge, maneuvering from one offshoot to the next until we gain the awareness needed to proceed to the center.

The offshoots represent positions we typically experience on our journey: *Contact, Disintegration, Reintegration, Pseudo-Independence,* and *Immersion/Emersion.* Within each position is an inner loop. The inner loops represent what happens when we operate from a single position over an extended period of time. Our circling can last for days, weeks, or even years. There are no dead ends, however, and so changing course and heading back toward the main road is always possible.

Two offshoots involve more complex navigation than the others. *Disintegration* and *Reintegration* are high-stakes positions because each manifests in two directions—one that moves us into antiracism and another that takes us further into entrenched racism. Getting stuck in defending whiteness or entrenched racism is what we most want to avoid, both for ourselves and for others in our community.

Each of us travels a unique journey within this roundabout. Some of us may travel the entire roundabout, entering each of the offshoots in succession. We may gain the skill needed to successfully navigate the traffic and operate closest to *Autonomy* for an extended period. Others may skip an offshoot altogether. Typically, we move from here to there and back again. As we do this, the road and its various offshoots become more familiar. With attention and effort, we gain nuanced perspective and skill that makes it easier to get back to *Autonomy* after something disrupts our flow and causes us to veer off course.

The freeway and the roundabout analogies are not the same. The freeway focuses on outward, *external* action, while the roundabout focuses on *internal* identity development. Yet, a relationship between them exists. Our position on the roundabout influences whether we join the freeway or not. Someone in *Contact*, for example, has not joined the freeway and may never do so. If we move forward on the racial identity journey in a way that leads us onto the freeway, our position on the roundabout will affect how we drive on the freeway. The interaction between our internal sense of self and our outward action will clarify as we explore what happens for us within the roundabout.

The chapters to come explore each position within the roundabout. As you read, we hope you will begin to observe your own movements. The point is not to judge ourselves if we have been circling within a particular offshoot's inner loop. Instead, we want to become familiar with the different positions, what characterizes each one, and how each reflects the typical emotions and behaviors of White people. We can then use this awareness as a tool to help us interact with and influence the people we encounter. Helms cautions us, however, that we cannot force a change in someone else's identity journey.[46] Instead, we want to act as models, demonstrating what is possible and supporting people to gain the awareness necessary to operate from a positive, antiracist White identity.

Navigating the Journey

Neither the racist far right or the majority of antiracists craft messages with the White identity model in mind. And yet, certain messages happen to align or misalign with the concerns we face at particular positions on the roundabout. This makes the messages more or less effective with people operating from those positions. For example, messages that provoke White people's fear of being rejected are felt particularly acutely when we are in *Reintegration*. Depending on how we are navigating that position, we may fear losing our White friends or disappointing People of Color.

With this in mind, the chapters ahead explore messages that compete to explain race and racism as well as suggest approaches you can use to meet people where they are as they navigate those messages. We offer approaches that we have found most helpful, fully aware that they are not the only ones that may work. In a broad way, these chapters help us make sense of what we encounter and experience at the various positions on the roundabout. Each chapter includes the following:

- *An Overview*: A brief summary of what the position typically entails, including the issues White people generally grapple with while operating from that position.
- *Far-Right Messages*: Examples of far-right messages that can resonate strongly with White people in that position, and the reasons why. We also offer approaches to support someone navigating that position. Please note that the approaches are guidelines and not absolutes.
- *Antiracist Messages*: Examples of antiracist messages that are often ineffective with White people in that position, and the reasons why. We also offer approaches to support someone navigating that position.
- *Reflection*: Two types of reflection questions include:
  - *Thinking of Yourself*: What is your personal experience with the position and messages explored?
  - *Thinking of Others*: How might the messages affect the White people around you?

The appendix offers a chapter-by-chapter reference table listing the various positions, dilemmas, messages, and suggested approaches.

Journeying with Characters

We recognize that the roundabout and its various offshoots may seem complicated at first. This is why we invite you to get to know four characters. We will journey with them as we explore each position.

Meet Ryan

Ryan is a 17-year-old White, male, high school senior who uses he/him pronouns. He loves watching sports more than playing them and is interested in a career in music. He spends a lot of time on the internet, watching livestreamed videos and scrolling for content to share with friends. The mid-sized city where Ryan lives is about 85 percent White. The high school he attends reflects the city's population. Ryan is a solid student, takes honors classes, and mostly hangs out with White peers, with the exception of Jazz Band, a club where he is forming relationships with some Black students. He attends a Christian church with his family most Sundays.

Meet Tyler

Tyler is a 20-year-old White, male, college sophomore who uses he/him pronouns. He attends a large, predominantly White state school and lives in an off-campus apartment with a group of White, male friends. He is majoring in communications and is considering advertising as a potential future career, although he recently became interested in law after taking a political science course. Tyler grew up and lives in a White suburban area adjacent to a large, diverse city. He attended a Christian church throughout his childhood. He has a childhood friend, Dani, who is Mexican American. They have a shared interest in comedy.

Meet Madison

Madison is a 31-year-old White, female, part-time graduate student who uses she/her pronouns. She works for a local not-for-profit community center. Her job involves working closely with a racially diverse staff with whom she has become friendly. Over the past few years, Madison has become increasingly aware of how racism negatively affects People of Color.

Madison's graduate school courses and her conversations with co-workers of color challenge her to reflect on her whiteness. She feels responsible for challenging other White people to reflect on their whiteness and address racism. She does this primarily through posting on social media and engaging with people online.

Meet Alexis (Alex)

Alex is a 45-year-old, White, female, veteran high school humanities teacher who uses she/her pronouns. She has significant experience with issues related to diversity, equity, and inclusion. She has spent many years working in racially diverse areas where she often discussed race with people from a wide range of racial backgrounds. Alex is open and comfortable in these conversations.

Alex loves teaching history and literature through a lens of critical inquiry, hoping to inspire students to think deeply about the past and how it informs the present. A particular focus for her is how people make sense of their world and how that affects their decision-making. After years spent learning about social justice issues through activism and joining a group of White, antiracist people that regularly talk about race, Alex is committed to helping other White people develop an antiracist practice.

SELF-REFLECTION ALONG THE WAY

In our experience, Helms's and Tatum's work has been liberating, helping us reduce the fear, anxiety, and confusion we initially experienced on this journey. We hope their work, as extended through this book, will benefit you as well.

To make the most of the experience, we invite you to pause to reflect, perhaps journal or engage in other forms of self-reflection (drawing, meditation, conversation, etc.) along the way. A few important questions to consider include:

- What feelings or thoughts arose for you as you have read so far? Try to identify what prompts those feelings or thoughts.
- Do you already feel turned off by these first two chapters? If so, take note of your feelings without judgment.

3

Encountering the Other

Contact

Click. Click. My White family members lock the doors to the car as we wait for my uncle. "This is not a good neighborhood."

The only difference I see between this neighborhood and my family's is the Black people walking around. I, Christine, am in Contact.

Most White people begin the racial identity journey in Contact, which is characterized by a White person's belief in racial innocence and race neutrality. From this position, when we encounter issues of race personally or through media, the idea that we are colorblind preserves our sense that we exist outside of race. At the same time, we may be curious about and/or slightly fearful of People of Color.

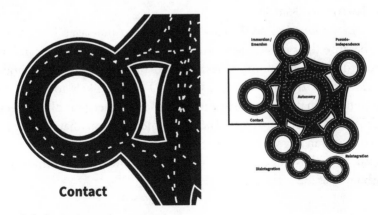

Figure 3.1 *Contact.* ARTIST: LIZ WILTSIE

When we meet Ryan and Tyler, they are operating from a *Contact* frame of mind. Neither believes being White is meaningful. As well-intentioned people, they try to be colorblind to ensure that they are not racist. Although both Ryan and Tyler have had some friendships with People of Color, they tend to think about race only when friends or peers of color bring it up. Even then, they typically brush off comments they hear from People of Color about race, believing race does not matter.

Because of the media Ryan and Tyler consume, their internalized views about some groups of people, particularly Black people, are somewhat negative, albeit unconscious. The overall societal messages they have ingested portray Black people from urban areas as scary. Their internalized negative view is particularly focused on those who do not conform to society's expectations and are angry at White society. Ryan and Tyler are critical because their life experiences and their families' Christian worldviews reinforce the idea that people who make good choices succeed and are rewarded. They believe people who do not succeed have made poor choices, have not tried hard enough, or are being punished for their sinfulness.

> *Dear Reader*: Do not be surprised if you find that you believe some of the messages advanced by the far right and shrink away from those offered by antiracists. This is common. Try to avoid self-judgment.

FAR-RIGHT MESSAGES

People in *Contact* are particularly vulnerable to messages from the far right because their messaging aligns with an individualistic lens and narrative grounded in colorblindness, a kind of "commonsense," unquestioned racism.[47] In other words, Ryan and Tyler are likely to feel swayed by arguments that offer easy-to-understand rationales that blame People of Color for racial disparities. These arguments claim that focusing on race or racism in any way, but especially to explain racial inequities, is racist itself. The following two examples highlight how entreaties that rely on colorblindness are often successful.

Message: Being Colorblind Is American[48]

The far right is not colorblind. However, they use the idea of race blindness to convince people to uphold the racial status quo by claiming that simply paying attention to race is racist. They attempt to prove their point by celebrating and amplifying the voices of People of Color who agree with them and who argue against the existence of systemic racism.

One day scrolling online, Ryan lands on a video that shows a White conservative commentator giving advice to a Black man who says he does not want to be seen as a victim. The commentator tells the man to insist that people see him as an individual because "everyone wants to be treated as more than their skin color." This leads Ryan to another video of the same commentator claiming that capitalism is colorblind.

Intrigued by the content, he follows the commentator on social media. This leads him to a website that emphasizes the value of colorblindness as framed by Dr. King's words: "I have a dream that my four little children will one day live in a nation where they will not be judged by the color of their skin but by the content of their character." The site argues that people who focus on race are the real racists dividing America today.

Ryan's belief that colorblindness prevents racism aligns with other messages on the site claiming that systemic racism is not real. So the assertion that individual effort determines a person's success feels right to him. Ryan believes it is possible that people focused on race are trying to make excuses for sinful People of Color who cannot succeed on their own.

- How have these messages about colorblindness and individual success influenced you over the years?
- What could help Ryan make sense of a video of a Black person arguing for colorblindness?

Cultivate Curiosity

Questions are an essential tool of engagement. They help us build relationships as well as allow us time to slow down, deal with our emotions, and think about if and how to respond strategically. Our curiosity allows us to learn more and to tailor our responses, when appropriate, to engage further.

Alex, the teacher with extensive experience discussing race, would avoid immediately countering Ryan's views. That would be the best way to shut him down. Instead, she would pose questions to find out more about him and how his beliefs developed. This would help her make a connection and find a path into a deeper discussion. Alex might ask the following:

- What in Ryan's life reinforces the idea that race doesn't matter in people's lives?
- What attracts him to the people and groups he follows online?
- How does his religious upbringing affect how he interprets what happens to people?

Hearing how he responds to those questions, Alex can explore the following:

- What does colorblindness mean to Ryan?
- Why does he think it is a good approach?
- Does he ever feel conflicted about it?

Alex would seek to understand Ryan's perspective and the emotions he has attached to this ideal before offering an alternative perspective.

Offer Perspective about People of Color and Colorblindness

Alex can also engage Ryan in discussion about how people within all racial groups hold different points of view. Just like all White people do not believe the same thing, People of Color also have different perspectives.

- What does it mean for Ryan to hear People of Color arguing for or against colorblindness?
- Does he take People of Color arguing against colorblindness as seriously? Why or why not?
- What does it mean if we believe a small minority of People of Color advocating for colorblindness and dismiss the views of thousands of other People of Color? What makes some People of Color more believable or trustworthy than others?

- What if the problem named by the majority of People of Color is real? How might the colorblind view limit our ability to recognize it?

Alex would avoid overwhelming Ryan with conceptual information about systemic racism. That can come later. First, it is important to help Ryan foster his understanding of racism as widespread and real for a significant majority of People of Color.

Offer Perspective on Other Forms of Oppression
Alex could also engage in a conversation about a form of oppression other than racism. She might ask Ryan if there is an experience of marginalization he or his loved ones experience. Perhaps his uncle uses a wheelchair and feels particularly disadvantaged by how people and society treat him. If Ryan is able to acknowledge the systemic ways injustice exists for one group, he may be more open to how systemic dynamics impact People of Color.

Message: Join the Fight to Protect the Innocent
According to the far right, the nation must protect its children from a liberal school system that indoctrinates its students in an effort to prioritize "minorities" and make White people feel guilty. This is often combined with false claims that schools are trying to influence kids to become LGBTQIA+.

As a young person who feels comfortable almost anywhere and views himself a critical thinker, Tyler likes to explore provocative ideas. One day, he walks past a booth in the campus center and sees a flyer that says, "Protect Children from Indoctrination." Tyler stops to hear more. The speaker, a student from the Republican Club, expresses concern about how "radical liberals" influence education from grades K–12 through college. Curious, Tyler listens.

The club leader rails against "race-based ideologies," everything from critical race theory and whiteness studies to *The 1619 Project*, and how these curricular approaches hurt White children because it shames them and calls them racist.[49] Tyler recalls feeling uncomfortable when his history classes covered slavery, the taking of Indigenous people's lands, abuses of the Chinese during the Gold Rush, Japanese American intern-ment, and the Jim Crow era. Yet, Tyler never felt personally connected to any of that. Tyler views these as past issues that no longer affect today's generation. He certainly does not want White kids to feel like racists for these historical events. Tyler thinks, "If that's what teachers are doing, that's not right."

Without a deep, more complex understanding of how race and racism function in the United States and why, Tyler is enticed by the speaker's invitation to attend a meeting that weekend, where they will coordinate actions against a local district's equity program.

- What experience do you have with the claim that liberal teachers are trying to indoctrinate students?
- What would you say to Tyler if you had the chance to speak with him?

Build Relationship

Alex can express curiosity about Tyler and his thinking in order to build trust. Some questions to ask include:

- What do you think indoctrination is?
- How do your Christian values affect how afraid you are of kids being indoctrinated?
- What made you feel uncomfortable in your history class? Why?
- What concerns you about how history is taught?

As Alex listens to Tyler, rather than arguing with him, trust can grow.

Engage Critical Thinking

Having built some trust with Tyler, Alex can lean into Tyler's sense of himself as a critical thinker. She can offer other ways to view race-based ideologies and the history behind them. For example, they could look at *The 1619 Project* to explore how it adds to the scholarship on enslavement in US history. They can explore models of indoctrination, such as that in Communist China, and ask whether these models truly apply in this situation.

ANTIRACIST MESSAGES

Much of the antiracist messaging on social media highlighting systemic racism makes little sense to White people in *Contact* because of their belief that bigotry is an individual's problem. Complicating the situation is that when we operate from the middle positions of racial identity (such as *Reintegration*, *Pseudo-Independence*, and *Immersion/Emersion*) and criticize what we perceive as racist, we tend to offer rigid and harsh messages devoid of context and empathy. This often repels people in *Contact*.

Message: Being Colorblind Is Racist

In the book *Racism without Racists: Colorblind Ideology and the Persistence of Racial Inequality in America*, sociologist Eduardo Bonilla-Silva explains how colorblindness justifies racial injustices. The idea is that people and institutions use language that prevents racism from being a possible explanation for racial inequities. Yet, by paying no attention to racism, it allows racism to continue uninterrupted.[50] Many antiracists familiar with this dynamic find it important to disrupt the colorblindness narrative.

Ryan encounters this as he follows more people who highlight the value of colorblindness and the dangers of "racial consciousness." He comes across responses by Madison, who has been busy attacking colorblindness as ignorant and racist. Quoting Bonilla-Silva without context, Madison's language comes across as aggressive and smug to Ryan.

Madison's posts also offer no alternatives to the individualistically oriented arguments he's recently read to explain racial inequities. Unfortunately, the only message Ryan takes from Madison is that antiracism is judgmental and divisive. This strengthens Ryan's position that race should not matter and people who focus on race are the problem.

- What messages have you received about what it means to be racist, not racist, and antiracist?
- How could you explain the value of race consciousness to Ryan without belittling his appreciation for colorblindness?

Educate Yourself

For some people in *Contact*, learning a more complicated version of US history may help the person understand the ongoing significance of race and racism. Before doing this, however, Alex should consider: What is missing from her own education? What more does she need to know? Alex can then guide Ryan toward resources to fill in common gaps without being overwhelming. The goal is to reinspire Ryan's curiosity.

Offering to learn together provides a way to explore the impact of historical injustices without acting as the expert. It allows us to learn and build relationships at the same time. Together, we can explore how learning more about Indian boarding schools, the internment of Japanese Americans during World War II, and the forced deportation of Mexican Americans help us to understand racism today.

Offer Perspective

Once Alex engages with Ryan and hears his perspective, she can share some stories, tailoring them to fit the moment. For example, she can share her own experience of realizing that colorblindness didn't work the way she thought it did. She can share the story about how her belief in colorblindness prevented her from seeing the racism her Chinese American friend experienced at school. Alex's insistence that race didn't matter in the face of the racism her friend experienced damaged their friendship.

One resource to offer Ryan is *The Other Wes Moore: One Name, Two Fates*. The book tells the tale of two Black men named Wes Moore and the ways their lives turned out differently from one another.[51] This story may seem too focused on the individual for those operating from later identity positions because it does not address systemic racism. However, for people in *Contact*, this kind of resource explains how race can make a difference in a person's life. This lays the groundwork for the later, more complex work of learning about systemic racism.

One thing Alex has learned over time is that when people are in the early stages of their learning, it's best to avoid suggesting denser texts found on many antiracist reading lists, such as *The History of White People* by Nell Irwin Painter.[52] This is an excellent resource, but the extent of its evidence contradicting colorblindness can feel overwhelming and lead to the person rejecting the information altogether.

Keep in mind that Ryan and Tyler swim in the common narrative of American idealism. If Alex focuses solely on all the racism that People of Color have faced as a way to get Ryan or Tyler to admit the reality of racism, she will not undermine the stereotypes that a colorblind attitude lets fester. Instead, she might unwittingly reinforce some of the far-right messages about "victimhood." This can happen because Ryan or Tyler can look at all the historic wrongs, such as slavery and genocide, and conclude that the healthiest thing to do is move past the long-ago trauma and just stop talking about it.

That said, filling in the gaps so that Ryan or Tyler can understand that today's racism is alive and well and connected to history is necessary. It is important to balance the hard history with education about the resilience, resistance, and agency of People of Color in the face of racism. Narratives about People of Color's achievements undercut the far right's messages of sinful, lazy People of Color mired in victimhood who are blameworthy for their position.

Message: Of Course, You Are White and Racist

People learning about racism often have "a-ha" moments that open them to an entirely new way of interpreting the world. This can lead people to notice racism everywhere they look and, as a result, believe that all White people enact racism, whether overtly or subtly. This results in many newly active antiracist people delivering the message: "Of course, you are White and racist."

After attending the meeting to plan a rally against "race-based ideologies" in schools, Tyler shares information about the upcoming event on social media. The response from people he hardly knows is swift and damning. A number of people call the Republican Club racist for promoting the rally. Tyler is confused because his experience at the planning meeting was positive. Although it was predominantly White, a few People of Color were there too, so he does not understand what the problem is. When Tyler counters by saying that it's racist to judge all White people, even more people attack his position, calling him the real racist. Tyler is offended and cannot make sense of the accusations.

- When have you felt offended by messages that equate being White with being racist?
- How would you help Tyler understand the situation?

Cultivate Curiosity

First, Alex would take the conversation with Tyler off the thread to avoid undermining the voices of the People of Color who have already responded. Then, in addition to asking Tyler about how his beliefs formed, Alex might also ask what Tyler believes racism to be. She can ask about his personal experience with racism and listen for an opening for her to share personally as well.

This is particularly important because Tyler may be stinging from the negative experiences online. Giving him a chance to share the impact of being shut down and validating his positive intent is important groundwork, setting the stage for Alex to share contrasting, expanding stories as their conversations continue.

Offer Perspective

To help Tyler consider why people suggest that White people as a group are racist (without him becoming defensive), Alex can offer personal stories. What moments surprised Alex while she was learning about the breadth and depth of her own internalized racism? When did it happen? What happened? How did it feel? How did Alex come to accept the reality of it?

Alex can share her own experience with racist jokes, either as the sharer or the listener. She can explain how she rationalized the behavior by arguing that "it's not that big of a deal" and "Black people joke like this." Then, she can explain that these rationalizations no longer made sense once she understood the impact of the joking. These kinds of confessional stories, when told authentically and with empathy for oneself, are powerful and tend not to trigger defensiveness because they are not accusatory.

Embrace Both/And Thinking

Stories are particularly effective when they demonstrate how to use *both/and thinking* and provide a healthy model of what it looks like to learn about and disrupt racism within oneself. For example, Alex can talk about being *both* a good person *and* having participated in racist joking, which is not okay. She can then talk about how good it feels to stand in more integrity now that telling racist jokes is off the table. Sharing examples that illustrate how a shift in understanding and behavior results in a positive sense of self reduces the chance of triggering shame, which leads people to dismiss important ideas.

Message: You're Ignorant

Judgmental messages, such as "you're ignorant," push people in *Contact* further away from antiracism rather than drawing them in.

Both Ryan and Tyler feel hurt by the antagonism they feel coming from antiracists online, and they respond with variations of "I don't see race" to defend themselves. For example, Madison responds to one of Ryan's posts, calling out the colorblind approach as allowing racism to continue. She adds, "Such ignorance. You have no idea what you're talking about. You want to learn about racism? Google it!" After this exchange, Ryan does not become more receptive or curious. He feels defensive, shamed, and mistreated.

Unfortunately, leaving people to "google it" too often leads White people to far-right propaganda, which deepens their miseducation. Consider Dylann Roof, the white supremacist who murdered nine African Americans in the 2015 Charleston church massacre. The previous year, during the trial of George Zimmerman after the killing of Trayvon Martin, Roof googled "Black on White crime." Those results escalated his fall into active white supremacy and violence.[53]

White people in *Contact* do not have enough knowledge to assess the accuracy of information on their own. Because of this, they can easily accept messages that reaffirm stereotypes and racism already infused throughout society. When they make a misstep, reactively charging them with racism rather than supporting their understanding can turn them off from antiracism altogether.

- When have you received or delivered condemning antiracist messages? What happened?
- Whom do you feel most aligned with so far—Ryan, Tyler, Madison, or Alex?

Offer Perspective

Many antiracist people forget or distance themselves from the details of their own racial identity journey—the aches, the pains, the defensive moments, the arguments, and the refusals. For this reason, many people operating at the middle positions of identity development, as illustrated by Madison, lash out at those who operate in the early positions.

Antiracists with a more developed positive antiracist identity, like Alex, reflect on the difficulty they had in unlearning racism and can support others in the process. Doing this involves providing people like Ryan and Tyler with opportunities to learn about the realities of other racial groups, rather than relying solely on one-dimensional depictions. If time and the relationship allow, it can be helpful to open new ways for people in Ryan or Tyler's position to experience other racial groups. For example, attending cultural events or joining arts or sporting activities that cultivate a sense of teamwork can be useful.

Build Relationship

In Bryan Stevenson's book, *Just Mercy*, he calls us to "get proximate" to those we do not know.[54] For people in *Contact*, engaging with People of Color is a way to learn through direct interactions. Ryan and Tyler need more experiences with people who have different lived experiences, people who disprove the claims of the far right.

A first step in this direction is reading *Just Mercy*. The book provides an important education on its own. A second step may be Alex helping Ryan or Tyler to locate opportunities to get proximate to others. A challenge is that simply pointing a finger in a particular direction and saying "there they are, go get proximate" is not good advice. Unsupported experiences with proximity can result in reaffirming racial stereotypes and preconceived judgment. For example, a White teacher in *Contact* may proclaim that Black people don't care about education because he worked in an all-Black school and knows from experience.

A lens foggy with racism leads to inaccurate interpretations. Because White people coming to racist conclusions ultimately harms People of Color, proximity requires community support. If Alex recommends that Ryan or Tyler hang out at a venue populated by mostly Black people without more guidance, they might witness behavior that becomes their evidence that "those people" are problematic. To avoid this, Alex can support their understanding of cultural differences. A strong relationship would allow her to provide feedback as they process their experiences in proximity.

REFLECTION

Dear Reader: You've made it to the end of this chapter. We appreciate your engagement in these scenarios. Before you go, we ask you to consider at least two of these questions, perhaps while journaling or engaging in another form of self-reflection.

Thinking of Yourself:
- What feels familiar to you about the *Contact* position?
- Do any particular moments stand out?
- When have you used or experienced messaging described in this chapter? What happened?

Thinking of Others:
- Who in your life might operate from a *Contact* frame of mind?
- How do you recognize far-right or antiracist messages affecting people in your life?
- What do you need to practice to be able to ask questions of people in the *Contact* position?
- How might religious beliefs related to sinfulness inform a person's understanding of race and racial disparities? How might that affect how you engage with them?

SUMMARY OF ENCOUNTERING THE OTHER: *CONTACT*

In *Contact*, we feel neutral, colorblind, like race does not affect us in any way. We may feel curious or fearful about People of Color, but do not give it much thought.		
Far-right messages we are susceptible to in this position: • Being Colorblind Is American • Join the Fight to Protect the Innocent	Antiracist messages that are harmful in this position: • Being Colorblind Is Racist • Of Course, You Are White and Racist • You're Ignorant	Suggested approaches: • Ask three to five questions before offering your own ideas • Share personal stories that offer different perspectives • Share stories of People of Color to expand awareness

4

Moral Dilemmas

Disintegration

Sitting on a bench outside the boys' locker room, the high school senior and I talk for the first time. He and I are the only two sprinters on our track and field team headed to the state meet, the only two still training after school every day.

"It's not the same for me at this school. Do you know how hard it is to be one of just a few Black people here?" he asks. I shake my head. I have no idea.

For the first time, someone I know talks of being ill-treated because of race. I feel sad for him and disappointed about how he thinks of the school. I, Shelly, am torn between a sense of self-satisfaction that he is sharing his story with me and a strong desire to dismiss what he says as exaggerated. The inner tug does not feel good. I am in Disintegration.

The primary feature of *Disintegration* is internal conflict. According to Helms's model, White people enter this position when they encounter a set of moral dilemmas, a set of conflicting beliefs that provoke the stress called cognitive dissonance. White people do not necessarily experience every one of the moral dilemmas during their first major pass through this position. However, each of the dilemmas tends to arise eventually. This chapter focuses specifically on the either/or nature of the dilemmas—how there is a sense that only one of the conflicting ideas can be right—and what it can look and feel like to wrestle with this. Chapters 5 and 6 then explore how these dilemmas can cause us to move in two

 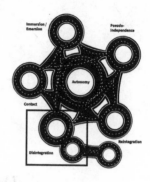

Figure 4.1 Disintegration. ARTIST: LIZ WILTSIE

directions: a *disengaging* that seeks to normalize whiteness, and/or an *engaging* that moves us toward antiracism.

Ryan and Tyler enter *Disintegration* as they each experience disrupting events that cause them to consider that race may play a larger role in people's lives than they thought, and they begin to question their assumptions about how the world works. Some describe this experience as "the rug being ripped out from under them," because of the way it launches people into a sense of emotional turmoil.

We invite you to make connections while reading about Ryan and Tyler's experiences. When have you experienced or witnessed these dilemmas? How do you relate to their stress points? How did your experience differ? How has your spiritual or religious worldview informed your experience?

While every racialized interaction can influence a person's life to some degree, the lessons White people take from their experiences in this position may be particularly consequential in setting them on a track to engage with or disengage from antiracism. As you read about Ryan and Tyler's experiences, consider how significant and useful it would be to have a supportive person to provide guidance.

RYAN ENCOUNTERS MORAL DILEMMAS

To fulfill a senior year service requirement, Ryan volunteers to give music lessons for an after-school youth program located at an elementary school in a neighborhood with a majority Black, Hispanic/Latinx, and Hmong population. Although Ryan continues to enjoy live videostreams and podcasts uplifting the colorblindness ideal, he cannot help noticing inequities for People of Color. Stark is the contrast between the well-resourced schools Ryan has always attended and the disrepair evident at the elementary school he visits. Over several months, engaging with students and parents weekly, Ryan has come to enjoy working with the kids. Two students have captured Ryan's heart, Davon (Black) and Kaj (Hmong).

Colorblindness Dilemma

Ryan's belief in colorblindness comes into question while hanging out with some White friends. After Ryan shares a story about his music lesson with Kaj, a couple friends start to make fun of Kaj, holding their fingers slanted against their eyes while laughing about Hmong kids not being able to read the music. Ryan likes these friends, so the racist comments surprise him. Or is he just thinking differently now? Doesn't colorblindness mean people wouldn't joke about race? Ryan is upset and not sure what to do.

Ryan hits a bump in his relationship to colorblindness again in his history class. To help understand segregation within cities and suburbs, his teacher shows a video about the links between housing covenants, violence, redlining, and the New Deal. He learns that the vast majority of People of Color were forced into segregated areas with fewer resources by discriminatory laws and policies. Ryan has always believed that people just chose to live where they wanted—that it was only a matter of preference and that race had nothing to do with it. Ryan now feels conflicted and isn't sure what to believe.

The colorblindness moral dilemma arises when White people who hold a strong belief in colorblindness face evidence that race does matter and results in the inequitable treatment of People of Color.

- What is your relationship to colorblindness? When did you realize that race matters?

Love and Compassion Dilemma

Over time, Ryan learns more about Davon and hears a particularly upsetting story about Davon's uncle when the police mistook him for a suspect in a robbery. Davon witnessed several officers aggressively arresting his uncle, ignoring the uncle's claims of innocence. It took over a day for him to be released, without apology, once they caught the actual perpetrator. The uncle came home with multiple bruises and lacerations. Davon's fear and confusion hits Ryan hard and activates his compassion for Davon and his family.

Ryan has always experienced his church as a place of love and compassion. There is a big emphasis on helping the less fortunate; in fact, that philosophy helped Ryan choose his service hours at the elementary school. One Sunday, a White guest pastor preaches that antiracism is part of a secular, anti-Christian movement that is leading the country away from God. This message seems to make some sense because race shouldn't matter, but Ryan still feels like something isn't quite right.

As the congregation shares coffee afterward, Ryan overhears a conversation between two White neighbors about a recently released video showing a White police officer punching a Black man. The men say terrible things about the Black man getting what he deserves. Their lack of compassion sticks with Ryan hours after church has ended, and he can't help but wonder what they would say about Davon's uncle.

The love and compassion moral dilemma catches people when they experience a strong lack of care for People of Color from White people who otherwise claim to be loving and empathetic.

- When have you witnessed a lack of love and compassion for People of Color by other White people?

Inaction Dilemma

As Ryan's sensitivity heightens, he feels bad for not interrupting people who say racist things. Ryan has long heard some White classmates using the "n-word" in the cafeteria when students of color are present. Ryan knows a few Black students through Jazz Band and finds out that some Black students went to the administration about the use of the word.

Unfortunately, the Dean's office believes the White students' denials, so no consequences are issued. Even hearing his Black friends' anger and disappointment, Ryan does not offer support. The situation leaves Ryan feeling a twinge of guilt, although he wonders why no other White students spoke up either.

The inaction dilemma raises confusing feelings of guilt and shame for not taking action in the face of racism.

- What is your experience with feeling conflicted about failing to take action against racism?

TYLER ENCOUNTERS MORAL DILEMMAS

Tyler prides himself on his intellect and engaging with people having different beliefs and experiences. As Tyler engages more on issues of race and racism, with which he has not had much personal experience, he struggles with some of the pushback he has been receiving. After the backlash against him promoting the rally about liberal indoctrination, Tyler continues his relationship with some of the guys from the Republican Club on campus. Through conversations with club members and some of the free speech advocates he has begun to follow online, Tyler's interest in free speech deepens, especially in the world of comedy, which he loves.

Morality and Equality Dilemma

One day, Tyler meets up with his longtime friend Dani, who is Mexican American. Because they both belonged to the Improv Troupe in high school, they often share and watch videos with one another. At this get-together, Tyler shares his frustration that political correctness is shutting down free speech in comedy. As an example, Tyler shows Dani a clip that has been getting a lot of attacks. In it, the comedian jokes about the ways to not get shot by the police, making fun of many high-profile killings of Black men by the police. Dani does not find it funny.

In response, Dani asks Tyler if he's ever noticed how differently White men with guns are treated than men of color. She asks him about the difference in police preparation and response to the Black Lives Matter movement over the summer of 2020, which was intense and militarized, compared to the police preparation and response to the insurrectionists who attacked the Capitol in January 2021.

Tyler is surprised by Dani's seriousness and caught off guard by her example. Tyler believes strongly in the American ideal of equality and struggles not to dismiss Dani altogether. Uncomfortable, he changes the subject.

In the morality and equality dilemma, White people find their deeply held belief that the United States is a moral country that values equality challenged by evidence of inequality for People of Color and a lack of morality in caring about that mistreatment.

- What is your personal experience with the morality and equality dilemma?

Freedom and Democracy Dilemma

Tyler and Dani are on a text thread of friends in which someone shares a clip in which the comedian jokes about the efforts to replace the term "illegal aliens" with "undocumented immigrants." Tyler responds with a "ha-ha." Later, in person, Dani asks Tyler why he thought it was so funny. Tyler focuses on the jokes and how people who break the law deserve to be made fun of.

Dani shares that she has recently gotten very involved with an immigrants' rights group. Tyler is surprised and asks Dani why her interest in this never came up before. She shares that Tyler has not seemed to appreciate how her experience as a Mexican American is different from his. She expresses fear about being honest with him but decides to take the risk because of their years of friendship. Dani is undocumented; her parents brought her to the United States when she was two years old. This unleashes a painful conversation between the two where Tyler hears about the negative impacts of US immigration policy on Dani's life and her lack of freedom to pursue citizenship and college.

While Tyler struggles to understand the life restrictions Dani is experiencing, he continues to hang out with his White roommates, who believe strongly in US exceptionalism. At a party with this group, a partygoer mentions that she had spent the day registering voters. Tyler's friends recognize the neighborhood as a Latino neighborhood and begin to make jokes about registering "illegals" and using other racist slurs for Latinx people. One person goes as far as to say, "you will not replace us" and throws a Nazi salute to rounds of laughter. Tyler smiles uncomfortably but does not laugh, as Dani's situation is in the back of his mind.

In the freedom and democracy dilemma, White people who believe that freedom and democracy are fundamental to the United States begin to recognize current injustices for People of Color and/or learn about systemic racism in history.

- When have you questioned the US commitment to "freedom for all" and its democratic principles in relationship to race?

> *Dear Reader*: We invite you to pause and recognize that grappling with these dilemmas is an important part of our journey. Experiencing confusion is normal. Our internal struggle often leads to pivotal moments that help us learn more about ourselves, the world, and what we hold dear. When we keep an open mind, these moments help us become our better selves.

Individualism Dilemma

During a lunch with some of Tyler's conservative White friends, a conversation erupts about a White professor who asked the class what it means to be White. They mocked the question and emphasized, "I'm not White. I'm just me." They complained about the professor's identity politics and how she reduces everyone to their race rather than seeing them as individuals. As a person who values his individuality, Tyler can see their points and doesn't agree with the professor's approach.

Curiously, as the topic turns to the experience of Black students on campus, which was also discussed during the class on identity, Tyler notices that his friends immediately start saying, "if these Black kids want to succeed, they need to work harder and take education more seriously." On one hand, Tyler agrees with them. Messages about Black people being lazy fits with what he has heard over the years. On the other hand, in the back of his mind, he remembers Dani making a point about how often communities of color are only referred to as groups, not as individuals. He feels drawn to dismissing her comment, but isn't sure.

The individualism dilemma catches White people who believe that they should be viewed as individuals and judged on their own merit, but start to see that People of Color are often viewed and judged as a group.

- How does individualism impact how you think about yourself compared to how you think about communities of color?

REFLECTION

Dear Reader: We appreciate you engaging with these important moral dilemmas. Before you go, we invite you to consider at least two of these questions, perhaps while journaling or engaging in another form of self-reflection.

Thinking of Yourself:
- How have you wrestled with any of the dilemmas? What happened? How did you feel at the time? How do you feel now?
- What helped you gain insight into the dilemmas you faced?
- What pushed you away from antiracism?
- What pulled you toward antiracism?

Thinking of Others:
- Who in your life might be actively grappling with the moral dilemmas described in this chapter?
- What are your typical responses to people caught in these dilemmas? Do you feel superior because you know more than they do? Scorn at their "ignorance"? Empathy for their struggle?
- How might a person's spiritual or religious worldview affect how they experience the dilemmas?
- What personal stories might you share with others who are confronting these dilemmas?

Summary of the Moral Dilemmas: *Disintegration*

When we encounter racism, we confront moral dilemmas that move us into *Disintegration*. We question the accuracy of our vision of the world and how it works.

Key Dilemmas:

- *Colorblindness*—Does race make a difference in people's lives?

- *Love and Compassion for All*—Why is care not extended to people equally?

- *Inaction in the Face of Racism*—How does not acting against racism cause it to continue?

- *Moral and Equal Treatment for All*—Why are some people treated badly because of their race?

- *Freedom and Democracy for All within an Equitable Democracy*—Are US policies really designed to support everyone?

- *Individualism*—Are all people actually treated based on their individual merit?

Defending Whiteness

Disintegration

"I would not teach Heart of Darkness *with its damaging portrayals of Black people to my students," my White practicum teacher proclaims.*

"But it's an exceptional piece of literature. We can't not read it just because it deals with hard issues!" I respond.

I feel caught—I don't want to hurt Black students and I don't want to give up my great White authors. I, Christine, am in Disinte- gration, *defending whiteness.*

According to Helms's model, the moral dilemmas encountered while in *Disintegration* create inflexible either/or binaries that require people to choose a side. This leads us to either disengage from our concerns over racism and defend whiteness or engage further and turn toward antira- cism. The choosing of a side occurs cumulatively as we resolve uncomfort- able feelings by interpreting various situations in a way that offers a sense of clarity, reducing our inner tension.

If we use White norms to interpret events and justify the status quo, we no longer feel the need to talk about race. This allows us to return to a sense of internal calm and assurance that the world still works as previously understood. Whether occurring consciously or unconsciously, disengaging and adopting the interpretation most comfortable for White people results in a defense of whiteness.

How will Ryan and Tyler resolve their cognitive dissonance? One way is to refute the evidence of racism so that the dilemma goes away. If there is no racism, there is no dilemma. For example, Ryan can pass

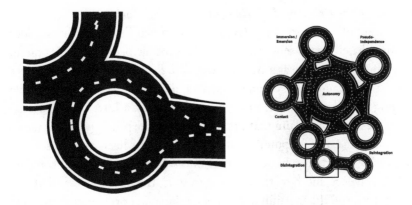

Figure 5.1 Disintegration: Defending Whiteness. ARTIST: LIZ WILTSIE

off his friends' mocking of Asian eye shape as a harmless joke. Tyler can decide that Dani's circumstances and the experiences of Dani's family are due to them breaking the law. Ryan and Tyler might deepen their attachment to meritocracy and individualism, deciding that only personal choice explains racial disparities.

If their questioning persists, another option is to avoid situations that raise issues of race altogether. Ryan may experience a natural end to the dissonance once he completes the required service hours in the after-school program. Tyler might spend even less time with Dani. Disengaging from interracial situations and media that presents information about race and racism allows the dilemmas to disappear. Separating themselves from upsetting racial information, Ryan and Tyler would be primed to move toward more active racism.

In this chapter, we look at messages that are likely to push people like Ryan and Tyler toward disengaging, allowing them to normalize or defend whiteness. We also look at some approaches that might prevent them from moving in this direction.

FAR-RIGHT MESSAGES

People in *Disintegration* with a tendency to withdraw and/or defend whiteness are particularly susceptible to messages from the far right. The following four examples explore how the appeals work with people in this position.

Message: White Privilege Isn't Real, but It Is Real Racist

The concept of white privilege, developed by scholar Peggy McIntosh, does not immediately make sense to most White people because it relies on an understanding of racism as a system—a system that the far right claims does not exist.[55] Because the systemic understanding is not yet in place while wrestling with the moral dilemma of colorblindness, it leaves Ryan susceptible to messages that claim that the concept of white privilege itself is racist.

Through a far-right pundit that Ryan follows, he hears about a scandal at a nearby suburban school where White students were asked to reflect on their privilege and how they benefit from it. The pundit insists that it is racist to focus on the melanin in someone's skin and not their character. He asserts that disparities are not based on race, that other "real" factors besides skin color are what matter. He names "two-parent privilege" as the real explanation for inequity. If Black families were more intact, he argues, they would have better outcomes. He throws out statistics about poor White people and wealthy Asian people to claim white privilege doesn't exist.

While Ryan's empathy for Davon and Kaj and their families may place him on the cusp of learning more about privilege and structural advantages, the interpretation that race is not a factor in inequity can be a seductive way to end the stress he feels and pull him the other way. He may be drawn to this argument and conclude that race is not a factor—that a lack of fathers and other poor choices explain what's going on with the community around the elementary school. This would fit with the language he hears at church about family values, personal responsibility, and the idea that God-fearing people experience less difficulty.

Should Ryan attach further to these arguments, he'll find more examples claiming to show how People of Color get advantages that White people don't, such as affirmative action. He will also encounter more calls to protect White people from the racism of white privilege and critical race theory. This has the potential to influence him away from antiracism.

- What thoughts, emotions, and beliefs come up as you think about white privilege?
- What support might Ryan need as he wrestles with identifying what factors impact a person's life?

Cultivate Curiosity

Ryan would benefit if someone like Alex were available to ask him questions about his thoughts and feelings about the situation, support his critical thinking, and explore what questions he has about the lesson and about white privilege. What feelings does he have about the concept? Does it make him feel defensive?

Tackling the questions together about what "two-parent privilege" is and why the pundit might bring it up in a discussion of white privilege would also help. How is having the benefit of two parents different than being subjected to systemic racism? How does this idea trigger judgment based on a religious belief about marriage?

Alex could also point out that, although the pundit suggests that simply paying attention to race is racist, there are other definitions of racism. How else might Ryan think about what racism is? Discussing how different people have different definitions of racism would open Ryan to different ways to consider the pundit's claims.

Embrace Both/And Thinking

Alex might also explore with Ryan the possibility of multiple factors, individual and systemic, that can impact families of color when they face racism. For example, is it possible that having two parents is beneficial *and* the existence of additional factors, like economic policies, that make a difference in people's lives? Is it possible for Ryan to hold his religious beliefs as valid *and* recognize that looking at the situation solely through a "family values" lens creates too narrow a view?

Part of the discussion might include turning the question around: Why might the pundit want to frame the issue as an either/or situation? How does that further a particular narrative or point of view? Over time, Ryan might adopt a more complex perspective so that he can see the idea of white privilege as a concept that helps us understand how systemic racism works, rather than as racism itself.

Message: The Real Issue Is People of Color

When people feel the tension of the dilemma of morality and equality, they search for messages that directly answer their questions about whether race really does make a difference in people's lives and how. Because understanding systemic racism is challenging due to its complexity, far-right messages about People of Color being responsible for every bad thing they experience offer reassuring answers for those looking to end their confusion.

The White friends that Tyler spends more time with on campus continue to share right-leaning and far-right positions that dismiss unequal treatment based on race. They look at the high-profile deaths of men of color and vilify the victims. The far right claims that these men get what they deserve because they do not follow the rules, whether this involves resisting arrest, selling single cigarettes, passing counterfeit bills, using drugs, failing to educate themselves, and other actions.

The far right returns to familiar explanations: these communities don't value family (lack of fathers), they don't value education (so they don't do well), and they don't care about Black-on-Black gun violence (which, they say, is the real issue—not police brutality). The more extreme members share the false claim that race is biological—that there is scientific proof that White people are more responsible and intelligent.

After months and months of hearing these messages, Tyler feels himself distancing from Dani. It's hard not to see her family simply as lawbreakers. Especially now that Dani is involved in Black Lives Matter and her immigrant rights group, Tyler finds himself more and more thinking that she's not taking responsibility for herself and just wants to play the victim.

- Have you participated in or listened to White people focusing on the problems of communities of color and how they are to blame for those problems?
- How would you engage Tyler in conversation about his feelings and his desire to distance himself from Dani?

Build Relationship

Having someone like Alex available is critical, as she could explore Tyler's feelings about Dani. Why does he value her friendship? What does he value about her as a person? How are those things still true about her despite her documentation status? What has he learned about her family's experience that might complicate the message that undocumented immigrants are the problem?

Cultivate Curiosity

Why are Tyler's White friends so sure of their perspective? What experience do they have with communities of color? Why might they feel so strongly about People of Color being problematic? What emotions are at the forefront for them, and for Tyler?

Embrace the Both/And

Like the example above, Alex could tap into Tyler's sense of himself as a critical thinker and explore the ways in which personal choice *and* the ways that systems work can both be at play as they wrestle with these important societal questions together.

Message: Racism Is in the Past—Get over It

When people search for answers to the moral dilemma of freedom and democracy, the message that all negative aspects of US history were fully resolved through the civil rights movement can prove powerful.

Tyler believes strongly in the American ideals of freedom and democracy. These beliefs have served him well; being an American makes him feel good and proud. His White friend group invests heavily in the belief that the United States has nothing to rectify or resolve when it comes to our nation's racial past.

So, when Tyler encounters an argument in history class that links current economic racial inequalities to laws and policies of the US government, he feels genuinely troubled about the racism. But his friendship circle dismisses the issues, finding other narratives to maintain a pristine vision of the United States. When the issue of reparations comes up in class, Tyler feels drawn to the students who argue against it. The idea that his family was not even here during slavery resonates deeply. Why should he and other White people have their taxes go to people who weren't enslaved and who live in the best country in the world?

Tyler starts to think more and more about the message that Black people just need to get over it and stop being victims. He's primed for the argument from the far right that White people need to be protected from unfair retaliation for what is over and done with.

- What emotions come up for you when thinking about the impact of historic racism today?
- How might you respond to Tyler if he shared his thoughts and feelings with you?

Build Relationship and Emotional Capacity

A critical insight Alex brings with her is that many White people fear that we will be treated as badly as People of Color have been in the past if we work to eliminate white privilege. Although this is not often talked about, this fear often exists right under the surface and may drive White people into a defensive posture. While that fear may be apparent to Alex when listening to Tyler and his other White friends, that is not the emotion she would identify and start with if she speaks with Tyler. She needs an entry point that does not highlight racism.

Instead, Alex can explore Tyler's strong pride in the United States. How does that pride make him feel? Why does he feel that way? Is it possible to be proud of his country and acknowledge some of the racist parts of its history, like enslavement? Helping Tyler feel connected and heard by Alex can keep him talking to her. This is essential so that they will be able to tackle the other fears that exist just under the surface.

Message: I'm Not Racist, but . . .

The colorblindness moral dilemma is a tough one to navigate, particularly because White culture has long taught that being colorblind is a way to combat racism. Therefore, when people navigate the thoughts they have about race and racism early in their journey, they tend to use the phrase, "I'm not racist, but . . ." to engage the race conversation while distancing themselves from racism. When in *Disintegration*, this can be an authentic attempt to resolve the tension while discussing confusing concepts.

In a conversation with his White friends, Tyler shares his story about discussing reparations in class and says, "I'm not racist, but it really seems like Black people just want handouts." This prompts one of his White friends who sometimes shares white nationalist content to respond, "Of course, you're not racist. You're seeing reality."

Tyler's friend is taking a cue from the playbook of Don Black, a white supremacist and founder of Stormfront, which for decades was the internet's most influential white nationalist website. Black admitted targeting White people who say, "I'm not racist, but . . ." as a recruitment strategy.[56] The far right does an outstanding job helping White people feel better about their fear of "speaking the truth" during a time of "political correctness." They activate a sense of moral righteousness by claiming that antiracism suppresses freedom of speech to protect minorities and that this is unfair to White people. That moral righteousness can feel good and draw White people closer and closer to white nationalism and white supremacy messaging.

- Have you ever said, "I'm not racist, but . . ."? What are your reactions to knowing how the far right exploits this line of thinking?
- What guidance would you offer Tyler about what it means to adopt this view as reality or "the truth"?

Take Care of Self

Many antiracist people experience the phrase, "I'm not racist, but . . ." as merely a preamble to a racist statement. This can lead us to lose our center and focus on challenging the person on the issue, turning the conversation into a debate. This is unlikely to draw someone in *Disintegration* away from racism.

Knowing that a group like Stormfront names this as a moment ripe for far-right recruitment, instead of allowing our own desire to confront or challenge to take over, this is a moment to take care of our own emotions and lean into compassion so that we can keep someone like Tyler engaged in conversation.

Cultivate Curiosity

Alex would need to stay curious with Tyler. Why did he feel the need to say, "I'm not racist, but . . . "? What concerns does he have about being perceived as racist? What conflicting feelings does he have about the issue he raised? What makes him see the issue as he does, and is he open to different interpretations?

> *Dear Reader:* While it's true these strategies are important to use when someone is reachable in *Disintegration*, it is not necessarily true when someone has retreated into whiteness and is operating from *Reintegration.* The "I'm not racist, but . . ." statement may no longer reflect genuine concern and may just be a cover to avoid being called racist. These moments warrant a different orientation, one that balances our need to care and connect (for the sake of not pushing the person further into racism) with the understanding that we do not want to engage in a way that validates racist beliefs or wastes our time with someone trolling us. It takes time and practice with mindful questions and listening to assess another person's motivations. Is that person genuinely conflicted? Or simply trying to push racist beliefs?

ANTIRACIST MESSAGES

The dynamics that happen in this section are some of the ones that keep us up at night. This is because when using a *Disintegration* frame, even people leaning toward defending whiteness have not yet made up their mind. They are searching. They may be searching for an easy answer that feels good and neatly resolves their tension. However, in this position, there is an opening. Potential exists to redirect, to turn the small glimmer of recognition that racism affects people into a larger, more substantial flame. Unfortunately, some antiracist approaches used with people defending whiteness can snuff out that small antiracist spark.

Although we feel extremely concerned about people in *Disintegration* and want them to experience exchanges that pull them toward antiracism, no one can force someone on the racial identity journey. What we can do, though, is ask questions, listen, and share our experiences in ways that make the complexities of antiracism more understandable. When a person is feeling the internal turmoil of *Disintegration*, the quality of interactions they experience with antiracists can be consequential. In this position, we need to approach people with strategic thoughtfulness and a recognition of the emotional turmoil the person is experiencing.

Message: Stop Being Fragile! That Is Your White Privilege!

White Fragility, by scholar Robin DiAngelo, offers important analysis of how systemic racism has socialized White people to avoid conversations about race and racism. Because society does not require us to develop racial stamina, when we are confronted with evidence of racism, we engage in a variety of strategies including tears, rage, defensiveness, and silence (among others) to stop the conversation.[57] White fragility accurately describes a lot of our behaviors in the early and middle positions of racial identity, although DiAngelo does not use this language.

Unfortunately, many antiracists use the language of white fragility to criticize people who are in *Disintegration*. While those lashing out may believe this is helping to end racism, it is not. In fact, it often drives away White people at this and other middle positions. It also results in fewer of us joining the racial justice freeway and negatively impacts People of Color. (Please note: We'll address when it *is* helpful to engage with DiAngelo's work on white fragility in chapter 10.)

Tyler runs into this message after engaging online with a story about a conservative news pundit's argument that the Democrats are trying to replace White votes with votes from "third world countries." Tyler feels that it is unfair to discount White people's votes just because they are White. He tweets out the story and his feelings about it. Madison, the antiracist eager to call out racism, jumps at the opportunity to name how ridiculous it is to think that fighting for voter rights is unfair to White people. She says his focus on what's fair to White people is his white fragility and privilege. She asserts that it's White people like him that allow racist voter suppression to continue.

At this point, Tyler does not understand what Madison is saying. It just sounds like an unfair critique that really is targeting White people in the ways the pundit says. Even more, Tyler feels like he should just stay quiet rather than argue with someone like Madison. He knows he'll be able to talk to his other friends about how unfair it all is. Madison has missed an opportunity.

- How have you witnessed or experienced people using terminology that you or others do not understand?
- What could Madison do differently if she wants to pull Tyler toward antiracism?

Cultivate Curiosity

If Madison wants to act strategically and try to connect with Tyler, she should express curiosity about his emotions and ideas. She can ask him what he believes, and where those ideas come from. Tone matters here; it's important to not ask the questions as a challenge or an interrogation. Where does his sense of unfairness come from? What is familiar about unfairness to him and his reaction to it?

Exploring Tyler's belief system may reveal that his concerns are not solely about race, but also about religion. He may believe that immigrants are diluting the country's Christian population. His exposure to Christian nationalist rhetoric may prevent him from viewing the issue through a racial lens focused on privilege.

Build Emotional Capacity

Discomfort and disequilibrium are necessary parts of White racial identity development. Supporting people to move through their discomfort is part of normalizing emotions. Madison can explore what strong emotions come up for Tyler when he thinks about unfairness in general, then move to the emotions about concepts like white privilege or white fragility. This would help her understand what supports he needs. She can listen to his stories, including those that focus on how he has lacked privilege or how he fears for the future of the nation.

Tyler's tweet shows that he is open to the argument that White people are being oppressed by voter rights reform. Generating curiosity will provide Madison a chance to determine the degree to which

Tyler is wrestling with a moral dilemma versus feeling hardened into a racist position.

It is important to note that Madison will have to do some of her own work about how she feels about herself and other White people before she'll be able to engage authentically with this type of dialogue. Someone like Alex, who has been pushing herself to understand her own racial identity and how she relates to others, will be in a better position to engage Tyler in this type of conversation.

Offer Perspective

Once trust has been established through curiosity and listening, Madison can share some of her own experience of the upheaval that comes with encountering ideas about fragility for the first time. Notice the difference between Madison sharing her own process versus trying to convince Tyler how privilege or fragility is operating in his life. He's not yet in a place to be open or have the skills to engage in that conversation. The point is to validate his confusion while gently providing a message about how Madison finds the concepts to be useful in her life and not racist.

Madison could share her own confusion when she learned that something she had been taught as true wasn't actually true. For example, she learned from other White people that the book *The Bell Curve* proved White people to be academically superior to Black people.[58] When she first heard that it was privilege that allowed her to believe that was true, she felt upset. But through conversation and support, she decided to find out more about race and racism. This inspired her to explore other mistruths she might have learned.

Stay Strategic

To be clear, we're not saying to never discuss white privilege or white fragility. Instead, we're offering a strategy that lays the groundwork for those later conversations when someone like Tyler is in a different frame of mind, after he has been shepherded through *Disintegration* and *Reintegration*. This might take some time. If you do not have the type of relationship that allows for such a long-range strategy, it is still important to focus on being curious and asking how a person came to those beliefs and asking if you may share your own experience.

Please note, it may seem counterintuitive to put off the conversation, particularly given how popular the privilege/fragility concepts have been and how they have made their way into mainstream conversation. The point is not that they are dangerous or problematic concepts. The issue is the need to avoid overwhelming the person in *Disintegration* so that you can stay in relationship and support them in developing a more complex and nuanced analysis of what they are experiencing.

Conversations about white fragility and white privilege can happen when we are ready to reflect on our personal relationship with racism. That is a more advanced discussion. While in *Disintegration*, we want to expand the person's awareness of widespread racism and help them reimagine their world into one where large-scale racism does in fact exist. We need to create a foundation of knowledge and emotional support under them that will allow them to navigate the fragility/privilege conversation later.

Message: Get Systemic

Antiracists often default to only a systemic approach when talking about race. However, White people who have entered *Disintegration* and are defending whiteness are typically not ready for a systemic analysis.

In Tyler's history class, he witnesses an exchange that sticks with him. During a class discussion on inequities in the healthcare system, the professor shares statistics that show Black and Brown people have poorer health outcomes. As the professor reviews the data, she provides systemic analysis of poverty, insurance, and health outcomes. One student challenges the professor's interpretation of the data as being evidence of racism within healthcare. The student argues that the poor health outcomes of People of Color are a result of their poor personal choices.

Some classmates in the middle positions of racial identity counter that the student is missing the point and must think in terms of systems. Some even mutter how racist the student is. Tyler finds their systemic argument unpersuasive and their claims of racism off-putting. The argument for individual choice is compelling to him and aligns with the other conversations he has been having.

Focusing on data to help people see systemic racism often fails in *Disintegration*. The correlational nature of much of the data, showing that disparities exist but not *why* they exist, make it easy for someone with an individualistic frame to interpret the information in a way that reinforces the individualistic view, particularly as confirmation bias takes over.

Confirmation bias occurs when we notice, accept, and make conclusions based on information that tells us what we already believe. People will focus on the information that supports their current view and ignore or discount the information that does not. When presented with evidence of systemic racism, people can easily dismiss it. The far right presents a great deal of "evidence" online to help people reject antiracist viewpoints and entice them into more deeply racist stances.

- How have you witnessed or experienced data being used to argue that racial inequities are due to systemic racism? What happened?
- What other strategies might help when engaging Tyler?

Take Care of Self

Someone like Madison will experience an intense emotional reaction to the racist lines of argument that follow from the individualistic frame. She's likely to be one of the people calling out racism. It's not that her thinking is wrong; it is that naming it at this moment is not going to convince the student who offers the individualistic interpretation or the people like Tyler who are listening.

We need to build our emotional resilience to stay calm when upset by what we perceive as racism. To do this we need to connect with other white people so that we can experience our genuine anger and frustration and work together to share strategies to help influence other White people. We can use mindful inquiry to ask people how they developed their viewpoint and to explore their emotions. This can help us avoid using shame-based approaches that can drive people further away from antiracism.

Build Emotional Capacity

Exploring the emotions underlying a person's attachment to the value of "personal responsibility" is important. Typically, there are fears we need to identify that draw people to these ideas. For example, Tyler is starting to fear having to pay for other people's bad choices. If Madison is able to stay centered, she can offer positive feedback and validation as Tyler examines his relationship to the moral dilemmas.

Taking a person's emotions into account can help us know when that person is ready for us to share about systemic racism. For example, if someone already fearful of People of Color looks at statistics from the criminal justice system, the disproportionate number of incarcerated Black and Brown men will only reconfirm their belief that men of color are more dangerous and prone to crime. Instead, exploring the influences that led to their fear can help untangle the emotions that stop them from accepting a systemic analysis.

Offer Perspective

Once Madison understands the emotions and beliefs underlying Tyler's frame of mind, she can use storytelling to broaden his perspective. Storytelling that carries emotional weight is typically more effective at shifting a person's interpretive frame than attempting to prove an idea using data. If Madison knows People of Color who have experienced harm related to the trends of racial disparities, sharing those stories would be useful. Madison could also share her experience coming to understand the impacts of racial disparities and how these have affected her.

Madison may not yet recognize the way socialization into whiteness harms everyone. However, if she did, she could invite Tyler to consider that everyone would be better off if society closed racial gaps in education, housing, health outcomes, and other areas. She could share how the book *The Sum of Us* by Heather McGhee explains that we are all harmed by allowing racism to continue.[59]

This may be particularly useful if Madison combines this message with a discussion of how many White people are also struggling today. Madison may not be ready to deliver these complex messages about shared struggle and the idea that we all need to break free from socialized harm. However, this is something for her to work toward because these messages are more likely to draw young white men who are struggling to make sense of their own place in society toward antiracism.

Embrace Both/And Thinking

It is useful to state *both* that personal responsibility is important *and* that systemic racism is real and affects the lives of People of Color. Everyone has personal agency, even within a racist system. Everyone can make choices for themselves to navigate an unjust system as best they can. Both individual responsibility and systemic racism can happen at the same time.

We can hold people accountable for their choices *and* recognize that a racially unjust system makes it harder for some people to navigate and succeed within our society than others. We can value a focus on the content of someone's character *and* recognize the impact that race has on people's lives. Both are true, and this understanding can go a long way in helping people shift toward the "engaging in antiracism" side of things.

Moving to this both/and thinking can be difficult for Madison at her position in her identity development, though, because she has some lingering guilt and fear that lead her to avoid anything that is perceived as a critique of People of Color. Acknowledging any aspect of People of Color's personal responsibility in this situation would make her feel like she is blaming People of Color and avoiding a systemic analysis. She will need more support to be in a healthy space to understand the importance of both/and thinking.

Someone like Alex, with a healthier sense of her antiracist identity, will be able to offer the following both/and: Some People of Color make choices that undermine their well-being; this is true for people in all racial groups. And there are historical and systemic issues that create barriers for People of Color which help to explain the persistent racial disparities we see today.

> *Dear Reader*: Please note how much context matters when deciding to engage in a public conversation about White people's feelings. Helping a White person process the individualism dilemma in a multiracial space can cause deep harm to People of Color. So be very thoughtful about how and when you have these types of conversations with struggling White people. It's okay to wait for an opportunity to talk to someone privately in order to avoid harming People of Color.

A CASE STUDY MOMENT: JEWISH PEOPLE AND THE CONFLICT OF WHITE SUPREMACY

Christine experienced a formative moment during the 2016–2017 school year when a young, White Jewish student shared in class, "I'm so sick of this school making me feel guilty for being White. I can understand why people want to join the alt-right, and I'm Jewish."

Antisemitism is at the core of white supremacist ideology worldwide as expressed in its fundamental messaging and its violence, such as the 2018 Tree of Life massacre in Pittsburgh in which a white nationalist killed eleven people and injured six.

White Jewish people experience the complexity of simultaneously not being seen as White by hatemongers and being seen as White by antiracists. This means White Jewish people are primary targets of hatred, yet also seen as racially privileged, all while experiencing the reality of anti-Semitism. Jewish People of Color experience a different layering and targeting of anti-Semitism and racism, as they are targeted as both Jewish *and* as People of Color.

Antiracism steeped in building relationships and developing White racial identity supports people if and when they feel guilt. This is particularly important so that White people never excuse or ignore anti-Semitism. Christine learned from her experience with her student to avoid underestimating the power of the alt-right and white nationalists. It deepened her practice individually as a teacher in her classroom and collectively in her work with other faculty members, reinforcing her recognition that she had to provide positive identity development to guard against anti-Semitic and racist appeals.

REFLECTION

Dear Reader: you've made it to the end of another chapter. Before you go, we ask you to consider at least two of these questions, in a journal or another method of self-reflection.

Thinking of Yourself:
- With whom do you most identify in this chapter, Ryan, Tyler, Madison, or Alex? Why?

- Which stories or ideas resonate most? When have you faced similar situations? What did you do? What were the results?
- When have you defended whiteness? What helped you turn toward antiracism?

Thinking of Others:
- When have you tried to engage with someone about racism? What happened? If you were in that situation again, is there anything you would do differently?
- What are your typical responses to people who defend whiteness? Do you respond with anger? A feeling of hopelessness? Curiosity?
- How do you navigate your emotions so you can hear people's stories, even while they defend whiteness? What helps you listen and engage strategically?

SUMMARY OF DEFENDING WHITENESS: DISINTEGRATION

In *Disintegration*: Defending Whiteness, we explain away the racism we encounter and dismiss any concerns about race; we tell ourselves the status quo is fair.		
Far-right messages we are susceptible to in this position: • White Privilege Isn't Real, But It Is Real Racist • The Real Issue Is People of Color • Racism Is in the Past, Get over It • "I'm Not Racist, But . . ."	Antiracist messages that are harmful in this position: • Stop Being "Fragile!" That Is Your White Privilege. • Get Systemic	Suggested approaches: • Ask questions to understand why people think/ believe as they do • Use both/and thinking to talk about the complexity of the moral dilemmas • Normalize the emotions we feel when facing moral dilemmas • Share personal stories to help people recognize that stereotypes and bias are the source of racial fears

6

Toward Antiracism

Disintegration

"This child would benefit from antidepressants," the White psychologist and psychiatrist agree. "The problem is not in the child," the Black mentors push back. I watch the ongoing exchange as if it is a tennis match.

I am a volunteer research assistant, helping to observe and assess Black and Hispanic/Latinx elementary school students. Initially aligned with the White psychologist who trained me, I am now skeptical of her approach. The Black mentors' arguments draw me in.

I do not want to be on the wrong side of this argument. I, Shelly, am in Disintegration *and moving toward antiracism.*

Because the dominant version of White culture we experience in the United States is deeply invested in individualism and colorblindness, individuals in *Disintegration* experience daily reinforcement that racism is not as bad as people suggest. Fortunately, maintaining this status quo is not the only way to resolve the cognitive dissonance of *Disintegration*. White people can choose to confront race and move toward antiracism.

This "toward antiracism" side of *Disintegration* provides relief from the moral dilemmas; however, acknowledging racism introduces new challenges. People may recognize more of the past and present racism than they did previously, yet not understand how the complex web of interrelated systems operates. For this reason, part of the work in this position involves cultivating an emerging recognition of what whiteness entails and how it is based in assimilation, oppressive power, and white superiority. Frequently, in the desire to reject white supremacy, we can

Figure 6.1 Disintegration: Toward Antiracism. ARTIST: LIZ WILTSIE

reject the existence of White culture altogether, and as a result, believe that only People of Color experience the richness of culture.

While in this stage, we often feel anger, guilt, shame, sadness, and fear. Fear emerges as we want to interrupt racism, yet worry about losing our relationships with other White people in our lives. We also fear casting too wide a net around whom to consider racist, often teetering between rejecting White people (and all things related to whiteness) and holding onto the belief that not all White people are racist. We cannot imagine that the term *racist* could apply to ourselves or those we love.

In our relationships with People of Color, we may mean well, and yet we tend to feel so badly for people who experience poverty, criminalization, and violence that it engenders a sense of pity such that we only perceive the downside of what it means to be a Person of Color in the United States. In doing so, we can fail to recognize the strength, achievements, and beauty in the lives of People of Color. This often causes us to adopt condescending ideas that lead to counterproductive action.

At the same time, in reflecting on our history, we may romanticize some People of Color. For example, we may believe we are being complimentary, and yet we treat Indigenous people as historical figures instead of real people with immediate concerns related to well-being, land rights, religious freedom, and economic development. In this way, our romanticizing prevents us from perceiving their current struggles for justice.

It is essential to realize that choosing the "toward antiracism" side of *Disintegration* is far more challenging than defaulting to the status quo. This is partly because as we make more decisions in this direction, we experience constant pressure to stop being "so serious" and to abandon talking about racism. As a result, it takes continual reinforcement to maintain this trajectory. Having community support that models how to resolve negative feelings without abandoning a focus on race is critical.

> *Dear Reader:* This might be a good time to rest and refuel. Take a moment to breathe. The road ahead may inspire new learning or self-reflection that feels stressful. As you proceed, remember that you are not alone. Many are on this path with you. If you feel isolated, reach out and connect with others who aspire to antiracism. Traveling this road together has provided us, your authors, with important moments of healing. It can do the same for you.

How likely are Ryan and Tyler to land on this side of *Disintegration?* What support can help? How much effort might it take to overcome the messaging of their friends and family that reinforce the status quo? In this chapter, we look at some of the messages that may prevent someone like Ryan and Tyler from engaging with race, as well as responses that can support a step toward antiracism.

FAR-RIGHT MESSAGES

The emotional challenges we experience in this position leave us vulnerable to the far right's claims that White people should view ourselves as victims of unfair racialized backlash. What follows are two far-right messages that align with the heightened concerns of this position and can draw people away from antiracism.

Message: No One Can Take a Joke Anymore

The far right attacks people who stand up against hate as "woke social justice warriors" or "snowflakes" who cannot take a joke. They take it further, though, suggesting that anyone criticizing a joke is the real racist trying to constrain people's behavior. In their view, People of Color intentionally target White people to manipulate and control their speech. It results in people asking, "Why should we give up our freedom of speech? A joke is just a joke, right?"

Ryan faces this question as racism creates strain at home and with his friends. He notices racist undertones when his parents talk (often jokingly) about the news, and his friends tell racist jokes more often than they did in the past. He has started interrupting them, saying he doesn't find it funny. He even told his friends once that he wants them to stop joking about other racial groups. They laughed at him, calling him "the PC police" for being too sensitive.

He now wonders if his friends tell the jokes just to bother him. When one of them starts in with a series of jokes one day, Ryan says, "Just stop it. It's racist, and I hate that you keep saying this stuff." For a moment, all his friends get quiet. But then one says, "You know, you're not fun to be around when you're like this. Lighten up." Another adds, "I'm not sure who's gotten to you, but we're not hurting anybody. Nobody can say anything around you anymore. You're turning into a snowflake." Ryan is both frustrated and confused. His friends are mad at him. Interrupting their jokes isn't making things better. "What's the point?" he wonders.

- How have you experienced this claim that interrupting racist jokes is the same as stifling people's freedom of speech?
- What can help Ryan navigate his competing desires to take a stand against racism and maintain his relationships?

Offer Perspective

Explain that the free speech argument is an attempt to deflect from racist language used. The use of the term "snowflake" implies that the person trying to disrupt racism is being oversensitive. And yet, those who refuse to recognize the impact of their words typically display significant oversensitivity when defending their use of hurtful speech. The difference between positions lies in whose feelings and interests are perceived as valuable.

If we cannot identify this dynamic and gain clarity on our own stance, we remain susceptible to the challenge and can default into letting racist jokes continue. The effect is to maintain the status quo. Without support to see this pattern and resist it, Ryan is likely to shrink back, perhaps still experiencing empathy for People of Color, but more quietly and privately.

Questions Ryan can use to expose this pattern include:

- What makes that joke funny?
- How is it wrong to care that a joke hurts someone?
- What does humor without racism sound like?

Build Relationship

It can be hard to feel like you are the only one resisting. The social pressure to go along with racist situations is often called *white solidarity*. In this case, the solidarity asks for the status quo to continue—White people can make racist jokes without consequence. To deal with this pressure, Ryan can find solace in cultivating closer relationships with his Black friends from Jazz Band and people like Jamie, one of his fellow White volunteers from the after-school program who identifies as nonbinary and is savvy about race issues.

This does not mean that Ryan should distance himself from his current friends and family. Instead, deepening relationships with people in his life who match his values can help him develop the resilience and courage to stand true to his newly emerging antiracist principles. Jamie, particularly, might offer advice on how to more successfully talk about the harm of racist jokes.

Because *Disintegration* is so confusing, if our closest family and friends do not readily support our early moves toward antiracism, we probably need to expand our social circle. What clubs or organizations in our local community focus on service or justice? Who in our immediate vicinity is interested in social or racial justice issues? Now that we are asking new questions about the world, we may have more in common now with people taking part in these activities than we did in the past. Just like Ryan's experience at the school, volunteer efforts may help us connect with people who have asked themselves similar questions and have useful experiences to share.

Message: Why Bother to Help If They Hate You Anyway?

The far right is adept at amplifying White people's emotional distress so that antiracism will not appeal to us. As part of this effort, the far right takes People of Color's understandable and legitimate anger, particularly among Black people, and uses it to claim that any anger directed at White people is unfair and equates to hatred. Some call this *reverse racism*.

Consider what happens after Dani reaches out to Tyler after over a month of the two not speaking. Although hurt and sad about how Tyler has changed, Dani hopes to reconnect with him. Reaching him by phone, she says, "We've been friends for forever, and I don't want to lose you." After reminding him of his attendance at the Republican Club's meeting earlier in the year, she asks him to go with her to one of her activist meetings. "Please just give it a try," she says. "I want you to understand me." Missing the fun they had together, and softened by Dani's outreach, Tyler reluctantly agrees.

When Tyler tells one of his roommates about his plan to go to the meeting, the friend scoffs, "Why the hell would you do that? Those people don't want White people there; they hate us." Tyler suspects his roommate is probably right, but Tyler decides to go anyway to try to save his friendship with Dani. (We'll explore what happens to Tyler at the meeting in the "Antiracist Messages" section of this chapter.)

This far-right perspective questioning why we should bother to help is not foreign to Ryan either. He has heard the same message from the podcasters he follows. He remembers hearing a White guy talking about activists at a Black Lives Matter meeting telling him, "We don't need you here." He went on to say, "That was the end of me trying to help Black people. Clearly, it is anti-White and racist." Remembering this, Ryan feels tentative about attending a community meeting at the elementary school. Jamie convinces him to go with them. The room is filled with mostly Black parents and a few mostly White teachers. As Ryan makes his way over to Jamie, he sees the parents' eyes on him and feels out of place.

Over the course of two hours, Ryan learns a lot about why the school needs money and feels drawn in. They detail how racism is at the heart of the lack of funding and rally for a major fundraising campaign. He also hears significant anger. One Black man in particular yells from the back of the room that they should look around and take notice of who gives a damn. Riling up the crowd, he says, "We can't expect anything from anyone but ourselves. White people are too damn racist, they ain't never gonna change. And I sure as hell don't trust them to do right by our kids." The man gets a standing ovation from about half the crowd.

Ryan is self-conscious. On one hand, he is there, so he might count as giving a damn. On the other, he might be just another racist White person to them, which seems unfair. As the meeting ends and they stand to leave, Jamie asks Ryan what he thinks.

- How does the claim that People of Color hate White people play in Ryan's emotional turmoil? How might it stop further movement into antiracism?
- How might Jamie help Ryan process whether it is "fair" for People of Color to be mad at White people (in general) for ongoing racism, even when they show up to "help"?

Offer Perspective

White people have a long history of injecting ourselves into movements led by People of Color, taking over, and creating significant problems.[60] In short, although there are many ways we can be useful and important solidarity partners, White people, as a group, have not historically generated much trust. Jamie knows this history and shares it with Ryan to help him understand why People of Color might be uninterested, skeptical, or downright antagonistic toward White people who show up to a community or activist meeting.

Without this understanding, we can fall victim to far-right claims. This is what happened to Christine while she was attending Temple University and tried to join the acts of civil disobedience the Black Student Union was organizing after a racial profiling incident. When a Black organizer pointedly told her they did not need her help, plenty of White voices around her suggested that this is precisely why she never should have even tried to lend her support in the first place. Their voices sent her into a more reactionary position and back toward whiteness. The claim that Black people just want to be mad about the past and mad about White people stayed with her for years.

Christine wishes she had some White folks in her life at that time to help her understand that there were other viable interpretations of that moment. She wishes she had understood that racial justice organizing depends on relationships and that White people need to earn trust rather than expect it or assume it is freely available. She expected a celebration of the fact that she was offering to help, and at the first sign of resistance to her desire to help, she crumbled and stepped away from racial justice for several years. She only returned years later after receiving encouragement. Something like this could easily happen to Ryan if he has more encounters with understandably frustrated People of Color and lacks someone like Jamie to help him process his feelings and interpretations.

Embrace Both/And Thinking

When in *Disintegration,* we do not yet fully grasp the level of violence, oppression, and harm endured by People of Color throughout our nation's history (up to and including the present day) and the resulting feelings it engenders. The resulting lack of empathy allows us to feel unjustly accused when People of Color speak of White people as a general group.

Jamie, being more solid in their racial identity journey, can help Ryan process his feelings and interpretations about the meeting's events using a both/and approach. For example, White people have been *both* the cause of massive historical and ongoing pain in the Black community (making Black people's anger and lack of trust completely understandable) *and* each White person is a unique individual who can deviate from that pattern. Both are true. It is up to each of us to demonstrate our ongoing investment in ending racism if we want People of Color to trust us.

Build Emotional Capacity

Ryan needs support to manage his fears of People of Color rejecting him. Jamie can help Ryan by validating his feelings and asking self-reflective questions that help him to depersonalize these moments:

- How have you experienced rejection in the past? How did you get through it?
- How do we hear People of Color's anger and/or rejection of us as a "typical White person" without taking it personally?

ANTIRACIST MESSAGES

In this section, we highlight three anti-racist messages that often backfire when introduced to people in *Disintegration*. Part of our concern is that although each of the messages has an important foundation in truth and conveys an essential antiracist principle, we typically do not understand them at this critical juncture. This means the messages can easily snuff out a burgeoning interest in antiracism.

Message: Stop Being a White Savior

A major factor in the long history of White people undermining racial justice is the pattern of assuming that we are more knowledgeable than People of Color and that our efforts are of primary importance. Whether we realize it or not, this is white superiority, and it prompts us to turn our upset feelings about People of Color's circumstances into action attempting to "save" them. However, simply telling people in *Disintegration* to "stop being a White savior" is likely to backfire, because what we hear is that trying to help is wrong.

Ryan encounters this message in response to his efforts to support the school community's fundraising campaign. Thankfully, after the evening meeting Jamie and Ryan attended together, Jamie helps Ryan process his discomfort and stay engaged. So, when the group announces an ambitious fundraising goal, the first thing Ryan does is post widely on social media and local message boards.

Ryan figures the best way to entice people to donate is to make sure friends, family, and his wider affluent White community feel shocked about the school's situation; he includes overly dire descriptions of the community of color and overhyped statements about how the White community can help and are key to the success of the fundraising effort. A few of Ryan's White female friends reply favorably, expressing sadness about the kids' situation and appreciation that Ryan cares so much.

A different reaction comes from Madison upon seeing Ryan's post. Madison replies that Ryan should stop acting like a "White savior" and that Ryan's message is dripping with white superiority that reinforces whiteness. Many people like and share Madison's critique; these responses get far more traction than Ryan's original post. Ryan is upset that his attempt to follow Jesus's kindness is being twisted. He feels his Christian principles are under attack. As far as he is concerned, Madison's post is the problem.

It is important to point out that Madison's analysis is not necessarily wrong. Ryan's approach involves significant missteps that are offensive and undermine the larger goal of correcting the inequities the school community faces. The issue is that the message about being a "White savior" who has internalized superiority does not land as intended. First, his desire is to help and the criticism that trying to help is equal to feeling superior does not make sense to him. Second, Madison does not realize how the use of the "savior" idea might land for people steeped in a Christian worldview. For example, some Christians may feel pride in emulating Jesus, while others may take offense at being compared to the one and only Savior.

- When have you witnessed or experienced criticism related to someone acting like a "White savior"? What were the results?
- When have you felt like you were uniquely positioned to be of help? What happened?
- What can help Ryan stay engaged and continue learning?

Cultivate Curiosity
Hopefully, Jamie can follow up with Ryan to ask his motivation and intent. How are his actions an attempt to resolve one of the moral dilemmas?

What makes this important to him? Is he inspired by compassion and care? Understanding his deeper motivations can help him untangle why he felt the need to overdramatize People of Color's circumstances and realize the harm that may have caused.

Build Relationship

Madison could deliver the critique within a broader message that affirms the value of White people thinking about, talking about, and acting against racism and its effects. Although White people cannot and should not expect People of Color to affirm our efforts, that does not mean other White people cannot affirm our efforts while providing guidance. For example, Madison could affirm Ryan's initiative and pair her criticism with a genuine offer to help Ryan understand how to write more accurate posts, encouraging him to find alternative language that doesn't play on stereotypes.

Embrace Both/And Thinking

To prevent an overreaction that interprets any effort to support People of Color as White saviorism, Jamie can emphasize that White people do have a role to play in antiracism, *and* our approach can help or hurt. In other words, Ryan can be involved without falling into White saviorism and/or centering whiteness. He just needs more support to do that effectively.

Ryan would benefit from exposure to positive White antiracist role models. Unfortunately, in the attempt to avoid centering White people as saviors, many people avoid teaching or sharing about White people involved in antiracism, including abolitionists and those involved in the civil rights movement. This leaves many with the idea that there is no role for White people to play in ending racism. If we can embrace the complexity of the *both/and*, we can highlight inspiring role models without overemphasizing our role.

For example, many people know the story of Ruby Bridges, the first young Black girl to integrate an all-White school in New Orleans. Fewer people know the name of the White teacher who traveled to teach Ruby Bridges when no other White people would. At a racial equity conference, Ruby Bridges was a keynote speaker and asked the audience to join her in asking the Secretary of Education to honor her White teacher, Barbara Henry, with a statue. Bridges spoke passionately about the need for interracial efforts to end racism, demonstrating how we can provide White people with positive antiracist role models without falling into a savior narrative.

Message: You Need to Be Accountable

White people in this early position tend to struggle to know when to get involved and when not to get involved, when to speak up and when to stay quiet. We often feel confused about how to show up in a way that people appreciate. Then, when we try to act, we are likely to do it poorly and step on toes because all of this is very new. Confronting the message that we should "be accountable" can be overwhelming and cause us to turn away unless we have support that helps us know what accountability means.

Ryan feels confused a lot of the time. His efforts to interrupt racism are tanking, and he elicits criticism every time he posts something on social media. The most recent dust-up over the fundraiser almost sends Ryan over the edge with frustration, although Jamie helps him calm down and understand the mistakes he made.

Days after Madison's original response about the fundraiser, she follows up with a post telling Ryan that if he is trying to be antiracist, he needs to be accountable for the harm he caused. She says he needs to be transparent and tell the community how he will repair the harm. This does not make any sense to Ryan. What does it mean to be accountable? Who is the community he is supposed to be accountable to? What exactly is the harm he needs to repair? While Ryan recognizes that he messed up, and he feels badly about it, how is he supposed to make up for it?

Madison's ongoing criticism, offered without concrete, helpful suggestions, all seems like too much. In Ryan's mind, Madison is acting like his original post caused some kind of massive trauma. He can't imagine that being true. He feels under the microscope again. He is frustrated, bothered by Madison and the comments she inspires, and ready to give up. Feeling overwhelmed, he stops working on the campaign.

- What does "being accountable" mean to you? What would you do if you were Ryan?
- How would you support Ryan to understand what accountability can mean and what it could require of him?

Cultivate Curiosity

A useful conversation for Ryan would involve asking him to think about times in his past when something didn't go as planned, when he needed to apologize for messing up. What did it feel like to make it right? How did he resolve any feelings of guilt or shame?

Embrace Both/And Thinking

In the face of Madison's challenge, Ryan needs support to understand that messing up means we need to improve and do things differently. This does not make us bad people. We can *both* be good *and* mess up at the same time.

Offer Perspective

Jamie might be able to help Ryan understand what accountability means by helping him make connections with moments in his life when he felt responsible for something or to someone. For example, does he feel responsible for showing up to teach his after-school music class every week? What if he didn't show up? What would he need to do to make it right?

Jamie could help him realize that in a similar way, People of Color count on White people to show up to engage in antiracism in a way that is not harmful. When we make an error, we must find out if we caused a negative impact and need to engage in some repair, and then do better going forward.

Build Relationship

The question of whom we are accountable to and how to be accountable is a complex one. Ryan would benefit from an introduction to a local or national White collective that has experience supporting people as they grow into antiracism. These groups are where we make mistakes together while posing questions, articulating new ideas, and considering how to act in new ways.

Groups like these also help us navigate what accountability can mean, because there are different approaches. AWARE-LA (Shelly's antiracist home) provides regular in-person and online dialogues that have a long history of supporting White people to take their next steps and recover after making a mistake. This kind of group could help Ryan get feedback on ideas before he takes action and help him understand what accountability means, why it is important, and how to navigate its expectations.

Christine developed the term *loving accountability* to ensure that conversations about accountability include a focus on love *and* justice to help her think about the way she only saw accountability as beating up other White people and herself. Loving accountability means holding space and grace for people to be valued as the imperfect humans that we are while we correct and repair our missteps.

Ultimately, accountability happens within relationships. Ryan could talk with the person running the school campaign to share the error he made, what he learned from the experience, and how he plans to go forward in a better way. That person can then let him know if anything further is needed from him. Sharing his process in a follow-up post might make sense, if the person running the fundraising campaign agrees or suggests it.

Message: Yes, All White People (Are Racist)

People draw on different definitions when discussing racism. For some, racism means acting with racial hatred. For others, racism is when prejudice becomes institutionalized by those in power. Antiracists typically view racism as layered, existing internally, interpersonally, culturally, institutionally, and systemically. People who recognize the layers realize that all White people (by virtue of living in a racist society) are socialized into racism and that we are complicit with it daily. This perspective prompts many antiracists to deliver the message that "all White people are racist." Unfortunately, this message delivered to people in *Disintegration* often does not have the intended result.

Consider what happens with Tyler. Two weeks after his last conversation with Dani, Tyler makes good on his promise to go with her to an activist meeting. Talking in the car on the way to the meeting, Dani expresses that she appreciates him keeping an open mind. She lets him know that although the group organizes across race, they frequently meet "in affinity" for part of their meetings. She explains that they separate into two groups, White and People of Color, and that the groups help them do their activism work more effectively. Tyler thinks it sounds strange, but he says nothing. Although skeptical, he wants to continue being friends with Dani, so he hopes this meeting will surprise him in a good way.

When they arrive, the group seems friendly enough. Of the 25 people there, about a third are White. None of the Black or Latinx people sneer at him like he feared. The meeting begins with an opening round of introductions and several short presentations meant to charge up the group. Tyler notices that they use some of the same rallying cries the Republican Club uses; for example, both talk about the importance of "leading with love" to successfully recruit people. He remembers how one of the Republicans mentioned being strategic about love to battle the false perception of them as hateful. Tyler figures maybe these activists are trying to do the same thing.

Halfway through the meeting, the leaders announce that the group will break into affinity. The White folks stand and head to a separate room. Dani smiles and says, "have fun." Tyler follows, nervous but more relaxed than he was earlier.

In the affinity group, a man begins a warm-up exercise, asking each person in the circle to name how they have been complicit with racism in the last week. Tyler is third in line to share, and what the first two people say doesn't make sense to him. Feeling unsettled, he says, "I have not been racist this past week. I'm not racist." One of the women sitting next to him says, "If you really think about it, you'll come up with something because all White people are racist, even you." Tyler is both perplexed and put off, saying, "Actually, I don't think all White people are racist. And I think that's a racist attitude."

The room visibly reacts by bristling, rolling their eyes, or taking in a deep breath. As far as Tyler is concerned, he knows some racists, and he is nothing like them. After a pause, the woman next to him gets the circle going again. He's confused by their examples of racism. For example, one person said she was complicit with racism when she assumed the supervisor of an organization was White when it turned out that she was Black. To Tyler, that isn't racism, it's a fair assumption because White people are generally successful in the United States.

The only thing that keeps Tyler from leaving early is that Dani drove. He's pretty sure this is the end of the road for him and Dani. For the rest of the meeting, Tyler stays quiet, except for a few moments where he could not help but pose questions to poke holes in people's assumptions about People of Color experiencing racism all the time. If the group seemed friendly at first, they are not now. The experience solidifies his view that these are the "guilty White liberals" his parents talk about.

When the meeting ends and Tyler and Dani are back in the car, Tyler lets Dani know that, although her group believes they are fighting racism, they are reinforcing it. He tells her about his experience in affinity, how negative they are about White people, and how he never wants to go back. Dani holds back tears, recognizing that bringing him to the meeting backfired.

- What thoughts and feelings arise as you read this story?
- How could the affinity group have provided a different experience for someone like Tyler?

Build Relationship

The White affinity group members operate from a different racial identity position than Tyler. For a different outcome to occur, someone first needs to recognize that Tyler's disintegrated position makes the group's activity inappropriate for him.[61] Second, they should generate empathy for him and decide if Tyler is a potential ally worthy of time and effort. This might include taking Tyler off to the side for a one-to-one conversation or allowing the meeting format to shift so Tyler can participate in a small break-out group with people willing to work directly with him.

If we struggle to find empathy for Tyler, consider that he took the time and energy to come to the group. It might help if we remember the moments when we struggled to understand racism and the vulnerability it took to put ourselves out there. How did people empathize with us to help us on our journey? We can channel the time, energy, and patience they used with us so that we can show up for someone like Tyler.

Cultivate Curiosity

After assessing with empathy, connecting with curiosity is key, even with White people who do not yet "get it." Asking Tyler the following questions may encourage deeper sharing, as they show interest in him and his experience:

- What motivated you to join our group today?
- How do you define racism? What makes someone racist or not racist?
- Where does that belief come from? Why is it important to you?
- What experience have you had with racism?

Stay Strategic

If a White affinity group easily dismisses someone like Tyler, they risk pushing him toward a retrenchment in whiteness and racism. People of Color expect White people to engage other White people to pull them *away* from racism, not move them toward it. We need to use all the tools in our toolbelt to do this, including providing empathy to people in *Disintegration*. It is also more reflective of antiracism's goal of us becoming more humane with one another to end racism.

If antiracists want to pull more people toward antiracism, we need to be strategic and empathetic. This means connecting with people who say racist things without immediately telling them they are racist. We need to begin at the beginning. Many on the far right have an explicit strategy of recruiting people bit by bit, connecting with people's concerns as they lead them toward increasingly bigoted positions, slowly over time.[62] Antiracist people need to be similarly strategic, building trust over time and engaging in relational organizing, if we want more people to choose our side.

Embrace Both/And Thinking

Introducing the idea that we can be *both* good people who do not intend to harm others *and* that we can do and say racist things (and have done them) can support people to stay engaged.

The point is to honor a person's sense of self as a fundamentally decent person even while introducing the idea that we are imperfect human beings who unintentionally have and do cause harm. To do this, we need to be prepared to stick with people while we interrupt the either/or idea that we are either good or bad people.

We can share our own specific examples of moments when we have recognized our racism while also viewing ourselves as good, decent human beings. A helpful idea comes from abolitionist culture which Bryan Stevenson, author of *Just Mercy*, amplifies when he observes, "Each of us is worth more than the worst thing we've ever done."[63] While his focus is on incarcerated men of color on death row, we can apply it to helping people through the challenging feelings we experience when we begin to recognize our socialized racism.

Build Emotional Capacity

When talking with people who do not recognize the reality of implicit racism, posing questions that lay the emotional groundwork for the person to accept this idea can help. For example, what emotions come up when discussing the various things People of Color find racist? What does it mean to be thought of as part of a racist White group? When you think about yourself and your own needs, what would help you avoid becoming defensive, angry, or depressed if someone associates you with racism?

We can also assist people in depersonalizing the issue by helping them recognize that we can be both individuals and members of our racial group at the same time. While we want people to view and treat us as individuals, we may trigger feelings associated with decades or centuries of racialized trauma, reminding People of Color of a pattern associated with whiteness, like assuming a Person of Color is not the supervisor in a company. In those moments, we are making a racist assumption and that assumption is tied to a very long, harmful history, which makes our error about more than just a single assumption.

The challenge is that, while we are using this frame of mind, it is hard for us to recognize how we do harm. This is why engaging with people further along the identity journey is important. Connecting with antiracist people willing to help each other while honoring each person's value supports people in *Disintegration* to stick with the antiracism path.

REFLECTION

Dear Reader: You've made it to the end of another chapter. Before you go, we ask you to consider at least two of these questions, in a journal or through another method of self-reflection.

Thinking of Yourself:
- What emotions arose as you read the stories in this chapter?
- How do Tyler and Ryan's experiences relate to your own? What is your reaction to Madison? What do your reactions tell you about your own journey?
- What or who in your life supports you to keep moving toward antiracism?

Thinking of Others:
- How do you hope to interrupt racism in the future? What insights do you want to remember from this chapter?
- Which suggested approaches feel most challenging? What would help you implement them? More knowledge? Skill? Emotional balance? What steps can you take to prepare yourself?
- How might a *both/and* approach help you avoid acting harshly toward people who are at the beginning of their journey?

SUMMARY OF TOWARD ANTIRACISM: DISINTEGRATION

In *Disintegration*: Toward Antiracism, we feel conflicted by what we learn about race and its effects; we realize the world does not operate like we thought it did.		
Far-right messages we are susceptible to in this position: • Why Bother to Help If They Hate You Anyway • No One Can Take a Joke Anymore	Antiracist messages that are harmful in this position: • Stop Being a White Savior • You Need to Be Accountable • Yes, All White People (Are Racist)	Suggested approaches: • Pose questions about people's experience with the moral dilemmas • Try to understand why people think as they do; what underlies their beliefs? • Build people's capacity to see themselves as associated with racism through personal stories

7

Retreating into Whiteness

Reintegration

"We don't need you here," the Black activist points to me, the White woman offering to join their civil disobedience on campus.

I leave the protest planning, and I also leave the movement. I retreat into the comfort of the White voices who tell me, "They just want to be upset. You shouldn't have tried to help anyway." This experience draws me, Christine, from Disintegration *into* Reintegration *toward whiteness.*

If *Disintegration* is where White people fall apart, *Reintegration* is where we put ourselves back together. The fundamental question here is: How will we do that? Although we typically veer back and forth in *Disintegration* between "defending whiteness" and moving "toward antiracism," when we land more solidly, that is *Reintegration*. Whether consciously or unconsciously, we develop a more anchored position that provides a longer-lasting resolution to moral dilemmas. In *Reintegration*, we either retreat more fully into whiteness and White culture, or we move closer to forming an antiracist identity. Which side will we choose?

If we retreat into whiteness, this often leads to more overt racism. We have considered the racial terrain and determined that individual racism is not widespread and systemic racism does not exist. We blame People of Color for racism: "If only they were not so loud, so dangerous, so illegal, then they would be successful." From this position, we believe People of Color are the ones who blame everything on racism and there is no way to reason with them.

Figure 7.1 Reintegration: Retreating into Whiteness. ARTIST: LIZ WILTSIE

White people in this position are the ones who claim that "the most discriminated people in this country are White, Christian men." If we are not wealthy, we are likely to reference poverty as a reason why we cannot possibly have white privilege. In this mindset, we will often say and do things that reveal a belief that White people are superior. As a result, we generally avoid interracial situations and will spend time with other White people who have similar opinions.

We hope to stop White people from landing in this position. It's far better to reach people in *Disintegration* or before. Here is why: Whereas people in *Contact* are either oblivious or skeptical about issues of race, and those in *Disintegration* are confused and conflicted, people in *Reintegration* have engaged with race enough to take a position. If the choice is the "retreat into whiteness" side, the decision is that White American culture is not only worth defending, but that it is exceptional—worthy of celebrating as the greatest—and that anyone who says otherwise is attached to wrong-headed views. This is an entrenched position.

And, as we've asserted, context matters. It's important to distinguish the position in which a person is operating: *Contact* vs. *Disintegration* vs. *Reintegration*. For example, in the late 2010s, many antiracists looked at every person wearing a red "Make America Great Again" hat and assumed the person to be a free-range bigot. That may be true for people who have retreated into whiteness and have reinforced their racist beliefs. However, many who wear MAGA hats operate in *Contact* or *Disintegration*, meaning they are not consciously invested in racism, at least not at first.

This can be very difficult for antiracist people to comprehend and, unfortunately, the impulse to dismiss people wholesale creates a missed opportunity. There is a decent chance to guide people in *Contact* and *Disintegration* toward antiracism. Yet, when people in those positions feel antiracists have already judged them to be racist, that can push them into *Reintegration* and toward a full retreat into whiteness and racism.

What do we imagine will happen to Tyler? He is the one whose experiences in *Disintegration* are most likely to move him in this direction. Even though he initially felt empathy for Dani and had brief moments of concern about racism in the United States, his experience with self-proclaimed antiracist people did not match his investment in treating people as individuals with personal agency.

This chapter details what happens as Tyler internalizes racism more fully. We look at the various messages that are particularly likely to continue Tyler's process of retreating into whiteness and examine some approaches we can use so that a pathway remains available for him to re-engage with antiracism somewhere down the road.

> *Dear Reader:* As you read this chapter, take note of your own emotions. Where do you feel angry, frustrated, sad, or hopeless? When do you feel encouraged, supported, and ready to try something new? When have you had similar thoughts or feelings as Tyler or encounters with someone like him? How do you react to someone like Tyler in your own life? Consider what it would take for you to help a person like him re-enter Disintegration so that he can reconsider moving toward antiracism.

FAR-RIGHT MESSAGES

For decades, white nationalists and white supremacists strategized to move the so-called Overton window, the range of ideas people are willing to accept within American mainstream debate, toward white nationalist talking points. The Trump administration succeeded in this beyond white nationalists' wildest imagination. The debate shifted in the late 2010s to such a degree that vast numbers of middle-ground observers on both the right and left side of the political aisle felt horrified by the rank racism, sexism, and xenophobia emanating from Trump and his followers. By the early 2020s, even Fox News opinion hosts, who for many years used "dog whistle" code words to signal racist views while couching them in race-neutral terms, began parroting white nationalist conspiracy theories in plain sight.[64]

This recent history creates a conundrum. The conversation on the political right incorporates harsher, more "in your face" racist viewpoints than in the decades between the civil rights movement and the Trump years. Does this mean that all people on the political right are avowed white supremacists or white nationalists? No, it does not. Antiracists have a hard time recognizing the distinction, however, because an antiracist analysis recognizes the clear overlaps. People on the right who continue to value individualism, colorblindness, and traditional American narratives about the nation's ideals of freedom, democracy, and equality typically do not see the connection to white nationalism and white supremacy.

What this means is that a wide variety of people operate in *Reintegration*, retreating into whiteness. It includes many with limited racial awareness who anchor themselves in traditional, conservative views of personal responsibility, limited government, and colorblindness as well as white nationalists, militia members, Christian nationalists, and others. In this way, it is important to understand how people aligned with this position, but who still believe they are not racist, remain susceptible to messages that can pull them into overt racism. What follows are four examples of claims that work to do this.

Message: Antiracism Is Anti-White

White nationalists and white supremacists regularly argue that "Antiracists say they are against racism. What they are is anti-white. Antiracist is a code word for anti-white." Their recruiting campaigns actually use the phrase "antiracism is anti-white" on banners, billboards, and stickers and this mantra has been associated with racist violence around the globe.[65]

Tyler becomes more susceptible to this claim after his experience at the meeting of activists, where he was asked to join a separate breakout group for White allies. When they asked all the White people to name how they were racist, Tyler believed the stories were designed to make the participants feel guilty. When Tyler asserted that not all White people are racist, the response he got felt inflexible and judgmental. He believed their foregone conclusion that all White people are racist allows no space for people's individualism. Tyler did not feel welcomed or seen and believed the affinity group members had already made up their minds about him, so there was no point in engaging. He suffered through it for Dani's sake but resolved to never return to a group like that ever again.

Once Tyler returns home and shares, his roommates are more than happy to make fun of the Whites-only group: "These so-called antiracist White people can't even be in the same room with Black people? Ridiculous!" Without a clear illustration of the purpose and value of affinity groups (and the essential support they provide), his friends can easily shake their heads and dismiss it as another illustration of the racism of so-called antiracist groups.

At this point, Tyler is susceptible to several messages, illustrated in the form of questions below, that white nationalists use to make the overarching claim that antiracism is anti-white. Notice that each question positions White people as victims and discounts the history and context that make these complex issues understandable.

- Why can People of Color have pride in their cultures, but White people cannot express pride in White culture?
- Why can People of Color expect White people to accommodate their culture, but it is wrong to expect People of Color to assimilate to American (White) society?
- Why do we have Black and Hispanic/Latinx history months, but we cannot have a White history month?
- Why is a Black Student Union okay, but it is not okay to have a White student union?
- Why is segregation wrong when it keeps out Black people, but it is okay to tell White people they are not welcome?
- Why is it okay to tell White people that they are all racist, yet claim People of Color cannot be racist?
- Why are only White people racist when People of Color say terrible things about White people?

All these questions build on each other, creating a false narrative that characterizes social justice principles and antiracist actions as assaults on White people. These questions represent some of the groundwork white nationalists lay as they work toward the claim that multiculturalism and immigration are leading to the "genocide" of White people, that a "great replacement" is happening, and "*those* people" are taking over the country.

Because Tyler does not feel connected to any White antiracist people, he is unlikely to read or hear anything that shows how antiracism is not anti-White. Because he no longer trusts Dani's judgment, whatever remains of their relationship is unlikely to provide Tyler with a pathway back to a nonracist or antiracist position.

- When have you wrestled with one of the questions/messages that the far right uses?
- How would you engage Tyler in the exploration of one of these questions?

Build Emotional Capacity

Hearing narratives that equate antiracism with being anti-White may impact you differently depending upon your position within the round-about. Resist the urge to fight or debate. Instead, self-reflect to identify your reactions. Center yourself as needed so you can stay engaged and move away from the white nationalist talking points. Consider the following reactions you might experience:

- Some of the questions posed above may resonate with you and, therefore, not allow you to offer a different perspective. For example, maybe it is hard to hear White people being made fun of in ways that you cannot do with People of Color. To resolve your confusion, engage with other White people who depersonalize the issue and reframe it using a larger historical perspective. Ask yourself: How does a broader understanding of history affect your feelings and beliefs about what is fair or equitable?
- You may be angry that White people seem so defensive and focused on themselves. You may want to tell them their

unwillingness to engage with antiracism is due to their privilege and fragility. You're probably not wrong; however, being in this "retreat into whiteness" position means they are unlikely to respond well to your assessment. The situation calls for a more strategic approach. For example, rather than retort that White history is taught all year long, explore their defensiveness. Ask questions to hear their perspective and share your different experiences.

Educate Yourself

You may be confused and unsure about how to counter the implications of these questions. In fact, you might not have an answer. If this is true for you, seek out perspectives of scholars of color and White antiracists to understand the context of these questions through an antiracist lens.[66] Learning more can help you stand strong in your own personal experience so that you can answer the questions honestly. For example, you can demonstrate that loving your own culture is not the same as saying yours is the best culture. You can also do the following:

- Learn how we can maintain cultural pride in who we are while also appreciating the contributions and values of many racial and ethnic experiences.
- Learn about the harmful impacts of predominantly white environments on People of Color and the resulting need for People of Color to have intentional places where they can be together for healing, celebration, fortification, community building, and other actions.
- Contrast the segregation of the Jim Crow era, with its foundation in white supremacy, against the cultivation of affinity groups, intended to help people heal from society's racism and move us toward a healthy multiracial future.

Message: Equity Is Un-American

The term "equity" is a trigger word for the far right. This is because the far right understands that equality and equity are radically different concepts. You may have seen the popular graphic below that shows three people of different heights trying to look over a fence. *Equality* gives each of the three people a box of equal size to stand on to see over the fence. One person never needed a box; one person can now see; and one person still cannot see. *Equity* gives each of the people what they need to see over the fence. One person needs no box; one needs one box; and one needs two boxes.

Teachers use this image to explain why giving all kids exactly the same thing (equality) is not necessarily the best choice because it does not address each child's specific needs (equity). Those on the far right view the graphic and its implications very differently. In the far-right estimation, people need to work for those boxes. Hardworking White Americans should not have to provide resources to undeserving People of Color—especially immigrants. The far right doubles down on the idea of equality (from an individualistic, colorblind point of view), and views calls for equity as a way to give free stuff to people who do not work hard enough for themselves. They translate this into the view that "racial equity" is an affront to American values such as ambition, self-reliance, productivity, meritocracy, and independence.

Figure 7.2 Equality versus Equity. Interaction Institute for Social Change;
ARTIST: ANGUS MAGUIRE

When engaging with someone steeped in these far-right ideas, very quickly the language can turn to claims that racial equality does not even exist because racial groups—particularly with regard to Black people—are not fundamentally equal. This also aligns with certain strands of Christianity that continue to refer to Black people as descendants of those who were cursed.[67] In sum, the far right views a push for racial equity as an attempt to make up for some groups' inadequacies, supporting those who cannot get ahead on their own. In other words, scratch the surface, and a belief in the superiority of White people lurks underneath.

Recall that a priority for Tyler has been personal responsibility and individual merit. This makes him a perfect target for this claim that any effort to create "equity" is an un-American ploy to undercut people's need to take care of themselves and pull themselves up by their bootstraps.

Tyler comes into contact with this claim when his conservative and far-right friend group excitedly shares an op-ed by a prominent Black conservative who argues that an equity focus is racist because it prioritizes the color of people's skin and does not value equality of opportunity.[68] In fact, he suggests equity demands an equality of outcome that is fundamentally un-American. He specifically critiques one city that offers support to poor Black, Indigenous, and Latinx families, but not poor White families, and attributes that to equity.

Tyler feels a deep sense of unfairness and anger, believing White people are being mistreated. He's angry that the activists that Dani is following would support un-American and anti-White programs. Tyler increasingly feels the need to stand up for White people.

- What is your personal understanding of the difference between equity and equality?
- How would you offer different perspectives to Tyler, knowing that he feels emboldened because a Black man offers the perspective that equity is un-American?

Cultivate Curiosity

Ask questions of someone like Tyler to understand their definition of equity, equality, personal responsibility, and related values. Ask about their understanding of history and, if relevant, the role religious beliefs play in the strength of their worldview. Avoid challenging or contradicting. Listen to understand their belief structure. What values underlie their beliefs? What experiences pushed them in this direction? What key moments stick with them that helped shape their view? Why is it important that a Black man holds these same views if race doesn't matter? Are there any points of connection you can build on that do not reinforce racism, but allow you to demonstrate your full humanity and areas where you share common values?

Embrace Both/And Thinking

After asking about the person's belief system, try to explore their ideas in a way that validates the value of each concept.

- How and when is equality important? How and when is equity important?
- How can embracing *both* equality *and* equity lead to a healthy future for people of all racial identities?

Educate Yourself

Read economist Heather McGhee's *The Sum of Us: What Racism Costs Everyone and How We Can Prosper Together* to learn how to articulate the costs of "zero-sum thinking." This book explains how failing to support public resources out of a desire to protect one's own "piece of the pie" unwittingly decreases everyone's access to resources and well-being.[69]

Message: Cancel Culture Threatens Free Speech and America's Foundation

The term "cancel culture" means different things to different people. To the far right, cancel culture is a tool of the far-left, designed to oppress conservative viewpoints on social media, on college campuses, and other outlets. The far right views efforts to tell a fuller history as attempts to indoctrinate students with anti-American, anti-White, revisionist histories. They view efforts to remove confederate statues as a further attempt to erase the brilliance of American democracy. In their view, these actions threaten the very ideals of our country, which we must protect at all costs.

Former president Trump once proclaimed that cancel culture is "designed to overthrow the American Revolution."[70]

While this language goes far beyond what Tyler might have initially thought rational just a few months earlier, now that Tyler is decidedly unimpressed with antiracism, his reflection on the social media backlash against the rally he helped plan with the Republican Club looks different. Tyler now believes that the reaction from the "rabid, antiracist leftist mob" is evidence of a culture that cannot tolerate free speech. This belief helps create a longer-lasting resolution to Tyler's anxieties and cognitive dissonance. Tyler also increasingly looks back at his US history course with the view that the professor is undermining our democracy.

- What does the term "cancel culture" mean to you?
- How would you respond to someone who believes "cancel culture" suppresses conservative views?

Cultivate Curiosity

Ask questions about who a person's political and historical heroes are. Without debating or arguing, explore what they value about those heroes and why. Acknowledge the contributions of those heroes. Demonstrate that you are willing to listen. Make connections whenever possible, acknowledging the depth of feeling the person has around these issues. You may completely disagree with almost everything the person says. You can still express that you understand that they are concerned and explain that you emotionally relate to what it feels like to be upset, passionate, and worried over something.

Message: Defend True Patriots

Kyle Rittenhouse is the 17-year-old White boy from Illinois who drove to Kenosha, Wisconsin, in August 2020 amid the peaceful protests and looting that occurred after the police shooting of Jacob Blake, a Black man. Rittenhouse made the drive to join a local militia to help protect property.[71] That evening, he killed two people and wounded a third. He was allowed to drive home on his own, and the police arrested him the following day. As his case went to court, Rittenhouse's lawyers characterized the Black community as dangerous, calling Kenosha a "war zone."[72] They cast Rittenhouse as an American hero defending American ideals while exercising his Second Amendment rights.

The lawyers did not come up with the narrative on their own. Within days of the shooting, the far right offered praise for Rittenhouse's actions. One tweet on Twitter showed an image of rioting and looting and stated, "This is the sacred ground in Kenosha where a 17-year-old child became a Minuteman and said, "'Not on My Watch.'"[73] The far right counts on people overlooking the men Rittenhouse killed, the person he injured, and the fact that he was alongside a known Boogaloo Boi while in Kenosha. (The Boogaloo Bois are white nationalists who want to use social strife to stoke racial animus and start a civil war.)

While Tyler is not a white nationalist, he now believes antiracists are too one-sided. Prioritizing anger at looting as opposed to the unwarranted shooting of a Black man, Tyler feels more aligned with Rittenhouse than with those who protest police violence. This puts him in the position of defending White people and business owners who take up arms against danger in their neighborhoods. From this position, whether intentionally or not, when Tyler speaks up in defense of Rittenhouse, he acts as a defensive shield for white nationalists, white supremacists, and anti-government groups claiming they are the true patriots. This dynamic helps convince antiracist people that there is no distinction between people like Tyler and white nationalists.

- What is the difference between Tyler and white nationalists? Can you explain it to someone?
- How might you engage with someone like Tyler?

Offer Perspective

After gathering the strength to listen to Tyler's perspective, which is likely based on stereotypes, assumptions, or false data claims, offer statements and questions that express interested concern, such as "I wonder if that is really true? How could we find out?" Sprinkle in your own experiences and understandings using a both/and frame that extends the perspective into new territory for the person. Avoid falling into attack or debate mode. Share your experiences with an intention to connect. The point is to complicate the person's viewpoint while maintaining engagement. As David Campt, author of the *White Ally Toolkit*, often says, treat conversations with "race skeptics" like a first date; your goal is to get a second date.[74]

ANTIRACIST MESSAGES

Because this position involves White people actively celebrating whiteness, interactions easily trigger antiracist people's emotions in ways that make it hard to stay calm and strategic. Too often, we also fail to understand the underlying dynamics, which leads us to rely on delivering messages that are generally unhelpful with people in this form of *Reintegration*. The result is that we often feel like we are beating our heads against brick walls. Although avoiding delivering the four messages explored in this section is unlikely to pull someone away from this position, at least it avoids making things worse.

Message: The United States Is Founded on White Supremacy

A White person retreating into whiteness will not respond well to a long list of all the racism in the United States. Whether offering historical or contemporary examples, demonstrating how fundamental white supremacy is to the nation will not work.

Consider Tyler, who finds relief from the cognitive dissonance of our nation's complex history by focusing on facts and narratives that uplift White people as heroes. Unless someone interacting with Tyler acknowledges White people's positive contributions, Tyler will close himself off and find comfort in stories of American exceptionalism.

When a Black scholar comes to campus to talk about the nation's white supremacist roots, a far-right group posts fliers all over campus protesting the talk. Tyler feels drawn to the far-right arguments. In particular, he appreciates their focus on how the Founding Fathers understood the problems of slavery but had to be practical in their approach to ending it. It makes sense to him that the young nation first had to succeed before slavery could be abolished.

The antiracists on campus strip apart this line of thinking, focusing on the racism embedded in the arguments that delayed freedom and proposed that, once freed, the formerly enslaved should be sent back to Africa. Their arguments do not resonate, and Tyler feels more and more emboldened to defend the Founding Fathers against the antiracists and finds more far-right arguments to support his position.

- How does the statement, "the United States is founded on white supremacy," land with you? Do you embrace it? Do you resist it?
- How might you offer multiple perspectives to complicate the American exceptionalism mantra Tyler is attached to?

Cultivate Curiosity

Ask questions about who Tyler's political heroes are. Explore what he values about those heroes. Acknowledge the contributions of those heroes. Consider that Tyler's religious worldview may play a role in his attachment to ideas such as Manifest Destiny. Explore the degree to which Tyler believes White people's superior political, economic, and social position throughout colonial and early US history was ordained by God.

Embrace Both/And Thinking

When trying to lead a person to a more complex, nuanced view of history and their heroes, use a both/and approach to both acknowledge the person and push their thinking at the same time. Some questions that offer this combination include:

- How was Columbus *both* a brave explorer *and* a cruel practitioner of genocide against the Taíno people?
- How was Jefferson *both* a leader of democracy *and* an enslaver who contradicted his own ideals?

You may need to do some personal centering to hold the both/and of these questions. You may also need to deepen your own understanding of history, learning from a wide range of scholars and projects. If you are not particularly religious, this might include exploring works that highlight the positive contributions as well as the critiques of Christianity's dominant role in US society, such as Paul Kivel's *Living in the Shadow of the Cross*.[75]

Message: Equity Is Much More Important than Equality

In our experience, many antiracist people do not realize that the language we use around equity does not reflect a commonly held value in US society. Many antiracist people ask, "Who can be against equity?" The answer: many people who are committed to equality (meaning "same for everyone") and individualism, particularly those influenced by far-right messaging. In fact, antiracist attempts to prioritize equity are a massive red flag for someone retreating into whiteness because of the far-right messaging that blasts equity. Notice that the far right and antiracists offer directly opposing messages on this topic: "equity is un-American" versus "equity is more important than equality."

Recall the figure illustrating Equality versus Equity. It illustrates that not everyone needs *equal* support. Instead, *equity* asks that people receive what they need to succeed. A White person retreating into whiteness is likely to view this as people expecting special treatment that they do not deserve, or teaching people to be dependent on the government. Ironically, people in this position likely view Franklin D. Roosevelt's New Deal or Lyndon B. Johnson's support of Medicare and food stamps as creating a system of entitlement that promotes laziness. This is ironic, because these programs helped many White Americans achieve middle-class status. This also explains why so many conservatives today continue to resist social programs that Democrats advocate.

This issue does not apply only to government or social programs. Tyler runs into messaging highlighting the value of equity at a campus job fair and recognizes it immediately as a red flag. Still thinking about the Black conservative's op-ed and worried about being treated fairly on the job market, he approaches a booth for a major advertising company. Just as he arrives, he overhears the White recruiter tell a Black student, "This article tells you how we do things. We hope you'll consider a position with us." Tyler looks down and sees the article's title: "We Value Equity, Diversity, and Inclusion."

Pointing at the stack of copies, he asks the recruiter, "So how would the company treat someone like me?" The recruiter says that everyone at the company receives fantastic benefits and the tools they need to do their job well. Tyler asks what "equity" has to do with job performance. She replies that some people need more support to feel included and overcome historical disadvantages, so the company has special programs to enhance racial and gender diversity.

To Tyler, this sounds like extra handholding for women and People of Color that would put him at a disadvantage. He asks, "So the company doesn't believe in equality then, right? It's all about making sure that women and People of Color succeed. No one worries about White men succeeding?" He knows he sounds aggressive, but he can't help it. He is angry and feels less optimistic about his own prospects.

- How have you witnessed or experienced people trying to uphold values of equality and equity at the same time?
- If Tyler came to you, upset and believing that equity means the job market discriminates against White men, how would you respond?

Build Relationship
Someone interacting with Tyler should avoid contradicting or debating. Use the conversation as an opportunity to connect and get to know why Tyler thinks and believes as he does. Attempt to locate shared values and tell stories that demonstrate that you are listening. This does not mean validating racist or sexist ideology; we can tell stories of when we felt mistreated, subjected to prejudice, or had our personal goals undermined, without justifying racist beliefs.

Cultivate Curiosity
Avoid assuming there is a shared appreciation for or definition of terms such as equity, discrimination, racism, or diversity. Ask what the person means when they use certain words. Avoid using terms that the far right considers leftist jargon, such as systemic racism, white privilege, and white fragility. It will only serve to antagonize. Use the same language the

person is using and offer differing definitions after establishing a connection with them.

Build Emotional Capacity

Try to engage others in conversations that explore the emotions felt in the face of challenges to ideals about individualism and meritocracy. Ask: What it would mean to them if our society does not operate based on meritocracy all the time? What do they think a world that values equity would look like? What do they feel is at risk for them?

Embrace Both/And Thinking

Once you have acknowledged their perspectives and emotions, introduce the possibility of both/and in conversation. How and when is equality important? How and when is equity important? How can embracing *both* equality and equity provide a supportive and healthy future for people of all racial identities?

Message: I Can Prove You Wrong (with Data)

When talking with someone who views White, Christian men as the most oppressed people in the United States or who make racist statements about communities of color, it is tempting to move into full debate mode and use data and statistics to try and prove them wrong. Antiracists do this almost reflexively, as we feel it is our job to disrupt racism and convince people of their flawed thinking.

White people in retreat look at the data provided by antiracists in a way that confirms the worldview they already have. This happens as Tyler exits the job fair. A career counselor stops him and asks him to fill out a survey about the event. He refuses, saying there is no point because, as a White man, companies are not looking to hire him. She responds by asking him to consider that 90 percent of Fortune 500 CEOs are White men, hoping to undercut the "White men are oppressed" narrative. This does nothing to change Tyler's perspective, as it simply reinforces that no one cares about him becoming successful as an individual. He remains convinced that women and People of Color have not been smart, capable, or resourceful enough to be successful and so they now demand and receive special treatment.

- When have you tried to use data to change someone's mind about something? What happened?
- How can we avoid falling into unproductive debate?

Stay Strategic

The dynamic in the *Reintegration* position on the roundabout is different from *Disintegration*. Recall that as Tyler moved through *Disintegration*, he talked with both Republican Club members and peers from his US history class. Although questioning the concept of systemic racism and feeling pulled toward status quo narratives, Tyler was open and searching for answers.

In *Reintegration*, Tyler's mind is now largely closed, and he is more likely to be fully loaded with competing data points and interpretations. Antiracist people too often believe White people in this position are "uneducated," when it is far more likely that they are "miseducated," accessing contrary, manipulated messaging—"alternative facts"—that function along with confirmation bias to solidify beliefs anchored in white grievance.

The widespread implications of this horrified Shelly one day while attending a Christian nationalist conference in spring 2019 as part of her investigation into white nationalism. A presenter offered "data" drawn from Google search results collected at different points in time to justify homophobic views and policy proposals. The graphs looked nice, and the numbers did move in the direction the presenter indicated. However, having sufficient background in research and statistics, Shelly understood that the underlying method of data collection made the conclusions wrong-headed and the claims unsupportable. People can create "data" that support anything they want and use it to offer compelling narratives that build on people's fears and confusion.

What does this mean for how we engage with Tyler? Aggressively debating with him is unlikely to do any good. Tyler is so steeped in individualism that he cannot view the data from a systemic perspective until he returns to *Disintegration*. He'll need support to work through the moral dilemmas again, facing the fears they arouse. He will need someone to get curious, listen, and connect to expand Tyler's imagination regarding what racism can mean, its harm, and why it is worth addressing. Now, though, Tyler is primarily concerned about himself.

Embrace Both/And Thinking

One way to engage someone like Tyler is to lean into the idea of racism harming White people, but from a different angle. While Tyler thinks equity efforts undermine his life chances as a White man, an antiracist lens offers that white supremacy is an oppressive system that harms all people, including White people. Understanding AWARE-LA's "White Supremacy System Model" could be useful.[76] This analysis could encourage Tyler to consider that the struggles White men experience in the workplace are not due to women and People of Color entering and taking the positions. Instead, they are due to an inhumane, inequitable economic system that allows for the exploitation of all employees, including White men.

While this train of thought could lead to a debate about the value of capitalism and accusations of Marxism, it could also plant important seeds. A primary both/and question would be: "It seems that racism hurts everyone. I wonder how White people suffer from racism in different ways than People of Color?"

Educate Yourself

The book *Dying of Whiteness* by psychiatrist Jonathan Metzl is a great resource to learn more about the psychology of people who retreat into whiteness and how it convinces them—White men in particular—to scapegoat People of Color, women, and others while making choices that results in us collectively experiencing harm and reduced prosperity.[77]

The ability to identify whether a person is attached to a Christian nationalist worldview is also critical, as this ideology incorporates a complex set of beliefs that go well beyond race. The book *Taking America Back for God: Christian Nationalism in the United States* is a key resource that explains why individuals influenced by this ideology (which is more about political power than religion) are so attached to symbolic patriotism, gun rights, anti-immigrant sentiment, and various elements of the culture wars.[78] Recognizing the rationales underlying Christian nationalists' interconnected set of concerns can help you generate an approach that attempts to inspire moments of *Disintegration* (as difficult as this may be).

> *Dear Reader:* We want to highlight a particular dynamic to pay attention to when considering whether or how to discuss systemic racism. You may have noticed that in chapters 3, 5, and 7 ("Encountering Others: Contact," "Defending Whiteness: Disintegration," and "Retreating into Whiteness: Reintegration") that we caution against pushing the systemic racism concept because people in these positions are generally leaning away from antiracism and are not likely to react well.
>
> We do recommend learning about and discussing systemic racism for people in chapters 6 and 8 ("Toward Antiracism: Disintegration" and "Emerging Antiracism: Reintegration"). In these positions, people are better able to integrate the concept and shift the way they interpret the world.
>
> We know these nuances can seem challenging to navigate. Allow yourself opportunities to practice. You will not always get it "right." We know because we're always learning, too. And every interaction will make the next one better.

Message: You Aren't Worth It

While most who act from a "retreat into whiteness" position are not die-hard white supremacists or hate-group members, they do offend antiracist sensibilities. To demonstrate how seriously we take antiracism, many of us block these individuals from our lives and our social media accounts. Oftentimes, we receive positive reinforcement that this is the right thing to do, that it is a rejection of racism, and that we are better people for doing it.

Unfortunately, cutting off communication may only push people further into retreat where they will do more harm. In sending the message that they are no longer worthy of our time, we also confirm their belief that antiracism represents a "cancel culture." This plays into their view that antiracists are hypocrites when we claim to value inclusivity. And although distancing from someone is a far cry from wanting society to dispose of them in an inhumane way, it does provide fodder for the far right to question how seriously antiracists (particularly those who advocate for abolishing prison or police) believe in extending care and redemption for all people, regardless of their offense.

Tyler has stayed connected to a friend he shares from the improv world with Dani, a White man named Robert. When a favorite White comedian of theirs comes under fire for mocking a Chinese American, using racial slurs and a fake accent, Tyler vigorously defends the comedian. Robert, however, slams the comedian and his anti-Asian racism, particularly in light of the recent escalation of anti-Asian hate crimes. After an emotional round of argument, Robert ends the conversation and his connection with Tyler, telling him that he doesn't want to be friends with a racist. While Robert feels good about his stance against racism, Tyler takes this as further evidence of how antiracists want to cancel anyone with conservative viewpoints.

- When have you stayed in a relationship with someone who defends racist speech or actions? When have you ended those relationships?
- What would you do in this situation if Tyler were your friend?

Build Relationship

For Tyler to shift out of his entrenched position, he needs someone to act as an open doorway so that antiracist viewpoints can enter his awareness, even if in a limited way. For this reason, we ask that you avoid automatically disengaging from the Tylers in your life. Instead, approach the situation as you might a brick wall that you hope will crumble.

Use questioning, listening, connecting, and both/and thinking to strategically pick at the mortar that keeps the racist bricks in place. Undermine the wall's foundation as best as you can over time. If you are successful, and holes in the mortar appear, you may inspire the person to shift back into *Disintegration*. If that occurs, the person will need support. Experiencing *Disintegration* is not easy.

Staying engaged with someone in this position is also not easy, as it often involves hearing views that are racist and hurtful. To maintain the relationship, consider that race or racism does not need to be the topic of every conversation. Choose your moments wisely. Spend time talking about neutral, non-race-specific subjects to keep each other's humanity front and center. This will be key, particularly if the person regularly accesses media characterizing People of Color and antiracist people as anti-American haters who want to destroy the country. The idea is to connect on a human level and demonstrate the falseness of the claims whenever possible.

Even if you need to lessen contact to care for your own well-being and focus in a different direction, try to stay in a relationship with the person while still being clear about your own values. This is when acknowledging the truth of their emotions and then offering a different perspective can be particularly helpful. It allows you to believe their feelings, yet suggest a counter to their problematic ideas.

And if staying in a sustained relationship is not viable, that is okay. It is important to prioritize your health and strategize about the best uses of your time and energy. Be thoughtful about this challenging and difficult decision.

Many People of Color have told us they expect us to do this hard work with those who enact racism. From this perspective, cutting people off is performative. It allows us to claim credit for taking a hard line, and yet we do not decrease the harm they perpetuate. We need to interrupt this pattern and make a stronger effort to avoid blocking people while we work to become positive role models who can support them into a different frame of mind.

Take Care of Self

To be clear, we are not asking people to go along with racist behavior or to endure abuse, gaslighting, or trauma. We are also not asking people to spend a lot of time debating with people in this position. We are simply suggesting that we consider that staying in a relationship with them and maintaining open lines of communication may allow us to interrupt some of the harm done to People of Color.

If you take on this challenge, know that you will engage more successfully on some days than on others. Some days you will need to excuse yourself, as the emotional toll may be significant. Deciding when and how to engage can feel hard. These suggestions may help:

- Choose the form of engagement that works for you. Perhaps live, in-person conversations help you connect better. Perhaps email exchanges where you can think before responding can help you stay centered.
- Develop a predictable communication cycle so that you can prepare emotionally and mentally.
- Shift focus if an exchange becomes too intense or you do not have the emotional bandwidth to stay centered. Say, "Today's not a good day for this conversation," and move on.
- Cultivate healthy boundaries. Excuse yourself from a conversation if you are being verbally attacked.
- Take a break from the relationship when necessary. Sometimes a step away for a time will allow you to return later with more emotional capacity.
- After challenging conversations, don't isolate yourself. Reach out to friends and community members who can hear your disappointment, sadness, and frustration.

Not everyone is able to stay in relationship with people in this position. If you are unsure of what to do, or if the situation is beyond your capacity, reach out to others to help determine who is best positioned to maintain the relationship. Work together to notice a potential moment ripe for change, and then you might help the person move out of retreat and back into *Disintegration*.

Educate Yourself

Tyler is not an avowed white nationalist, and neither are most people who retreat into whiteness. A helpful resource for determining how far down the rabbit hole of bigotry someone has gone and what to do in response is the toolkit, "Confronting Conspiracy Theories and Organized Bigotry at Home," published by the Western States Center. It describes five levels of indoctrination, ranging from accidental absorption to calls for violence, and provides a conversation guide to help you stay connected and react responsibly to someone expressing bigoted ideas.[79]

> *Dear Reader*: If the idea of engaging with someone retreating into whiteness feels frightening or overwhelming, we understand. We are not asking anyone (particularly those from marginalized communities) to put themselves at risk of injury or harm. Fascists are dangerous (particularly to People of Color, female-identified persons, Jewish people, Muslim people, and members of the LGBTQIA+ community), and it is important to recognize the difference between someone like Tyler, who's not a fascist, versus an active hate-group member, as they require different responses. Please seek assistance as needed.

A CASE STUDY MOMENT: ADDRESSING PEOPLE IN RETREAT WITHIN MULTIRACIAL AND GROUP SETTINGS

In a workshop about systemic racism, Christine led a group through a historical review of Chicago's forced and de facto segregation. After the history lesson, a White participant asked, with a bit of an edge, "When are you going to address the fact that the Black community is addicted to welfare?" At that moment, Christine had to decide whether to use the strategies we suggest above (cultivating curiosity, offering a both/and response, building relationship, etc.) or attend to the needs of the group.

In this tough situation, Christine decided to acknowledge the person, and then pivot in a different direction. She told the participant she did not intend to explore that question and added, "I wonder how it functions to focus on Black people and welfare when we look at systemic racism, when actually more White people are on welfare proportionally? When you have more time, perhaps you can explore where those narratives come from and how they impact people."

Christine's "acknowledge and pivot" response prioritized the needs of the group instead of giving attention to an individual person in retreat. She acknowledged the person's desire to make a point, while diverting them away from offering additional and, likely, disingenuous arguments. This strategy is helpful in many multiracial group situations, from workplace meetings to family dinners, because it allows you to interrupt moments when someone's speech may be causing harm.

With practice, you will learn how to judge when to insert yourself and how to work with someone. In a public conversation where People of Color are being harmed, a quick pivot to interrupt and redirect the flow of conversation may be in order. In a conversation among a group of White people, the group might benefit from you posing questions and diving deeper. In general, when we are in public, we must balance the need to interrupt harm with our interest in shifting people away from entrenched racism. In private, we can afford to take time and slowly support someone.

The participant in Christine's workshop needed a private, follow-up conversation after the session, one that introduced a both/and lens to focus on how systems affect people's lives. As more of us improve in our ability to engage in these conversations, we hope someone in that person's life can draw the person away from the "retreat into whiteness" position.

REFLECTION
Dear Reader: You've made it to the end of another chapter. Before you go, we ask you to consider at least two of these questions, in a journal or another method of self-reflection.

Thinking of Yourself:
- When did you feel angry, frustrated, confused, or hopeless while reading this chapter? When did you feel encouraged, clear, supported, or ready to try something new?
- When have you had similar thoughts or feelings as Tyler? What helped you process those thoughts or feelings?
- Which of the suggested resources might you explore to learn more about how racism negatively impacts everyone, including White people, or how religion might play a role in your approach to issues raised in this chapter?

Thinking of Others:
- How do you react to someone like Tyler in your own life? Do you flee, fight, or freeze?
- What would it take for you to help a person like Tyler re-enter *Disintegration* so that he can reconsider moving toward antiracism?
- What experience do you have with people influenced by a Christian nationalist ideology? How have you attempted to engage in constructive dialogue? What has worked or not worked?
- How will you take care of yourself and avoid putting yourself at risk if attempting to stay connected to someone with staunchly bigoted views?

SUMMARY OF RETREATING INTO WHITENESS: REINTEGRATION

In *Reintegration*, we recognize being White as a meaningful part of our identity and defend dominating White norms; we believe discrimination is more widespread against White people than People of Color.

Far-right messages we are susceptible to in this position:	Antiracist messages that are harmful in this position:	Suggested approaches:
• Antiracism Is Anti-White	• The United States Is Founded on White Supremacy	• Be curious and learn how the person's beliefs developed
• Equity Is Un-American	• Equity Is Much More Important than Equality	• Use both/and thinking to acknowledge how White people have contributed positively to our nation's history while sharing ideas that complicate that history
• Cancel Culture Threatens Free Speech and America's Foundation	• I Can Prove You Wrong (with Data)	• Offer stories that question whether prejudicial ideas are true
• Defend True Patriots	• You Aren't Worth It	• Seek to remain connected by avoiding direct critique of the person's heroes

8

Emerging Antiracism

Reintegration

With an hour to wait between the campus tour and scheduled interview, the tour guide points me toward the cafeteria. The door opens to reveal a room crowded with mostly White people eating and talking. I stop short, catch my breath, and take a step back.

Everything in sight reeks of dominating whiteness. The musty old buildings symbolize White supremacist elitism and exclusivity. I assume the people are all racist, but probably don't know it. "How could I possibly attend this school?" I wonder.

Emotionally, I am reeling. Having recently watched a documentary revealing the damage racism has wrought over the centuries in the United States and how it continues, everything associated with being White feels awful. I, Shelly, am in the throes of a Reintegration *moment, heading toward antiracism.*

In *Reintegration*, if people move toward antiracism, they begin to recognize the significance of being part of a White group. In doing so, they start to accept their association with the history of racism and ongoing, dominating whiteness. Strong emotions of guilt, shame, regret, fear, and/ or anger often come with this acknowledgment. Facing these emotions makes this a challenging, yet ultimately liberating path forward.

Liberation feels like a distant goal, however, because this position requires us to navigate a complex set of dynamics. While further along in our identity journey, we are simultaneously prone to dissonance each time we integrate a new idea into our emerging antiracist worldview. This

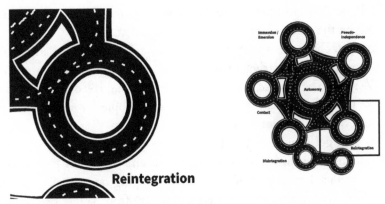

Reintegration

Figure 8.1 Reintegration: Emerging Antiracism. ARTIST: LIZ WILTSIE

means we can move back and forth between a disintegrated "defending whiteness" position and a reintegrated "emerging antiracism."

Part of the challenge is that it is very difficult to use both/and thinking while in this position unless we have support. We are newly grasping how systemic racism works, but our vision remains fuzzy, with individualistic interpretations remaining an easy default. For Shelly, visualizing the systemic nature of racism felt like repeatedly constructing a mosaic in her mind: sometimes, the pieces came together to reveal a complex, yet clear picture, while at other moments the image fell back into separate pieces.

At times, she could recognize how housing discrimination, criminalization of youth of color, and educational inequities worked together to negatively impact her elementary school students. Then, just hours or days later, facing a counterargument about people making the choice to move to less gang-affected areas, the clarity vanished. She would again question if systemic racism really existed, and in those moments could no longer see the full picture. Gratefully, she had a community around her that helped her glue the pieces into place over time, solidifying her understanding.

At this point, it is also hard to balance the ways our various identity positions lead to both advantages and disadvantages. We may realize that being White brings benefits; however, we may struggle to focus on those benefits if we are also a target of oppression—Jewish, female-identified, poor, disabled, and/or part of the LGBTQIA+ community. In other words, it can feel unsettling to focus on our advantages if we are used to focusing on the areas where we feel targeted and at risk.

Another challenge is that unlearning racism often feels like an assault on our egos, which can trigger painful emotions and an unsteady sense of self. We tend to beat ourselves up and/or feel beaten up by others. This can provoke us to verbally lash out at other White people for racist behavior or speech or for not living up to antiracist ideals.

We can get caught in this loop because while we may now recognize systemic racism, we remain unaware of and/or do not look at our *own* internalized racism. Instead of acknowledging our own limitations and complicity, we attempt to distance ourselves from White people and whiteness. This means that, although we are a step closer to antiracism, our antiracist identity and action is not as healthy or effective as we wish.

Madison frequently operates from this position. She often feels the need to demonstrate a commitment to racism by hitting back at any display of whiteness. Madison is not alone. Most of us who have passed through this phase recall moments where we acted unhelpfully, prompted by our own difficult emotions.

Role models are extremely important here. Although our learning will take time, a respected mentor showing us a different approach to being White can help us avoid getting stuck. Thankfully, mentorship can come in many forms, from personal connections and trusted community members to podcast hosts and authors. What we need is someone to show us what it looks like to be a healthy, antiracist White person.

Filmmaker and visionary Shakti Butler of World Trust Educational Services provides White people important role models in her films *Mirrors of Privilege: Making White Visible* and *Cracking the Codes: The System of Racial Inequity*.[80] Both films offer windows into how to navigate personal, institutional, and systemic racism as white people.

> *Dear Reader*: Perhaps you recognize yourself or those you know in this description. We understand what a challenge this can be. Operating from this position generally feels awful. It is also off-putting to others, making us unlikely to draw people toward antiracism. This is why we wrote this book. We want you to know

that joining a collective of supportive, White antiracist people can help you move past the emotional
turmoil. Being around people with a healthy and
positive antiracist, White identity offers something to
look forward to and a path to get there.

Whereas the previous chapter explored Tyler's retreat into whiteness, this chapter focuses on Ryan and Madison's attempts to engage with antiracism. Madison has been operating here for a while without support. It is new for Ryan, as he recently became friends with a multiracial group at the after-school program, including Jamie, his White non-binary friend.

FAR-RIGHT MESSAGES
Those on the far right recognize the guilt and shame felt by many White people and use it to their advantage. "Why would people want to subject themselves to this?" they ask. Each of the two messages discussed in this section are particularly provocative for people in this position because of how they exploit our emotional upheaval.

Message: Damned If You Do, Damned If You Don't
The far right seizes on antiracism's demands and poses the question: "If you can never get it right, why should you even try? Why subject yourself to guilt, shame, and blame? You're a good person; why let people make you feel guilty and responsible for fixing every bad thing that has happened throughout history? Nothing you do will ever be good enough for them."

Ryan is susceptible to this message after he sees one of his favorite pro football players come under fire for an ad campaign that activists call "performative" and "condescending." The ad shows the White athlete as the hero with a snappy tagline offering a hopeful vision; Ryan appreciates the positive message. The criticism bothers Ryan because he can see himself doing and saying the same thing. Why wasn't the player getting any credit for trying? After all, he is using his platform to speak out, which he has been told to do. So, why is he now getting criticized for drawing attention to himself?

Ryan wants a list of dos and don'ts that can keep him out of trouble. When he shares his frustration with Jamie, one of his friends at the after-school program, they tell him it's more complicated than a list can explain and that the only way to get things right is to keep working on himself to understand racism better. This hits Ryan hard because he feels stuck in a cycle of failure, surprised when White people's efforts offend People of Color in ways he does not understand. In exasperation, Ryan blurts out, "Why can't you just tell me what we are supposed to do! Why does this have to be so hard?"

- How have you witnessed or experienced the idea that it is impossible to do anything right?
- What could help Ryan stick with it and stay focused on learning from his or other people's missteps?

Embrace Both/And Thinking

Jamie starts by acknowledging that antiracism is complicated. A list will not truly prepare Ryan to make informed decisions. To build a nuanced view, Jamie helps Ryan explore some of the competing messages that White people receive, such as these common ones shown in the table below.

Competing Directives	
White people need to speak up.	Don't center White people in the conversation because White people talk too much.
Follow the lead of People of Color.	Don't expect People of Color to teach you.
This work is not about you as a White person who benefits from racism; focus on People of Color who are the targets of racism.	White people need to do their own work.

The idea is to shift these seemingly competing messages into the complexity of the both/and frame. Ryan needs to hear where and when each of these statements is true. For example, it is true that White people should follow the lead of People of Color as we partner in the fight against racism, particularly when it comes to taking direct action in organizing, activism, and rallying for change.

At the same time, we should not expect the People of Color in our lives to teach us about ourselves and about racism. We need to take responsibility for accessing the resources we need. Ultimately, the more we learn, the more we realize when to engage and when not to engage and how to do it more effectively. What initially feels contradictory, over time becomes distinguishable directives full of important insight.

Build Emotional Capacity

Share stories of how hard lessons ultimately reduce anxiety. For example, with humility, Jamie can tell Ryan about a time when they stayed silent when they needed to speak up. Learning from mistakes is all part of the process and has helped them navigate race more confidently. It is liberating to have a clearer sense of when to stay silent and when to speak up, knowing that we have the skills to repair the situation. If we keep trying and make good use of feedback, success is possible.

Message: Why Are Our White Children Being Shamed and Taught to Feel Guilty?

Well before the movement against critical race theory, the far right argued that antiracism intends to make White people feel guilty. The most current iteration is that all efforts to educate about historical, systemic racism and ongoing oppression harms White children by shaming them. The claims by the far right are purposefully inflammatory, overblown, and misstate the reality. However, the message resonates and is effective because most people do not want to inflict pain on young people of any racial background.

Consider what happens when the local news in Ryan's city runs a story about parents at a nearby high school who staged a protest about a history teacher who is "tearing down America's foundations." When Ryan sees the story, he wonders why the parents are mad that their kids are learning about systemic racism, which he now understands. But the parents claim the teacher told their kids they should feel guilty about being White. This catches Ryan's attention. He doesn't think people should be encouraged to feel guilty. Is there a way to learn what they need to know without so much negativity? Ryan isn't sure.

- What feelings arise as you think about how teachers should present US history? How should teachers consider and support students' feelings as they learn about difficult topics?
- If teachers offer a less provocative version of history to protect White students' feelings, how might it affect students of color?
- What can help Ryan sort through his confusion?

Offer Perspective

That weekend, Ryan has an opportunity to talk about the news story with his uncle, a history buff, who is visiting from out of town. Ryan knows that his uncle often offers different perspectives on issues. They discuss some key questions:

- *How did this resistance to antiracism start?* Ryan's uncle explains how the local protest is part of a larger movement funded by far-right organizers who believe students should learn only the positive aspects of US history, focusing on American exceptionalism. They reject the concept of systemic racism. For them, there is no middle ground where it is possible to teach a more complete version of US history without shaming White students.
- *When did White people become the focus of worry?* When Ryan asks about teachers making White students feel guilty, his uncle shares that he doesn't believe most teachers try to make their students feel guilty. The trouble is that for decades, US schools have primarily offered a Eurocentric history that glorifies White historical figures and validates White students. When teachers offer a more complicated narrative that highlights the stories of marginalized people and offers more detail about systemic racism, it disrupts the "all-around goodness" that underlies the white supremacy narrative. They agree that omitting parts of history isn't right.

- *How are the needs of People of Color lost within this debate?* Ryan's uncle reminds him that those protesting express no care about the feelings of students of color when the contributions of their people are left out of history. They discuss how accurate history leads to a more nuanced understanding of how racism impacts People of Color today and an increase in empathy among White students.

Build Emotional Capacity

Ryan's uncle supports Ryan by empathizing with his tough feelings and helping him process his confusion. Within this conversation, he provides encouragement regarding how to be resilient in the face of difficult emotions, telling stories from his own experience.

An important message he delivers is that shame and guilt are not the same.

Shame refers to negative feelings we have about who we *are*. When we experience shame, we often feel like there is something inherently wrong with us. Shame does not prompt useful forward movement. No one should be encouraged to feel shame based on their group's history.

Guilt operates differently. Guilt refers to feeling badly about something we *did*. Ryan's uncle can share how we shouldn't feel guilty about what other people did. We have a choice to show up differently than the people from the past. We can get better at opposing racism, day by day.

While some guilt can be motivating, antiracist organizers and activists are clear that overwhelming guilt can lead to inaction. Continuing conversation, if and when guilt and shame do arise, is a key to building emotional resilience and maintaining action. Action with purpose and integrity, in and of itself, will reduce guilt and lead to a healthier antiracist life.

Educate Yourself

For parents and other adults supporting young people, Jennifer Harvey's book, *Raising White Kids: Bringing Up Children in a Racially Unjust America*, provides great advice about how to build an emotionally healthy White identity for young people.[81] To learn more about what teachers can do to support students, read the article "White Teachers, Know Thyself" by Jamie Utt and Shelly Tochluk.[82]

ANTIRACIST MESSAGES

At the core of antiracism is an effort to become more human with one another. An entire range of important principles help guide us in that direction. At the same time, one-sided or harsh versions of those messages undercut the humanization that our collective liberation requires. This is true of the four messages highlighted in this section as they play on our unresolved fears, guilt, and shame and cause us to attend less to people's experiences and development.

Message: Don't Coddle White People

Given that White people's needs have been historically prioritized over the needs of People of Color, antiracists often try to do the reverse and appropriately prioritize the needs of People of Color. This is especially true when White people say or do something that demonstrates ignorance or perpetrates racism and requires a correction. In this position of *Reintegration*, we believe that not coddling White people means we need to come at them full force. Unfortunately, sometimes we lose our ability to differentiate when to support a White person as they change and when to call them out. We interpret any support as coddling.

Ryan experiences this at a teach-in about critical race theory. As people gather for the event, he notices that he is one of the only White guys. The presentation given by the multiracial group from the Social Justice Club impresses Ryan. He decides to play "devil's advocate" to demonstrate his investment and critical thinking. Isn't it important to worry about guilt? Don't they think teachers presenting a neutral stance or a balanced perspective can help avoid making White students feel guilty? Don't they worry about divisiveness?

As far as Ryan is concerned, he is on their side. However, one of the White presenters, Jess, views Ryan as being contrary. Jess appears increasingly frustrated as Ryan asks his questions, one after another. After his third question, she says, "Please stop dominating. Why do you always have to know better?"

As the event ends, Ryan sits flustered and tries to compose himself. A White girl, Emma, comes over to ask if he's okay. Jess notices and says, "Emma, please don't coddle him," and leaves the room.

- What thoughts or feelings arise for you as you hear about Ryan's approach to the meeting and Jess's reaction?
- How can we balance the need to be honest about the racism and/or privilege we notice while also supporting and helping people who enact racism and/or privilege?

Embrace Both/And Thinking

Both/and thinking allows us to hold people accountable with love. Christine recalls when she felt she only had one option to avoid accusations of coddling—go on the attack. Shifting to both/and helped her realize that she could hold herself and other people accountable, and do it with love. She developed the term loving accountability to interrupt the either/or thinking this message created in her. It allows her to support people to process their feelings while also guiding them away from problematic behavior.

If Emma can maintain a both/and focus, she can help Ryan process the feelings that come up when he receives criticism. She can also help him understand that while his questions might be important to him, he did take up a lot of space in a haughty and somewhat aggressive manner. Ideally, Ryan will learn from the experience and act differently in the future.

Build Emotional Capacity by Checking In

We will make mistakes and feel a whole host of emotions as a result. Emma already begins acknowledging this when she asks Ryan if he is okay. If Emma talks one-on-one with him and focuses on his feelings, this is not coddling. Instead, validating that Ryan might feel embarrassed and then supporting him to keep processing his emotions sets the stage for growth. Some of the questions Emma might discuss with Ryan are the following:

- How does it feel to be told you're dominating?
- What feelings did you have as you asked the questions? What feelings do you have now?

Build Emotional Capacity Through Mindfulness

Antiracists often say we need to learn to "sit in discomfort." This helps us stay open to new ideas and critiques that push us beyond our comfort zone. Mindfulness practices are particularly useful, prompting us to identify our emotions rather than trying to fight or flee from them.

Mindfulness practices could help Ryan recognize what motivations led him to act as he did. He might realize that underneath his questioning was a desire to impress People of Color or the Social Justice Club members more broadly. The idea is for us to learn how to identify the emotions that prompt us to make the choices we make, which allows us to get better at noticing our motivations in the future. Building this self-awareness is what helps us avoid falling into well-worn, damaging patterns.

To help other people as well as ourselves, we can seek out mindfulness practices. Dr. Bettina Love suggests "White Teachers Need Anti-Racist Therapy" in a useful *Education Week* article, offering many important resources including the work of Anneliese A. Singh and Yolanda Sealey-Ruiz."[83]

Offer Perspective

Loving accountability asks us to acknowledge the humanity of the person who has done harm and support them in understanding the impact of their actions. Emma can lean into this as she helps Ryan explore why he felt so comfortable asking a rapid-fire series of questions, almost to the point of interrogation. She can ask him questions such as:

- Why did you ask so many questions? What was your intent?
- May I offer you some feedback about how you came across and the impact of your approach?
- Can we think about how you can be aware of your tone and how much time you take up in the future?

This dialogue would clarify Ryan's goals and help him achieve them without him falling into common patterns of White male domination.

Message: You're Not Doing Enough

Antiracists deliver the message that "you're not doing enough" when guilt and shame mixes with the real urgency we feel to act. Often used to motivate people to adopt some action, the combustible mixture of negative emotion and pressure to act beyond one's capacity can backfire.

Madison experiences this dynamic at an organizing meeting that brings various community partners to the community center where she works. They are advocating for a shift in public resources from incarceration toward drug treatment. At the meeting, Tricia, a local White activist, passes out flyers for a Sunday morning rally, emphasizing that everyone needs to attend and bring at least five people with them. Madison has spent extra time for the past few weeks making phone calls, sending coordinating emails, and lending support wherever she can. She is happy to help, although she is not planning to attend the rally due to other commitments.

As the meeting breaks up, Madison apologizes to Tricia, saying she wants to be helpful but cannot attend the rally—she is exhausted and needs the weekend to catch up with grad school homework. Tricia tells Madison, "Us White folks really need to show up for this. Dig deep. It's not like People of Color get to take a break from racism." Feeling guilty, Madison relents and commits to attending and recruiting others to attend as well, using the message, "If People of Color cannot rest, neither can we. That's our privilege."

- How do Tricia and Madison use guilt to motivate people into action in ways that are not sustainable?
- How do we inspire people to act without anchoring the motivation in guilt and shame?

Build Emotional Capacity

Doing more often means stepping outside our comfort zone, acting in ways that are new to us. It is important to say "yes" to this kind of stretching. On the other hand, tactics that guilt or shame us into pushing beyond our capacity can lead to negative consequences. Thankfully, many of today's organizers value and dedicate themselves to ongoing growth and action as well as leading healthy, sustainable lives. This is part of rejecting a dehumanizing, dominant White culture that values people only for their level of productivity. Madison needs someone who can support her to accurately assess her capacity, receive validation for the contributions she has made, and consider whether there are additional ways to help that fit within her capacity.

As shame and guilt are not sustainable motivators, it helps to understand that white supremacy and domination injure everyone, although to different degrees and in different ways. This allows White people to authentically identify our personal stake in ending racism. A model explains how the white supremacy system harms White people supports us to build clarity about our personal stake in the struggle, and supports our resilience and fortitude.[84]

Using this kind of model can allow Madison to generate participation without relying on guilt. For example, instead of telling people that failing to show up is an enactment of privilege, Madison might use "relational organizing" principles and express the joy of coming together to fight for the world we want to live in.

Embrace Both/And Thinking

Underlying the "you're not doing enough" message is an unhealthy either/or belief: *Either* you're participating in everything *or* you're not doing enough. Unfortunately, this belief leads to overwhelm and burnout and prevents people from living sustainable antiracist lives. The both/and is to *both* contribute what you can *and* achieve balance in your life through collective action. When a collective acts with mutual care and an eye on sustainable movements, they recognize their strength comes from people contributing as they can and not asking everyone to be involved in everything.

Message: White People's Feelings Don't Matter

White people have a long history of caring only about the experience of White people. In response, antiracists push back against this pattern to rebalance the scales, intending to focus on the feelings of People of Color. Sometimes, though, this can erase care for White people's feelings altogether.

Madison runs into this as the center hosts a final preparation meeting for the rally. Before getting to the tasks needed for the rally, the meeting opens with a grounding in the center's mission. Two community members take center stage, one Black and one Indigenous, to share testimonials about their personal experience with addiction, incarceration, and recovery.

In a planning frame of mind, Madison had not expected to hear such powerful stories, and she feels raw. At that moment, another White woman stands up, awash in tears, and thanks them for their courage, telling them that she is sure she would never have had the strength to overcome what they have endured and how badly she feels about what they have had to go through. There is a strong reaction in the room.

As some people move to comfort the crying woman with tissues, the facilitators announce that the meeting will separate into racial affinity, People of Color and White, for the next part of the meeting to process how the comments and attention to the White woman's pain erased the pain and powerful stories shared by the Black and Indigenous women.

In the White racial affinity group, the facilitator says that was not the time or the place to center White people's feelings: they suggest that in a multiracial context, White people's feelings do not matter. They spend the affinity time talking about the negative impact of White women's tears in multiracial groups and why they must be avoided.

After the affinity time, the larger, multiracial group reconvenes. Madison is deeply self-conscious, hyperaware of her desire to cry, and upset at how this affinity group felt like punishment. She can barely focus on the logistics discussed during the rest of the meeting. A half-hour later, Madison walks out of the room believing White people are never allowed to show their feelings in front of People of Color, and she is more afraid than ever about upsetting her co-workers of color.

- What thoughts or feelings arise as you read about Madison's experience?
- What can help Madison navigate her feelings and develop a more nuanced perspective?

Build Emotional Capacity

Racism dehumanizes, and it is okay for White people to cry and have deep, complex feelings about it. However, we do need to be aware of when and how we express our emotions in interracial situations, particularly with crying. In order to build our emotional capacity in the face of racism's horrible consequences for People of Color, we need to name the emotions we feel and create a container for processing them. Racial affinity is the place for this to happen without harming People of Color. It is the place to explore the variety of our emotions: the shock at learning the depth of racism for the first time, the guilt we feel about how People of Color suffer in ways that we don't, and the hopelessness of feeling that racism will never end, among many other reactions.

The facilitators made the correct call to move into affinity after the White woman's reaction. However, the focus only on what happened in the multiracial space was a missed opportunity. The White facilitators could have also supported the White people to process their emotions to build the strength and capacity to not center their emotions when bearing witness to the powerful stories of People of Color.

To prepare for these difficult moments, expose yourself to new information regularly (via articles, books, and videos) and process your emotions before entering interracial dialogue groups. You can also practice sitting with emotion rather than trying to make the emotion go away. Mindfulness practices can be particularly useful.

Resources like Resmaa Menakem's *My Grandmother's Hands: Racialized Trauma and the Pathways to Mending Our Hearts and Bodies* can help us support others as well as ourselves.[85] As mentioned before, additional resources include *The Racial Healing Handbook* by Anneliese A. Singh[86] and the work of Yolanda Sealey-Ruiz on a process called "Healing through the Archaeology of Self."[87]

Embrace Both/And Thinking

Like the facilitators in this scenario, many people take an either/or approach to White women's tears and people's reactions to them. As a White woman who cries, Christine struggled with this message at first. Over time, she came to learn that it is less about *if* she cries than *how* she cries. Does she cry and expect all the energy to shift to her? Does she expect People of Color to comfort her? She now has strategies to let people know that she does not need or expect People of Color to focus on her or comfort her. This is how she interrupts the long pattern of White women derailing interracial dialogues and centering themselves when they cry. Christine has also learned to seek the support she needs from other White people.

Message: Your Intent Doesn't Matter

Antiracists often deliver the message that "your intent doesn't matter." It is a version of an essential principle known as intent versus impact. The idea is that the impact of people's words and actions are more important than people's intentions. For example, if someone steps on another person's foot, the fact that it was not intentional does not change the fact that the action led to someone feeling pain. The impact warrants an apology. This "impact over intent" principle developed because there is a long history of White people saying, "That's not what I meant" or "I didn't mean to hurt anyone" to avoid taking responsibility for racial harm. The focus on our intention also prevents us from understanding the impact of our words or actions and causes further harm to People of Color.

When the intent-versus-impact conversation turns into a "your intention does not matter at all" message, the categorical dismissal of the relevance of White people's intentions can lead to missed opportunities. Madison encounters this at a staff celebration after she approaches a new Asian American co-worker, Chan-mi, and introduces herself. When Madison asks Chan-mi where she is from, the co-worker responds, "I'm in the community outreach department."

In response, Madison clarifies, "I'm sorry. I meant, what country does your family come from? I think the different Asian cultures are interesting." Chan-mi replies that her family is originally from Korea, but she and both of her parents were born and raised in Indiana. Madison responds to this by saying, "One of my friends is getting me into Korean soap operas. Which are your favorites?"

Chan-mi waves to someone across the room and excuses herself. Feeling sad about Chan-mi's lack of engagement, Madison sees Angie, a White co-worker, standing close by; Angie has clearly overheard the exchange. As Madison starts to explain that she really is interested in culture, Angie tells her to stop. "Look, your intent to connect doesn't matter. You treated an Asian American person like they are Asian first, and American second."

"But, I asked about her culture because I know I lack culture as a White person," Madison replies, starting to cry. With a tone of frustration, Angie tells Madison to "Please stop making this about you. Focusing on your intent is only going to make it worse." Madison is shaken and embarrassed and leaves.

- Who do you feel empathy for in this situation? Why?
- If you were Angie, how would you work with Madison to try and help her understand?

Embrace Both/And Thinking

On one hand, Angie is right. Our intentions do not matter to the People of Color we injure. Madison's underlying wish to connect and her effort to be self-deprecating doesn't matter to her Asian American co-worker. Madison needs to understand the historical weight of Asian Americans always being seen as foreign, as other, not as citizens.

And it does matter whether we intend to do racist things. It matters that our mistakes are bred from a lack of awareness, not intentional animosity or meanness. As a White person, Angie *can* hold space for Madison to process how her intent and her impact did not align. There is also an opportunity to explore a potential role of unconscious bias, in a supported way—one White person with another.

Building Emotional Capacity

Depersonalizing is an important strategy that can help us navigate defensiveness in hard situations. The idea is to recognize what part of a situation is about us and what part is not. On one hand, Madison can take note of what is not her fault by generating a wider perspective about the situation. In this instance, there is a long history of Asian Americans being treated as less than full Americans. If the co-worker is sensitive to this history, her reaction may be intense. That intensity is understandable, even if the depth of it is not all Madison's fault.

And Madison needs to take responsibility for her role in triggering any pain or upset she may have inspired in her co-worker. Angie can support Madison in considering if and how to check in with Chan-mi about the impact of her actions and how to repair any damage done.

Angie can also support Madison on how to not let her emotions overwhelm her. The less overwhelmed we are, the more we can recognize that these moments are not only about us. Shelly articulates this in detail in *Witnessing Whiteness* in the chapter, "Capacity Building."[88]

Offer Perspective

When we feel defensive, we need a process that helps us acknowledge what is happening so we can pull ourselves out of our spin. Lee Mun Wah, a long-time facilitator, offers a series of prompts in his book, *The Art of Mindful Facilitation*. These prompts can guide Angie if she wants to support Madison in understanding why she is reacting as she is.[89] Following this order of questions explores the role emotion plays in a person's reaction:

- What I heard was . . .
- Tell me more about . . .
- What are the emotions that you are feeling?
- What's familiar about those emotions?
- How did it impact you then? How is it impacting you now?

Once Madison understands what is driving her, she can focus on how her unhealed emotions led her to react so defensively.

> *Dear Reader:* Each of the messages discussed in this section contain important truths that require support for someone in *Reintegration* to understand. We need encouragement. Be an enthusiastic supporter for yourself and others. Acknowledge the emotions that come up. Express that White people's emotions *do* matter. Lean into the empowerment that comes with addressing feelings of guilt and the fact that we can help repair harm after we make mistakes.

Having an antiracist White community in which we can process emotions and confusion is what helps us recover from mistakes and avoid hurting people. To cultivate these relationships in your community:

- Identify someone who has more antiracist experience than you. Extend an invitation to coffee, tea, lunch, or to take a walk. Risk being vulnerable. Let them know you're new to these ideas. Ask if they are willing to talk with you as you learn more.
- Invite a friend or colleague to read a book or watch a movie with you on issues of race. Explain that you're looking for a partner as you learn about these issues.

If you have trouble identifying someone in your community, join an ongoing White racial affinity/White accountability group that meets online. AWARE-LA, Alliance of White Anti-Racists Everywhere-LA, offers welcoming meetings both in person and online. The organization is a friendly group that regularly helps people feel connected and supported.[90] If you have enough experience and guidance, you may want to start your own group. AWARE-LA's website provides resources for how to run a group via their White Antiracist Culture Building Toolkit.[91]

A Case Study Moment: Assessing Identity Positions

The annual White Privilege Conference regularly brings together over two thousand people of all racial backgrounds to discuss privilege, oppression, racism, and related topics. About two-thirds of attendees are White. Collectively, White attendees operate out of the full spectrum of racial identity positions representing a range of experiences and histories. Some have no experience with antiracism, some are professional DEI (diversity, equity, and inclusion) practitioners, and most lie somewhere in between.

Each evening, race-based caucuses (also known as affinity groups) provide opportunities for attendees to process their experiences with people of their same racial group. The White caucuses are a petri dish of racial identity interactions, with attendees in each of the racial identity positions we've explored so far.

For over a decade, Christine and Shelly have co-facilitated these caucuses, moments of situational affinity, where participants do not share long-term relationships. One night, a woman feeling significant guilt demanded that everyone in the circle of about 25 people feel the same depth of guilt she was feeling or else they were not good antiracists. She was clearly speaking out of a *Reintegration* frame of mind, emotionally overloaded and lashing out at everyone else.

The distressed woman needed support to manage her guilt and depth of emotion. Others in the group were reacting differently: some were angry at her demand, some grew numb in the face of such emotion, some tried to change the subject as quickly as possible. Others were visibly frustrated because a more complex, not guilt-driven, antiracist discussion was nowhere in sight, and they lashed out at the facilitators.

In that moment, Shelly and Christine chose to 1) validate the enormity of the feelings in the room, 2) gently push back on the demand that everyone have the same emotional experience, and 3) give space for others to react, anticipating that out of the 25 people in the group, many would have perspectives that would benefit those in distress.

This experience raises several important questions about engaging with a White affinity group made up of people in different racial identity positions:

- How do you assess the position you are operating from and what you might need?
- How can you assess what position someone else is operating from? How does their position impact you and your response?

The key to figuring out where you are lies in humble self-reflection. The higher the emotion, the more likely you are in one of the early positions. The ability to recognize defensiveness and reduce ego is what opens the pathway to accurate self-assessment and the ability to figure out what it means for you.

Second, assessing someone else is tricky and may reveal more about yourself than the other person. Most useful is to look for broad markers that help you identify if an idea comes from an either/or perspective and/or builds from feelings of guilt or shame. If this is true, it does not necessarily mean the information or advice the person is offering is bad;

instead, you may need to extract an underlying principle from their over-all message and brush away the part that is not useful. A key is to avoid becoming reactive and dismissive, allowing your own emotions to reduce the value of what someone offers.

We (Christine and Shelly) met at a White Privilege Conference. It changed both of our lives for the better. We are stronger and better for having attended, year after year, finding our own guides, finding each other. For those of you feeling all the feelings of the early positions, we hope you will stick with us. It is altogether worth it.

REFLECTION

Dear Reader: You've made it to the end of another chapter. Before you go, we ask you to consider at least two of these questions, in a journal or through another method of self-reflection.

Thinking of Yourself:
- What memories or feelings surfaced while reading about Ryan's and Madison's experiences?
- When have you felt strong emotions related to race? What were they? Do you know why you felt them? How did you process those emotions at the time? With hindsight, how might you care for the person you were at that time?
- How have guilt, shame, anxiety, fear, or anger affected you when interacting with other White people or People of Color?
- When have you felt confused or conflicted about how to act in an antiracist way? Who supports you to gain clarity? If you do not have support, how might you seek it out?

Thinking of Others:
- When have hard emotions and/or self-judgment caused you to deliver unhelpful messages to other White people? What happened? In the future, what would you like to do differently?
- What would it take for you to become like Jamie and support others to move through the emotions we face in *Reintegration: Emerging Antiracism*?

- How can both/and thinking help you support others to engage in antiracism with *both* a healthy sense of humility *and* self-worth? What might this look like in your life, workplace, or faith community?

SUMMARY FOR EMERGING ANTIRACISM: REINTEGRATION

In *Reintegration*: Emerging Antiracism, we recognize that we are associated with a long history of racism and often experience complex, upsetting emotions; we feel for People of Color and want racism to end.		
Far-right messages we are susceptible to in this position: • You Are Damned If You Do, Damned If You Don't; It Will Never Be Enough • Antiracism Shames White Kids and Teaches Them to Feel Guilty	Antiracist messages that are harmful in this position: • You're Not Doing Enough • White People's Feelings Don't Matter • Don't Coddle White People • Your Intent Doesn't Matter	Suggested approaches: • Acknowledge the difference between guilt and shame and the need to reduce shame for effective antiracist action • Use both/and thinking to understand our role as individuals within a system and how to embrace loving accountability • Offer support and encouragement, anticipating challenging emotions

9

False Confidence

Pseudo-Independence

"Do you ever notice that when you talk about your students of color, you sound like you believe you're the only White person who can teach them?"
My pulse quickens as my Black mentor asks me to self-reflect. I, Christine, am in the false confidence of Pseudo-Independence.

As people continue to learn and build skills during *Emerging Antiracism: Reintegration*, they often move into *Pseudo-Independence*. This is the first frame of mind where they fully integrate an antiracist sense of self and worldview. However, the "pseudo" signals that the confidence they feel about their antiracism is largely unfounded and diverts from additional learning and skill development. In fact, people navigate important obstacles here, resolving or avoiding problematic patterns.

> *Dear Reader:* We hope this book helps people move through this position quickly, because the patterns we experience here do not promote well-being and often undermine efforts to end racism. Thankfully, we can bypass a lot of what occurs here if we access supportive people and resources that move us to the next position, *Immersion/Emersion*. Even so, it is important that we identify the patterns we face here so we can help others as well as ourselves navigate them and avoid getting stuck.

Figure 9.1 Pseudo-Independence. ARTIST: LIZ WILTSIE

In *Pseudo-Independence*, while we now have a solid understanding of systemic racism and recognize that we are part of the White group, we still resist perceiving racism within ourselves. This prompts us to distance ourselves from those we believe are racist. We often think being a "good anti-racist" requires a highly critical, self-righteous attitude and so we attack anything we view as problematic. We also tend to put other White people down, justifying these performative displays as us adhering to antiracist principles.

One reason this happens is that we generally do not feel good about ourselves when we operate from this frame of mind. We are typically upset about being part of a racist system that benefits us and disturbed by our association with White ancestors and US history. Whether we realize it or not, we act out of a lot of unacknowledged guilt and shame.

The overattachment to being "one of the good White people" leads us to defensively ignore how our unconscious patterns may reflect the intertwined influence of white norms, white supremacy, and Christianity's cultural dominance. Having bathed in US cultural waters that value missionary-style proselytizing, hero worship, and messages about finding "the one Truth," we are often unaware of how this cultural milieu shapes our attitudes and behaviors, and how we come across to others. This results in us acting like "saviors" or as though we have the "one right way," even if we are not particularly religious.[92]

Our lack of awareness leads to the irony that we enact certain harms precisely because we believe we are the ones best positioned to "help." For example, we may perceive ourselves as an ally who is so rock-solid that we feel comfortable telling Black activists the "right way" to protest racism. Our projected overconfidence is infuriating to People of Color because of how often it comes with a refusal to recognize how we act problematically.[93] We remain unwilling to investigate how whiteness shapes our beliefs and actions, because we believe we have rejected whiteness.

At the same time, we often feel a constant fear of harming People of Color and have a fierce attachment to a perfectionistic desire to "get it right." This overwhelming concern about "what exactly is the right thing to do?" can lead us to do nothing. Our sensitivity can run extremely high, and if People of Color reject us, it can send us back into *Reintegration* or even *Disintegration*.

Another pattern is that we can feel overwhelmed by the vast reach of systemic racism and languish in hopelessness. When this occurs, we run the risk of narrowing our focus to individualistic actions that make us feel better. We can become the "White savior" who helps People of Color survive difficult circumstances or get ahead within the system. While we do this, we believe there is overall steady progress against racism. We experience positive feelings that we are contributing, and yet these feelings typically come at the expense of our ability to work in solidarity with People of Color who press for more wide-ranging change. In this way, this stance ultimately lends itself to complacency and supporting the status quo.

With all of this going on, it is easy to find ourselves stuck in patterns that are so common in antiracism's cultural milieu that we believe they represent how we should act and what we should believe to be good antiracists. The pseudo (false confidence) part of this manifests in several ways:

- We falsely believe we understand antiracist theories, yet we misapply them and undermine antiracist efforts without realizing it.
- We have trouble accepting critical feedback about our internalized racism.
- We fail to effectively convey antiracist messages because we do not recognize how underlying emotions of guilt and shame affect our delivery.

- We swing wildly between different narratives because we lack clarity in our racial identity.

Ironically, it is our false confidence that also prevents us from taking advantage of the support offered by White antiracists further on their journey.

Madison operates out of *Pseudo-Independence* most of the time, with frequent downshifts into *Reintegration,* and sporadic moments of *Disintegration* as well. This shifting between positions on the roundabout usually takes place when her co-workers of color offer a challenge, prompting her to spin for a while until she can unwind old assumptions and filter the issue through an antiracist lens. Madison interprets her co-workers' feedback through an either/or frame and is desperate to avoid criticism. What buoys her are moments when People of Color seem pleased by her actions and online posts. Part of what keeps Madison mired in this position is that she does not have a White antiracist community to model a healthier, more positive racial identity and antiracist practice.

This chapter highlights Madison's experiences, a moment when Alex operates from this frame of mind, as well as what could happen for Ryan if he receives support.

FAR-RIGHT MESSAGES

The underlying guilt and shame typical of this position allows far-right messaging to unsettle us. We are susceptible to it because of the negative feelings we harbor about ourselves as well as the fear we carry regarding our relationship to People of Color. This section addresses two messages that are particularly provocative when we operate from this frame of mind.

Message: You Should Be Able to Appreciate Your Ancestors Too

As we established, the far right grounds itself in either/or thinking that presents a one-sided mythology of our "glorious forefathers" and American exceptionalism. Thomas Jefferson, for example, is an unequivocal hero in their minds, lauded for authoring the Declaration of Independence. Their dedication to pristine characterizations is so intense that they vilify anything that provides a more complex or critical view. For example, they rail against critiques referring to Jefferson fathering children with an enslaved Sally Hemmings as repeated rape. Countering this, they tell White people that we should be able to appreciate our ancestors, exploiting the fact that most of us in *Pseudo-Independence* do not feel such prideful feelings; they poke at our sensitivities.

These far-right narratives can cause us to lose our footing because *Pseudo-Independence* is slippery. An all-or-nothing, either/or approach leads us to react to the overwhelming negativity of racism by rejecting the idea that White people have contributed anything positive to history. Because of the destabilizing effect on our sense of self, we are prone to falter in three ways. Madison struggles with all three.

First, in terms of US historical figures, Madison cannot answer back to far-right tales of glory because her relationship to this history feels raw and triggers significant inner discomfort. All Madison can see are the flaws in the nation's White founders. Thomas Jefferson is nothing but a rapist and enslaver, and Madison would be happy to see Monticello shuttered. Her wholesale rejection of him and other historical figures makes her appear extreme and one-sided to other White people.

Second, Madison has no relationship to White antiracist historical figures. Her graduate program explicitly tries to decenter whiteness, and so she only reads work by and about People of Color. While an important counterbalance to the Eurocentric approaches of her earlier schooling, it leaves her unaware of the antiracist heroes we have that she can be proud of and celebrate, like Anne Braden, Viola Liuzzo, and Virginia Foster Durr, among many others.

Third, Madison has complicated feelings about her own family ancestry. She knows that her grandfather loved her and taught her important lessons about thriving, yet he also thought Black people were inferior, not unlike Thomas Jefferson. She also knows her family benefited from discriminatory policies. This leaves her uncomfortable, questioning what she can be proud of from her own family history and, therefore, unable to respond to the far-right claims without feeling deeply conflicted.

Overall, Madison's one-sidedness and confusion means she is not as effective at drawing other White people (currently in *Disintegration* or *Reintegration*) closer to antiracism.

- How do you feel about White US historical figures as well as your own ancestors?
- What could help us and others be resilient in the face of far-right messages about our historical figures and ancestors?

Embrace Both/And Thinking

The situation would be markedly different if Madison were grounded in both/and thinking, which would allow her to appreciate that White people are human beings who live complicated lives in complicated times. This is not about excusing immoral behavior. It is about recognizing that all people have positive and negative aspects to their histories. Everyone is imperfect, and we can hold both our personal ancestors and our historical figures with a measure of empathy, even in their human imperfection.

What would it mean to understand Jefferson's contributions to the idea of democracy while holding clarity around the incompleteness of "all men are created equal," the racism and sexism of who was not included, and the failure to acknowledge the Iroquois Confederacy as influential in Jefferson's thinking?[94] How can we wrestle with Jefferson's condemnation of Great Britain's introduction of slavery to the United States in an early version of the Declaration of Independence (which didn't make the cut) and the ugliness of his own slave-owning, particularly when it comes to the rape of Sally Hemmings and the treatment of his enslaved children from that relationship? We can hold these complex both/and moments with integrity so that we're not excusing racist behavior, nor are we reducing a person to a single narrative about his or her life.

Educate Yourself

Investigate and share information about White antiracist heroes that we can be proud of and hold up as role models for how we want to be.[95] For example, Anne Braden worked in solidarity with Black people in the South to combat racial and economic injustice. She spoke about the responsibility of White people to work with other White people on issues of racism:

In a sense, the battle is and always has been a battle for the hearts and minds of White people in this country. The fight against racism is not something we're called on to help People of Color with. We need to become involved as if our lives depended on it because, in truth, they do.[96]

Having positive antiracist role models helps to balance our view of White people, rejecting the either/or thinking of perfectionism when it comes to complicated racist heroes as well as antiracist role models.

Message: People of Color Want Power over You

The far right also knows how to tap into White people's conscious and unconscious racism and the deep-seated fears that fuel it. One way this is done is by suggesting that People of Color want power over White people to get revenge. They go even further, saying that once People of Color have power, they will treat White people as badly as White people have treated them throughout history.

Consider Ryan, who overhears one of the Black Jazz Band members one day, visibly angry, talking about getting back at "that White piece of shit" and how the person deserves to "feel some pain for the first time in his life." This throws Ryan into a spin in a couple of different ways. Although Ryan only overhears fragments of the conversation, it presses on his fears of being lumped in with a broader White group. It also reminds him of how the far right pushes the idea that we should fear armed Black people because they want to hurt White people.

Ryan understands why Black people would feel anger toward White people in general. Now that he views historical, structural racism more clearly, he recognizes the damage racism has caused and feels badly for the actions of many White people in history. Indeed, he even imagines that if the roles were reversed, White people would want revenge. Although it's hard for him to admit, the far right's warnings about an impending race war, even if extreme, make some sense to Ryan. Except now, Ryan feels more aligned with Black people. Ryan feels confused about how to deal with these issues of power and fear.

- What experience do you have with these messages and the fears they generate?
- What can help us avoid getting drawn into overblown, racist fears?

Offer Perspective

We need someone in our life who can ask us questions that help us slow down and reflect on our reactions and reframe our thoughts. For example, we can start by noticing how we learn to celebrate the White colonists who took up arms to fight against British rule. Yet we are taught to condemn Black people, like Nat Turner, who fought for Black people's freedom. What is the difference? How do these cultural messages socialize us to fear Black people with guns?

We also can ask what makes us believe that we would want revenge if we were the targets of racism. Is our imagined reaction tied to a socialization that tells us it is righteous when White people take up arms to fight for our rights? Is it tied to a deep knowing that what White people have done to Black people is truly horrifying, and thus we project a level of rage onto Black people we believe we would feel? We can then ask what the implications are if we combine our projections of rage with a socialization that already tells us Black people are scary. How might this affect how Black people are treated today, particularly those who carry weapons?

Examining these issues can help us pull back our own projections and open the door to a more realistic vision grounded in the hundreds of years of Black people fighting and dying for the United States, seeking to make it and its citizens better, not taking revenge. Ryan's access to this kind of conversation can help him understand the ways history and messaging have prioritized the experience of White people in a way that gives a false impression of People of Color, Black people specifically.

ANTIRACIST MESSAGES

When we are in *Pseudo-Independence*, we know we are dedicated to antiracism. We believe ourselves to be the "good White people," the "good antiracists," the "good White allies." Upholding this view of ourselves feels exceedingly important and therefore any message that undermines our false confidence likely results in upheaval unless we have support to steady us.

For this reason, any time we receive messages that undercut our confidence (as unwarranted as that confidence may be), we need support from other White people to counteract our emotional unsteadiness. This can come in the form of supportive messages to take healthy steps forward. In the end, unresolved guilt, shame, and fear explain our typical reactions to the four messages highlighted in this section. If we understand what leads to our reactions, we can help one another stay focused on ending racism instead of harshly criticizing each other.

Message: All White People Are Racist

From an antiracist perspective, it is impossible to grow up within the fishbowl of US society without soaking up the racism within its waters. Whether appearing as overt bigotry or subconscious bias that runs contrary to our stated values, all White people have racism within us that we need to unearth and disrupt. An abbreviated and often harshly delivered message related to this is that "all White people are racist." Readers may recall that Tyler ran into this message while in *Disintegration*, and his experience in the activist group pushed him away from antiracism and toward retrenching in whiteness.

Madison receives this message while in a meeting with the director of the community center. She hears several colleagues, both White and People of Color, advocating for mandatory antiracism training for White staff, while rejecting similar training for staff of color. Madison interjects that not all White people necessarily need training and suggests doing an assessment to determine who should attend. A White colleague counters that all White people need it because all White people are racist. Madison leaves the meeting feeling defensive and worried about what people think of her.

Recall that Madison believes racist people are bad people, and she spends a fair amount of time trying to distance herself (at least psychologically) from racist White people. She understands that implicit racism exists and that it affects many people. However, she is confident that it does not significantly affect her or the people she respects in a way that negatively affects People of Color.

The exchange during the meeting sticks with Madison and she retreats into the heightened emotions of *Reintegration* for a while. To steady herself, she writes a detailed email to the director, a Latinx woman, listing a range of books she has read and actions she has already taken to counter racism. She also tries to reduce the lingering sense of shame she feels by doubling down on her online activity and catching people saying racist things. In doing so, she uses harsher language than usual to demonstrate how antiracist she is. These efforts reinforce for her that she is really a good antiracist person and that her co-worker holds extreme views.

- What feelings arise for you when you think about the idea that all White people are racist? Why?
- How can we help ourselves and others receive the deeper meaning of this idea (the need for all of us to investigate internalized racism) and avoid defensive, harsh reactions?

Offer Perspective

The fish in water analogy is helpful when learning about internalized racism as well as racist policies, like redlining, or discussing our relationship to systemic racism. Does a fish notice the water in which it lives? No. Like the fish, White people are accustomed to living in a world dominated by White norms. Whiteness saturates our social world and us along with it. Our position has sustained us in ways that we do not perceive. Because of this, we often need help to see what is right in front of us (like racist policies) as well as the ways that we are participating in racist systems (regardless of our intent or awareness). This can help us understand the thread of logic underlying shortcut statements like "all White people are racist."

Build Relationship and Embrace Both/And Thinking

Madison needs help resolving the shame she feels hearing this message. In particular, she needs support from other White antiracists. Her emotions are blocking her from recognizing how she's seeking validation from the People of Color at the center in ways that can potentially damage her relationship with them. Her neediness can signal that she's not ready to handle the emotions antiracism often generates. Her listing of her accomplishments makes her appear as if she does antiracist work for "credit" rather than for liberation.

More antiracist relationships with White people can help Madison understand that it is possible to examine one's own racism *and* maintain a positive view of oneself. By exploring her fear of being viewed as racist, she can practice acknowledging her participation in racism *and* maintaining her sense of herself as a good person. This will allow her to participate in new learning without defensiveness and develop more empathy for the White people she is attacking online. The fact that we swim in racist waters is not our fault. What matters is how we take responsibility for doing something about it.

Build Emotional Capacity and Stay Strategic

Understanding our emotions and motivations helps us realize when we're delivering messages for the wrong reason. While in *Pseudo-Independence*, Christine would state that she was racist in order to make the point that all White people are racist. She now realizes that she offered this self-critique performatively to get accolades and rewards from other antiracists. She felt proud when White people became upset because she interpreted it as evidence that she was having an impact.

With a more fully developed racial identity, Christine realized her pride was more about her ego and that, by driving more White people out of antiracism, she helped racism stay in place. Refocusing her emotional fulfillment on ending racism, she changed her practice. Watching Jay Smooth's video, "How to Tell Someone They Sound Racist," was a perspective-changing moment for her. He emphasized that we should focus on how words and actions can be racist rather than on a person's internal character (which we can't really know).[97] We all have the capacity to change words and actions.

Message: You Are Not Ready! You Need More Work!

When we are new to antiracism, we are going to get things wrong—a lot. We want to do well, yet we are not fully skilled. Unfortunately, when we operate from this position, at the first sign that we are doing damage, our underlying, unresolved emotions overwhelm us, and we can simply stop trying. In other words, we often respond to the message of "You are not ready! You need more work!" with inaction or by backing away, instead of dedicating ourselves to additional growth.

When the novel *The Hate U Give* by Angie Thomas became popular, Alex persuaded her department chair to allow several of the Humanities teachers to use the text to explore the historical context of Black Lives Matter and policing. At their majority White school, Alex feels that this is a perfect way to help the White students understand Black people's anger and shake the students out of their comfort zone and address their privilege.

Alex is not prepared to lead this effort effectively. She does not know how to protect the few Black students from feeling like representatives for their race, and she cannot skillfully respond to the few White students who loudly push back against the book's messages. Other White students express feeling horribly about what they are learning. Alex struggles to address the students' needs. In fact, her approach amplifies the problems, as she pushes the students to understand the Black characters' experience while failing to support her White or Black students in their own racial identity development. The students aren't yet in a place to understand.

While Alex is further along in her racial identity than her other colleagues teaching the book, she is unable to support them in their struggles. While most are well-meaning White people, they struggle to understand the racism they read about in the book. One White teacher even veers toward defending whiteness, highlighting racial progress to avoid some of the harder conversations, further upsetting two Black students in her class.

A few weeks into the unit, a Black teacher approaches Alex to alert her that several Black students have come to her for support. This teacher shares that Alex and the other teachers have no business teaching the book without a stronger understanding of racism. She asks why Alex thought she could handle this without checking in with her Black colleagues. Alex feels chastened, ashamed, and regretful.

Not knowing what else to do, Alex conveys the negative feedback to her White colleagues as a "cease and desist" order, telling them that the entire project was a mistake and that they need more work before trying anything like it again. They quickly finish the unit. Many of the students and faculty consider it a failure. Two of Alex's colleagues have such a bad experience that they refuse to collaborate with Alex going forward. While wrestling with her feelings, Alex commits to learning from the situation and why this effort went awry.

- What feelings arise as you read about this pattern of feeling dejected and shutting down after receiving criticism, instead of staying engaged and learning more?
- How can we support ourselves and other people to be resilient and stick with antiracism after we mess up?

Embrace Both/And Thinking

Rather than embracing an either/or in the face of mistakes made, we can use a "coaching" approach to name *both* what has gone well *and* where and how we can improve. We can support each other to find additional resources to grow. The important thing is to avoid taking the message of "you screwed up" as a reason to abandon people or antiracism efforts. A favorite teacher phrase is, "To FAIL is our First Attempt In Learning." It happens to us all, and what matters is that we do not give up.

People of Color who provide feedback to White people are not responsible for offering the hand-holding approach we recommend. This is work White people need to do with and for one another. For example, Alex would have benefited markedly had she taken the feedback from her Black colleague and relayed it to the other White teachers in a way that inspired additional efforts to improve their practice instead of pushing them away. This would have allowed them to live up to the "stick with it" mantra.

It is important that White people continue to act, even when we do not feel ready. Building our capacity to listen to critical feedback and stick with it, even knowing we are likely to cause harm again, is how we move out of *Pseudo-Independence*. In this way, we keep learning *and* taking action *and* attending to people's needs at the same time.

Build Relationship

Taking antiracist action often feels and is risky. Whether we are shifting what we do in our workplace, speaking up when we hear something problematic, or joining an action led by People of Color, we need to try out new behaviors. Facing the risks is far easier when we are part of an anti-racist group within our organizations and communities. A group provides support, so we do not run away out of fear or frustration. It helps people stay committed to learning together.

If your organization or community does not have an antiracist group, consider starting a conversation with the person most likely to also want such a group to start. Begin talking with others to see if they have similar concerns. Cultivate a sense of shared interest and work together to explore what is viable within your setting. Also seek outside support from those who have experience with antiracist groups. Consider joining a group like AWARE-LA or Constructive White Conversation to learn how to host affinity dialogues and potentially meet others who are starting their own groups.

Message: It's Okay to Make Fun of White People

Making fun of White people is an entrenched cultural pattern within antiracism. It is destructive in two ways. First, it pushes people away from antiracism. Who wants to join a group that will make fun of us for not knowing something or for making a mistake? Second, it keeps us from working on our own inner growth.

Madison spends a lot of time making fun of White people. She does it to feel closer to colleagues of color, appreciating that they trust her enough to joke about White people around her. She also does it to make points about racism online. One day, a White person tells Madison that she's an antiracist mean girl. Acting cliquey, Madison laughs it off and turns it into a joke about White people's fragility. Distancing herself from most other White people feels righteous, yet masks the doubts she has about herself. She has no interest in learning from other White people, and her behavior pushes many away from antiracism.

Weaponizing jokes against an one other can have other odd consequences. When Shelly revised her book, *Witnessing Whiteness*, a White reader participating in a focus group went so far as to suggest that she change the name of one of the interviewees in the book, Karen T. (a real person), to avoid the association with the popular social media meme.

White people joking about "Karens" contributes to this type of response and disrespects the way the word "Karen" functions for Black people and other People of Color. Referring to White women who weaponize their identity to get what they want as "Karens" serves as a shorthand about the safety level of a White person. This use of Karen has historical precedents in the "Miss Ann" of the antebellum era and the "Beckys" of the 1990s. Within each historical context, the name indicated that the woman would use her whiteness to protect her place in the racial hierarchy, causing damage to People of Color along the way.[98]

White people using "Karen" to mock other people does not advance antiracist goals. Instead, it encourages distancing and a lack of self-inquiry. We cannot perceive ourselves fully when we defensively insist that "we are not like them." This prevents us from reconciling our own guilt and does nothing to help us move forward in our own identity development. After all, the next step on the journey is *Immersion/Emersion*, in which we deepen our understanding of self. Doing so typically involves White people learning from other White people, which we will not believe is possible if we do not resolve our negative attitude about White people.

Ultimately, making fun of White people undermines our ability to build a larger collective of antiracist people and it plays into the far right's narrative that antiracism is anti-White.

- How do you participate in making fun of people? What feelings come with it?
- What can help ourselves and others resist that urge?

Build Relationship

Joining a community of antiracists can provide opportunities to self-reflect with support from those who are similarly striving to create an effective antiracist practice. The following questions are important ones to grapple with together:

- Why am I distancing myself from other White people?
- How is my own guilt and shame part of that distancing?
- What is my antiracist purpose?
- Is what I'm doing helping to end racism?

One thing Shelly appreciates about AWARE-LA is the organization's dedication to a nonshaming approach. Shelly joined in the early days before members realized their aggressiveness disrupted the ability to influence other White people. Tracking their own emotional reactions allowed them to uncover the guilt and shame underlying their attitudes toward other White people. The group judged those who were less racially aware because people with less racial consciousness reminded them of their past selves; they did not want to be reminded of how they had been prior to their awakening.

At that point, the group dedicated themselves to creating a supportive White antiracist culture that values people loving themselves. They extend antiracist messaging infused with care and empathy. They invite White people to bring their full, imperfect selves to the group, prioritizing the need to try and fail and to make mistakes in a shared effort to grow. This is an important strategy in the effort to expand the circle of antiracists.

In addition to joining a community, consider reflecting on the following questions:

- What parts of me still need forgiveness?
- What parts of me need healing from the racism I have participated in and/or benefited from?
- How do I nourish those tender parts of me?

Build Emotional Capacity

Loving and creating empathy for ourselves allows us to extend care and empathy to other White people. Search for guidance and wisdom as needed. For some, that guidance will come from religion. For others, it will come from other philosophical worldviews. Find what speaks to you. Dr. Ruth King's *Healing Rage: Women Making Inner Peace Possible* offers an understanding of different manifestations of rage so that we can heal.[99] Madison needs this kind of resource because her anger, sometimes masked as joking, signifies something deeper is going on regarding her sense of self.

Message: Stop Worrying about Whether You Are a Good Person

A common message delivered by antiracists is to "stop worrying about whether you are a good person." On its own, this is not necessarily a bad message. In fact, it can be extremely useful to stop worrying about this and pay more attention to how we can do a better job of undermining racism. What makes the message challenging is how it lands on people for whom this is a major concern. In *Pseudo-Independence*, this is a huge issue. If we leave people's emotional distress unaddressed, it may inadvertently leave them less likely to investigate their relationship to racism, exactly the opposite of what we intend.

Ryan has learned a lot over the last six months from Jamie, his non-binary friend, about how systemic racism functions, particularly regarding the school-to-prison pipeline and how it captures a high percentage of the young men in the neighborhood where Ryan and Jamie volunteer. One day, during his music lesson, Ryan sprinkles in motivational, cautionary suggestions about how the students will be able to escape the inner city and avoid going to jail "like most of the men in the neighborhood" if they keep practicing. Ryan's statements are deeply troubling on multiple levels, while also inflating the actual number of people going to prison.

That afternoon, Mrs. Gardiner, a veteran White teacher, returns to her classroom where the music lesson is taking place. She enters just in time to overhear Ryan's statements and calls him over. They have never met before. It has already been a long day for Mrs. Gardiner, and she feels protective of the students. She has no interest in being gentle with "this kid from the suburbs" who is getting credit for volunteering. She has been through this before and witnessed the kind of damage "clueless, do-gooder" volunteers can do.

Within earshot of the kids, Mrs. Gardiner tells Ryan that his comments are "seriously problematic" and she plans to speak with his supervisor. Flushing and defensive, Ryan tries to explain that he is only trying to help because he cares and wants the kids to be successful. Realizing Ryan has missed her point, Mrs. Gardiner responds, "It does not matter what you think you're doing, you're damaging my kids with racism, and it needs to stop." Ryan feels the sting. Not realizing the racist assumptions underlying his statements, he feels wrongly accused. He also feels humiliated, noticing the kids staring at him.

Ryan tries one more time to let the teacher know he is not the person she clearly thinks he is: "Wait, I'm a good person here, trying to do a good thing." Grabbing her things and heading for the door, she replies with, "Stop worrying about yourself and your goodness. Focus on ending the racism." Ryan is dumbfounded, angry, and shaken.

Mrs. Gardiner is right to disrupt Ryan and prioritize the students. However, she missed the opportunity to help Ryan understand the criticism.

- What thoughts and feelings do you have about the need to feel like a good person?
- How can we help ourselves and others stay engaged in antiracism when experiencing a hit to the ego?

Build Emotional Capacity

While we are in *Pseudo-Independence*, we have a hard time generating empathy for White people who say racist things, intentionally or unintentionally. However, we need to build our capacity for empathy in order to pull someone like Ryan further into antiracism. Otherwise, we can leave him emotionally struggling and open to far-right claims that antiracism is against White people and that White antiracists are never good enough.

Offer Perspective

Empathy will allow Ryan's friend Jamie to support him to navigate Ryan's hurt feelings and hear another perspective. What is Ryan telling himself about what happened? What does it mean to him that he made a mistake? What does "goodness" mean to him and where does it come from? What are the concerns, fears, or points of resistance he feels? How could Ryan support his students without using racist tropes that paint where they are from as a place that needs to be escaped and categorizing Black men as destined for jail? If someone like Jamie is not available and Ryan cannot process these questions on his own, he could head into a regressive spin that lands him back into *Reintegration*.

Providing support for Ryan's upset feelings is not coddling. It is about helping Ryan develop the self-awareness and inner strength to pick himself up and hold himself as a worthy person who is on the road to getting better at antiracism. It is about helping him understand his cultural influences, like his connection to the Christian ideal of being without blemish or sin, and how they impact his emotional reactions. The suggestions in the previous section about self-love apply here as well.

Embrace Both/And Thinking

Jamie can try using both/and thinking to help Ryan center himself and provide him with the more constructive explanation he needs. For example, Jamie can help Ryan hold himself up as a decent person, one who made a mistake *and* recognizes why Mrs. Gardiner had such a significant reaction to what he said.

> *Dear Reader*: Do you have a negative reaction to our suggestion that Ryan should fortify his self-love and sense of self as a decent person? After all, he just delivered damaging messages to a group of youth of color. Does it seem that we care too much for Ryan and not enough about the students? That is not our intention. We care about everyone, the students who are harmed and Ryan's capacity to do better. In this case, for Ryan to do better, he needs to be okay with the fact that making mistakes will happen. Making mistakes doesn't make him a bad person. What counts is what Ryan does in the face of mistakes, using feedback to correct errors and repair any harm done. This is true for us as well.

REFLECTION

Dear Reader: You've made it to the end of another chapter. Before you go, we ask you to consider at least two of these questions, in a journal or through another method of self-reflection.

Thinking of Yourself:
- Which situations and emotions faced by Madison, Alex, or Ryan feel familiar?

- When have you felt defensive about being associated with racism? When have you pointed fingers at others and been pleased that it takes the focus off you?
- What can get you back on the horse after a fall? How can a both/and attitude allow you to receive criticism *and* maintain a healthy sense of self? How might this help you avoid seeking validation from People of Color?

Thinking of Others:
- How do "savior" and "one right way" patterns affect the way you engage with others? How do these patterns play out in your life, workplace, or faith community?
- How and when do you tell others about their racism? What is your motivation? How strategic are you?

SUMMARY OF FALSE CONFIDENCE: PSEUDO-INDEPENDENCE

In *Pseudo-Independence*, we feel a false sense of confidence in our antiracist stance; we believe we skillfully do what we can to help People of Color, and we do not perceive ourselves as enacting racism.		
Far-right messages we are susceptible to in this position: • You Should Be Able to Appreciate Your Ancestors Too • People of Color Want Power over You	Antiracist messages that are harmful in this position: • All White People Are Racist • You Are Not Ready! You Need More Work! • It's Okay to Make Fun of White People • Stop Worrying about Whether You Are a Good Person	Suggested approaches: • Use both/and messages to support self-reflection that unearths the role guilt, shame, and cultural values play in attitudes toward ourselves, other White people, and People of Color • Join an antiracist community for encouragement, support, and inspiration

10

Transformation

Immersion/Emersion

Sitting in a circle of eight people, I scribble in my notebook, "It's not only me!" I underline it twice.

This is one of the first meetings of AWARE-LA, and I no longer feel alone. A wave of relief washes over me as I recognize that these people are struggling with the same emotions and concerns that plague me. I, Shelly, am invested in the work of Immersion/Emersion.

In *Immersion/Emersion*, people stand on firmer ground as they engage in an intertwined and cyclical process of *immersing* themselves in learning and then *emerging* into action. This is when they engage in deep reflection about what it means to be White and how they need to transform to live an antiracist life. Their role models now include antiracist White people and People of Color.

Our work in this position allows us to wrestle with racism's moral dilemmas with a nuanced understanding and a both/and mindset that prevents us from easily falling into the overwhelming, extreme emotions characteristic of *Pseudo-Independence*, *Reintegration*, and *Disintegration*. This improved grounding allows us to remain increasingly balanced and helps us generate greater clarity about our antiracist purpose, allowing our commitment to waver less often. Our increasing self-awareness and skill results in an increasingly healthy and more compassionate approach to others and ourselves. This allows us to feel more joy and gratitude that we are part of antiracism. *Immersion/Emersion* is overall a place of nourishment and empowerment. The learning we do here is truly liberating.

Figure 10.1 Immersion/Emersion. ARTIST: LIZ WILTSIE

This does not mean *Immersion/Emersion* is without challenge. One thing that can take us off track is that intense self-reflection and systemic examination can result in a not-so-healthy hypervigilance, and our self-criticism can become overly harsh. Continually searching for the error in our ways, we may not rest until we find something that demonstrates our internalized white superiority.

This leads to a few challenging patterns. One is that we can extend our hypercritical focus outward, constantly searching for and finding fault in others. We sometimes weaponize new information and overgeneralize its applicability as we criticize. Another challenge is that, as we run into contradicting philosophies and strategies from people we hold in high regard (like big names within antiracism, both People of Color and White), we believe we need to keep learning more before we can take action, leading to inertia. We can also retreat into a heady overintellectualism that allows us to avoid the emotional work we need to do. Part of what makes this pattern prevalent is that it goes hand in hand with the message that taking time for inner, emotional work is selfish and less important than action.

A new development in *Immersion/Emersion* is that certain messages that were previously off-putting are now useful. For example, the "all White people are racist" message makes a lot of sense now and helps us connect structural racism, internalized racism, our personal complicity, and our responsibility to make different life choices. The same is true for the "the United States is founded on white supremacy" message because we now understand how whiteness as a system is woven throughout US society and its structures. It is also here where the "you're not doing enough" message inspires useful action, and we can respond to calls to deal with our "white fragility" without defensiveness.

Because this is where we invest in self-reflection, we appreciate race-based affinity groups and learn from and with White people; we recognize that being part of a collective of White antiracists is valuable. Alex spends a fair amount of time here, feeling the relief of having a community around her to continue her learning. This is why she can regularly discuss racial issues using a both/and lens. This chapter also highlights the challenges of this position, as we witness Alex, Madison, and Ryan each working to navigate messages that can trip us up.

> *Dear Reader:* The fact that you are reading this book at all means some part of your consciousness is in *Immersion/Emersion.* You are working to consider where you are and what it means to meet others where they are. That said, each time we cycle in and out of this position, it can feel different. As you read, notice the parts that feel more or less familiar. Where do Alex, Madison, and Ryan's experiences illustrate your journey so far? Where do they offer a vision of your future?
>
> If the last few chapters have felt overwhelming, know that many do arrive at this position and feel a sense of relief and excitement. You can, too. We know many people fear that antiracist groups exist only to tell people they are wrong and bad. They are surprised to find like-minded, welcoming, warm people once they finally join a meeting. Liberation and joy await on this journey. We hope you continue with us.

FAR-RIGHT MESSAGES

In this position, we are most susceptible to far-right messages that call into question how we treat people. Since we believe that we work to improve society for everyone's benefit, any suggestion that we are mistreating or injuring someone can sting. This makes us vulnerable to messages that question our place on the moral high ground. As a response, we can spend a lot of time second-guessing antiracism's practices and ourselves in general. The result is a detour whereby we deflect attention away from the harms caused by racism and, instead, toward areas where we might legitimately need to improve but might not be the most urgent priority. This section highlights three far-right claims that too often lead us down this path, distracting us and wasting our time and energy.

Message: Stop Making Everyone Victims

Far-right media personalities claim that racial and social justice infantilizes everyone so that no one accepts personal responsibility anymore. A prime example is when people who are committed to free speech and personal liberty loudly reject attention paid to trigger warnings and microaggressions, claiming they are making people, students specifically, weak and unable to handle stress.

- Trigger warnings are cautionary notes that warn people about upsetting content that a resource might contain. The purpose is to allow people who have experienced a trauma (such as sexual assault) to avoid having it re-engaged.
- Microaggressions are the everyday slights, slurs, or offhand comments that reinforce bias and racism.

While we are in *Immersion/Emersion*, even though we may be better able to tolerate the complexity of racism, we can still find ourselves swayed by the either/or nature of this assertion about infantilizing people. Ryan experiences this when a teacher at his school offers a screening of a short documentary film focused on the rise of liberal censorship on college campuses. Ryan has learned about how White people deliver racist messages without their awareness. He now understands why Mrs. Gardiner was so upset at him that day during his music lesson, and he has developed a larger antiracist community.

Ryan joins his friends from the Social Justice Club at his school to watch the film, then speak against it. Before the screening, the hosting teacher explains that he wants to warn them about the assault on free speech they will face when they get to college.

To Ryan's surprise, the film offers compelling, real-life examples: one professor complains that "woke culture" has gone too far in terms of identifying microaggressions and demanding trigger warnings. He argues that however well-intentioned, these demands force professors to predict students' psychological state, make assumptions about what students can handle, and lowers expectations of students. The documentary claims that it is racist to teach "minority" students that they are victims who need protecting from White people.

Ryan feels torn because he finds some of the critiques valid. Does he view People of Color as victims needing protection from White people? Does the Social Justice Club's work on microaggressions contribute to him seeing People of Color as victims? Do antiracists oppress free speech? He feels a little off-kilter and knows he needs more conversation to figure it out.

- What thoughts and feelings arise for you as you consider this issue?
- What can help someone navigate this message about victimhood?

Embrace Both/And Thinking

Ryan's experience demonstrates the need to process this argument using a both/and lens. There is no need to default to the either/or position that pits care for people against personal responsibility. We can support both. One can *both* include trigger warnings *and* understand that traumatized people have autonomy in caring for their own healing as well.

Message: You're a Hypocrite

The far right's claim that antiracists are "hypocrites" can send us into a spin when we are in *Immersion/Emersion*. They say, "You say you want to be inclusive, but you are not inclusive of conservatives." This lands hard on us because we are in the process of learning from people who hold a range of philosophies.

We are concerned about making room for the points of view of many people, although we approach this issue from an *equity* perspective, which means prioritizing the voices and feelings of people from traditionally marginalized groups. The far right, on the other hand, claims they care about *equality* of voice—that all voices are the same—which to them means the far right can say whatever they want, whenever they want, and it doesn't matter who they injure in the process.

Alex falls into this trap after she posts on social media about a lesson on the history of LGBTQIA+ rights in the United States. She writes about how she interrupted one of her White, male students to stop his disparaging attacks against gay people and how she intends to carefully moderate his speech in the future to protect her gay students. A far-right troll attacks her, claiming she is a hypocrite who denies traditional conservatives the right to express their point of view. The thread gains a bit of traction, and it soon has over a hundred comments, with people arguing back and forth.

Because she believes in her responsibility to educate other heterosexual, White people and feels defensive about being called a hypocrite, she takes on one of the less troll-like people. She spends a great deal of time and energy creating replies that offer a both/and attitude, hoping to draw this person closer to her.

After several days and many hours of time, she realizes that she's not making any headway. This person is not taking what she had to say seriously. She feels strung along and realizes how he was toying with her, manipulating her fears of hypocrisy to take up her time and energy.

- Have you ever encountered the idea that it is hypocritical to prioritize People of Color's voices?
- Do you find it important to stop someone from saying hateful things about people from a marginalized group? What feels complicated about this?
- What can help Alex avoid reacting so defensively in the future?

Stay Strategic

Antiracists need to understand that far-right cries of hypocrisy are often not authentic concerns about all voices being included. A great check is to find out if they care about any voices other than those they agree with. How do they demonstrate this? It is important to keep in mind that inclusion is a corrective for a history of legally enforced exclusion of specific groups and people.

The far right and some traditional conservatives may feel impinged upon in moments when their voices do not receive priority; however, they are not a historically marginalized group. The feelings of discomfort they experience when they are in the minority are not the same as the legally sanctioned exclusion that marginalized groups have faced. The hypocrisy is that, when far-right groups claim they care about inclusion, they only care about White people's experiences.

Message: Antiracists Traffic in Cancel Culture

The far right has been on the cancel culture bandwagon for quite some time. Consider that the "War on Christmas" narrative was in play long before "cancel culture" became part of conservative vernacular. To the far right, acknowledging that not everyone celebrates Christmas by saying "Happy Holidays" or advocating for hiring Black Santas is an affront. Cancel culture applies to anything that calls for changes that promote inclusivity for marginalized groups. Their claims exhibit either/or thinking; you are *either* for "Merry Christmas" and White Santa *or* you are against them.

The reason this narrative is challenging for antiracists deep in *Immersion/Emersion* is that we can conflate the far right's complaints with the antiracist community's often complicated efforts to hold people accountable for racism.

Some things are clear. For example, Donald Sterling, former owner of the Los Angeles Clippers basketball team, received a lifetime ban from the National Basketball Association and a fine of $2.5 million for racist comments he made on a phone call. The egregious nature of the man's racism made this an appropriate outcome and upheld antiracist principles. "If this accountability is canceling, so be it," says the antiracist community.

Some accountability efforts are less clear. For instance, we can struggle to figure out how to treat emerging antiracists who make mistakes. We assume they must be different from people like Sterling, and yet we have trouble articulating how this might warrant different treatment.

Madison experiences this dilemma when a White leader of a partner not-for-profit verbalizes the n-word in a meeting. Saying, "I can't believe he would say, n_____," the woman repeated the word out of shock that a member of her staff intentionally said it during a meeting. Several of the Black people and other People of Color on her staff feel injured by her verbalizing the word and express their complaints publicly. Attempting to support the folks of color, a local White antiracist group rallies to hold the leader accountable and get her fired. They make no effort to help her learn from the incident or support her to repair her relationship with the Black community.

On one hand, Madison feels clear that White leaders should know better than to verbalize that word, whatever the context. So, consequences are warranted. On the other hand, Madison hears how white nationalists reached out to the leader, attempting to provide her with support, which she refused. Madison is conflicted that only racists are reaching out to the woman, not the antiracists.

Madison quietly struggles with how the far right and antiracists both seem to want to cancel people who've done wrong. Does antiracism promote either/or thinking that allows no room for nuance and growth? How does this fit with antiracists' calls for a culture where we do not "dispose" of anyone? Is there really room for restorative justice practices within the antiracists' version of accountability?

- How do we reckon with the ways that antiracists do cancel each other?
- Have you ever experienced confusion over how to hold people accountable for public mistakes?

Engage Critical Thinking

Madison's experience demonstrates how using an either/or mindset creates a false equivalency between the far right and antiracism, as though both sides traffic equally in cancel culture. This can obscure important truths about how they are different. We need to recognize false equivalencies and be able to name them. We also need to reflect on how we seek justice and hold people accountable for harm.

Recognize False Equivalencies

- *Far-right pundits' claims of cancel culture are often false and inflammatory.* In 2021, when the Dr. Seuss estate decided to discontinue publishing six titles that included racist images and/or had flagging sales, the far right claimed the radical left canceled Dr. Seuss. They did so despite the fact that Dr. Seuss has published over 60 books, most of which remain available. Also, when the makers of Potato Head toys dropped the "Mr." and "Mrs." from the packaging in order to be gender neutral (although all the same parts were included in the boxes), the far right argued that Mr. Potato Head was being canceled, even though it remained on the shelves.

- *The far right strives to limit antiracism yet does not see their efforts as canceling.* For example, in 2021 and 2022, efforts to ban books in schools and public libraries skyrocketed. They particularly targeted books about Black people and the LGBTQIA+ community.[100] Far-right groups do not recognize this as canceling the stories and people from those communities. It is essential to note that what the far right fears is being canceled, as well as what they are attempting to cancel, typically uplift Christian nationalist priorities: symbolic patriotism, heteronormativity, traditional gender roles, and white supremacy.

Seek Justice: Hold People Accountable

It is acting with integrity to hold people accountable when they engage in racist behavior via boycotts, protests, or other actions, regardless of their political persuasion. Actions do have consequences. And it is important to consider whether the consequences are grounded in justice and a belief in the person's capacity to make amends and change.

Antiracism's struggle with cancel culture against "its own" and others is, ultimately, an effort to hold all people to a higher standard of behavior, as imperfect as our reactions may be. These efforts should be grounded in justice and not in vengeance. We should avoid treating people as disposable when they make mistakes. Jumping on our own cancel culture bandwagon under the guise of accountability is a problem. Instead, we should ask: Will this effort to hold someone accountable reduce future harm? If not, we may need to reassess how we call for accountability.

Embrace Both/And Thinking

A both/and position offers a way through the murkiness of our complicated questions. It allows us to hold that it is morally good to expect people to act in nonracist ways *and* admit that antiracism does not offer perfect answers to complicated questions. Our hope is that both/and thinking will eventually help us answer questions such as: Is there a way to hold people accountable without them having to lose their jobs? What would it mean to allow people who make mistakes publicly to have the opportunity to grow and learn while remaining in their jobs? Can we envision implementing restorative justice principles culture-wide in response to all types of harm?

Educate Yourself

Turn to a scholar like adrienne maree brown, who explores cancel culture from an abolitionist perspective in *We Will Not Cancel Us*.[101] The book addresses how to be strategic in our efforts to end racism while honoring one another's humanity. This involves critically observing and interrupting the ways we dismiss people's value when they make mistakes in order to transform our culture into one that does not dispose of people. Her book, *Emergent Strategy*, also supports organizations seeking to approach visionary change while allowing for mistakes and ongoing learning in the process.[102]

> *Dear Reader*: You may feel empathy for people who make mistakes, particularly public figures who are called to task for racist behavior that occurred years earlier.
>
> You may wonder how we should treat people in these situations. To begin, we need to acknowledge that some people intentionally hide behind claims that they "care about all people" to avoid experiencing consequences for their racist words and actions.

This is a problem, regardless of their status or position. And we can distinguish this pattern from those who genuinely want to do better by focusing on three important factors:

1. Are they able to name the harm they caused and then apologize?
2. Can they articulate shifts in their understanding and what they have done differently since they made the mistake?
3. Do they nondefensively receive feedback and commit to concrete steps for moving forward in an antiracist way?

These three factors should be essential for people to retain their status. Individuals may need support in order to accomplish this, and we want them to have that support. However, when facing criticism, they should dedicate themselves to becoming antiracist and not focus solely on preserving their status. This is what we should want and expect of ourselves as well.

ANTIRACIST MESSAGES

In *Immersion/Emersion*, we may stand more solidly, yet we are still developing a nuanced perspective. We are concerned about what it means to be White, how we contribute to racial justice, and how to engage across race accountably. The four messages discussed in this section are those that can disrupt our ability to stand with sure-footedness and take committed antiracist action.

Message: You're Either Oppressed or Oppressive

Part of our learning in *Immersion/Emersion* involves investigating different sociological frameworks that help us understand how society and its institutions function as well as the relationship between marginalized and dominant groups. As we explore a range of voices, a foundational idea is that our socialized identities place us in an oppressor or oppressed position. We may be part of oppressed groups in some ways, while part of oppressor groups in others. For example, a White, working-class, transgender woman fits in the oppressor category in terms of race, while they are in the oppressed category in terms of socioeconomic class and gender. Each of us has our own unique constellation of identity markers that affect us.

Scholar Kimberlé Crenshaw developed the concept of intersectionality to name the systemic discrimination she recognized in the legal world. A group of Black women charged General Motors with discrimination. The court considered the issues of race and gender separately. A previous case showed that Black men were not being discriminated against, nullifying the race claim. The positions held by White women nullified the gender claim. As a result, the court overlooked the specific claims of Black women. Crenshaw argued that race and gender cannot be separated and must be evaluated together to achieve justice for the Black women.[103]

Crenshaw's work reminds us to consider the difference between systemic intersectionality—the ways systems treat us based on our identities—and the ways our own identities impact us personally. Investigating our relationship to our various identity markers helps us understand our relationship to systems of oppression as well as our own areas of internalized dominance and oppression. However, if we use this framework too rigidly, the binary idea that "you are either oppressed or oppressive" can leave us feeling stuck. We do not want to be oppressors. Is there no other option? This concern can hinder the emotional healing we need. The either/or framing also allows the far right's appeal to "stop making everyone victims" feel more resonant.

Ryan certainly feels torn. The Social Justice Club gives Ryan a chance to talk with peers about these issues. One day, the club sponsor leads the group through an exercise that asks them to identify the ways they are part of oppressed or oppressor groups, making marks in two columns. Most of the students in the club end up with marks in both columns. Ryan only has marks in the oppressor column.

The sponsor explains that society affords privileges to people in the oppressor category and disadvantages to those in the oppressed category, inviting them to reflect on how it feels to be part of their various identity groups. One Latinx student says she feels great about being Salvadoran American as well as being female but is pessimistic about anything changing because she does not believe White people will ever give up their privilege. One Black student says, "Yeah right, there's no reason for them to ever stop being oppressors. Why would they give up their power?" One girl offers, "Well, as a female I know how it feels to be oppressed. I am trying as a White person to challenge White people." Ryan says nothing, internalizing a message that the only thing he can ever be is an oppressor.

Ryan's negative emotions as an oppressor could sidetrack him and send him back into *Reintegration* or *Disintegration*.

- Have you ever thought about these issues for yourself? Where has it taken you?
- What would you want to say to Ryan to help him avoid becoming sidetracked?

Embrace Both/And Thinking

What could help Ryan is a more complex analysis that demonstrates that he is not just "an oppressor," but someone born into an unjust system who has a role in the fight for justice. Thankfully, there are a variety of models that can support this. One model that could help Ryan is the "White Supremacy System Model" from AWARE-LA, which highlights the personal stake we all have in working against systemic oppression.[104]

Another comes from the National SEED Project. Using the work of Marilyn Frye and Jondou Chase Chen, SEED examines how our identities can result in oppression as if in a cage and can also provide us nourishment and affirmation as if in a nest.[105] That nourishment can be both systemic and personal, providing us a way to see ourselves not just as an oppressor or as the oppressed. This is a powerful use of both/and thinking and could support Ryan as he continues to develop his antiracist White identity.

Message: White Culture Is Whiteness

While in *Immersion/Emersion*, we typically focus squarely on what it means to be White, how privilege shapes our lives, and how our way of being reflects White culture. Very often, we make no distinction between White culture (beliefs and behaviors shared by some White people) and whiteness (holding White culture as superior and using it to oppress people of other cultures). In fact, many would argue that there is no distinction possible, and will offer many reasons for why this is so.

At the White antiracist group meetings Alex attends, they discuss the work of Judith Katz, a White educator who outlines aspects and patterns of White culture, to help them understand their relationship to it.[106] One aspect that strikes Alex is a strict adherence to time. She is a clock-watcher, is never late, and prides herself on starting and ending everything on time. This reflection prompts her to feel a strange sense of embarrassment and shame.

With this new information, Alex begins challenging White people when they end meetings on time, telling them they are enacting whiteness. She also challenges the use of a timer for an activity as a manifestation of whiteness. Alex's new behavior confuses the White people she's criticizing.

- How would you describe the difference between White culture and whiteness?
- How can we use critical thinking to identify when White culture becomes oppressive?

Engage Critical Thinking

It is possible for a strict adherence to time to be oppressive. For example, it is oppressive when it is used to pass judgment on some people, often People of Color, but is excused for White people in positions of power. There are also instances when a strict adherence to time is not oppressive. For example, noticing whether there is equity in the time taken by People of Color and White people in a meeting can support justice. Thinking critically about our purpose in our use of time can help us recognize the difference between when it is oppressive versus when it supports equity.

One way for the White antiracist community to better support each other is to learn about other cultural experiences of time. For example, in some Latinx cultures, relationship time is prioritized over clock time when harm would be done to a relationship by ending an important moment to defer to the clock. For some Black cultures, event time takes precedence—the event takes the time the event needs to fulfill the needs of the participants. For some Desi Americans (South Asian Americans born or raised in the United States), the announced start time is not the actual starting time; it's the time to prepare for the event which will start as everyone eventually convenes. For the Tslagi people (called Cherokee by the US government), story time takes precedence in sharing wisdom of the elders; the story takes the time the story needs.

Critical consciousness allows us to make a distinction between when strict adherence to clock time dominates all other experiences—when it becomes whiteness—versus when it is a neutral expression of White cultural learnings handed down from some European ancestors, an expression that does not cause harm.

Message: Everything We Do Is White Supremacy Culture

The article "White Supremacy Culture," by Tema Okun, is so regularly used by antiracists that it deserves special treatment.[107] The article and its corresponding website provides a set of characteristics of white supremacy culture, along with suggested antidotes for how to create more equitable organizations that undermine whiteness. It is a wonderful tool. However, our hypervigilance toward identifying, naming, and interrupting every expression of white supremacy culture in our lives and organizations can cause us to turn this tool into a weapon. We aim it at ourselves as well as other people, often overgeneralizing. This occurs so regularly that Okun even explicitly asks readers to avoid weaponizing the concepts.

Alex experiences this in her White antiracist group as they work to establish their group's communication guidelines for emails and calls to action. A few group members passionately argue that their focus on written communication is a manifestation of white supremacy culture and worship of the written word. They claim that the use of guidelines is oppressive and that their communication should be only in video/oral form. Alex feels pressure to join their argument, as she does not want to perpetuate oppression. However, she also feels that perhaps they're going too far.

Some in the group feel unheard because they believe that guidelines that disrupt the worship of the written word can be created. They experience the critiques as rigid and condescending. Others in the group feel deflated and frustrated that this critique has changed from a thoughtful effort to be accountable to one another into a distraction that is taking energy and focus away from their goal to disrupt racism. Thoughtful critiques help us break problematic patterns, but when critiques become our sole focus, it is a detour.

- Where is the critique about avoiding "worship of the written word" helpful, and where is it unhelpful?
- How can the application of a both/and framework help to examine white supremacy culture and move the work forward?

Educate Yourself

Anchoring our understanding of white supremacy culture in the 2021 version of Tema Okun's article is advisable. Okun warns against using the tool as a weapon and provides a written word example:

> *I worked in one situation where the communications function had come to a grinding halt because a segment of the staff had decided that editing was white supremacist and, while yes, there are elitist and racist frames around proper language, the organization was locked in an either/or frame that was incredibly unhealthy and unproductive.*[108]

The group can ground the guidelines in the antidotes Okun provides. For example, the guidelines group members develop can ask that stories be valued in communication, that they avoid overly academic language as a default, and that they offer both written and oral sharing of information about what the group offers. The group can lean into the beauty of both/and to free up more energy and time for antiracist efforts.[109]

Message: Antiracism Has Rules

The hypercritical self-focus we often experience in this position can make us prone to interpreting antiracist principles as inflexible rules. On one hand, "following the rules of antiracism" can be a way to deal with the self-questioning we experience in the face of claims that we are hypocrites or that we are treating people badly. However, a rigid approach that tells us what language to use, how to interact, or who we can support can be hard to explain and can lead us into a spiraling quest to learn more and more to uphold the rules. This can lead to getting caught in loops where we try to determine the exact "right" thing to do, reducing our ability to both relate authentically across race and take action.

Ryan experiences this when the Social Justice Club at school creates a list of "antiracist dos and don'ts" and distributes it across campus. The list includes: 1) Do not ask People of Color to teach you; 2) Use your privilege for good; and 3) Don't be defensive about the word "racist." Because Ryan sits in the meetings when the group creates the list, he understands the rationale and thinks it is important to follow the list.

One item poses a problem for Ryan, though. He has been having interesting and revelatory conversations with some of his Black Jazz Band friends about race, and he has learned a lot. Is he supposed to stop asking them questions? Will he offend them just by asking? To avoid being more of a burden, he decides to make the Social Justice Club his place for learning. This causes him to hold his tongue in his conversations with his Jazz Band friends.

After a couple of weeks, one of his Black friends notices his silence and asks what is up. When Ryan tells him that he's trying not to burden them, his friend expresses disappointment that Ryan doesn't trust that he would be honest and tell Ryan if he was becoming a burden. The friend says Ryan should just act normally and treat him like the friend that he is. Ryan's use of the list as an inflexible set of rules for how to relate to People of Color backfires.

- Is Ryan's experience with how a "rule" can backfire familiar to you?
- What can help you or someone else adopt a more flexible approach?

Build Relationship

As we learn and act, we develop the nuance necessary to interpret the "rules of antiracism" in a way that does not deny People of Color their individual agency. For example, while we may recognize the need to take responsibility for our own learning, we can also inquire with our friends and colleagues of color to find out if they are interested in having conversations with us about race. The key is not expecting the answer to be yes, but not taking it personally if the answer is no.

Ryan could have told his Jazz Band friends about his effort to follow the list and his plans to educate himself. He could have told them that he appreciates what he has learned so far and does not want to burden them. Ryan's friends could then have decided for themselves how much they wanted to continue educating him.

Engage Critical Thinking

When we feel stuck between two opposing options, the stress can cause us to default to thinking either/or is all there is. This is particularly true if we seek the "right" answer to a complex question. In these situations, the answer may lie in a third option.

And sometimes a third option is not available. We are pulled between two competing directives and do not know how to resolve the conflict. In this situation, we need to make a principled decision and act. Then, we stay open for feedback, as it is likely that there will be issues we have not considered. Incorporating that feedback and using it to guide us the next time around helps us navigate hard choices. Over time, we get better at explaining what antiracist principle guided our decision while we can also admit where the choice may not perfectly address all concerns.

Message: Always Defer to People of Color

In *Immersion/Emersion*, White people often receive a great deal of seemingly conflicting messages from different people of color. Some examples are shown in the table.

Seemingly Conflicting Messages	
Follow the lead of People of Color.	Don't expect People of Color to teach you.
Educate yourself.	White people book groups are performative.
Expand your social circles to include People of Color.	Don't tokenize People of Color.
White people need to work with other White people.	White people working with White people is centering whiteness.

The issue with conflicting messages is not that one is right and one is wrong. The truth is that the advice is contextual and requires White people to use what they are learning in *Immersion* to emerge into confident action. However, White people can feel pressure to defer to whichever Person of Color is speaking to them in the moment. We often justify this deference as a general principle of being accountable. Ironically, a person who constantly shifts and changes based on what the Person of Color in front of them recommends will erode their cross-race relationships overall. People of Color know when we are not acting with integrity and fidelity. When we are unable to stand solidly and navigate opposing, seemingly contradictory advice, we can also shut down and return to earlier positions.

As Madison moves into a full-time position at the community center, she is now more sensitive about not acting in a way that displays internalized superiority and privilege when interacting with the People of Color who come in for services. For example, she has stopped offering unsolicited parenting advice to the clients waiting in the lobby area.

Part of Madison's new responsibilities include intake interviews with new and returning clients. One of Madison's co-workers, Janet, a Black woman, asks Madison to call her to conduct the interviews with any new Black clients. Janet believes the Black clients will be more comfortable and open with her rather than Madison.

Madison follows Janet's request. One day, she implements an intake with a Latinx client in view of the waiting area and then calls Janet to do the intake with a Black man, who had been waiting. Having witnessed Madison working with the Latinx client, he is offended when she calls for Janet. Before leaving, he asks to speak with her supervisor and complains about "the White woman racially profiling" him. After learning about Madison and Janet's agreement, their supervisor informs them that they cannot continue this practice.

Janet pulls Madison to the side later that day, wanting to brainstorm a way to continue ensuring that Janet does the intakes with Black clients but without being so obvious about it. She feels strongly that her racially conscious approach is the best way and laments that their supervisor does not fully understand Black people's trauma with White folks.

Madison is caught between the desires and needs of three different People of Color: Janet, her Latinx supervisor, and any individual Black client who walks through the door. Each has their own perspective, their own sense of what acting "justly" means. Madison believes she should "take leadership from People of Color" and "defer to the most marginalized." How should she navigate this situation?

- How have you encountered expectations about White people deferring to People of Color? What have been the outcomes?
- What would you say to Madison if she asked you for advice? What informs your ideas?

Engage Critical Thinking

In this situation, Madison needs to take a step back and consider for whom the antiracist action is taking place. The client is the person of focus. Everyone in the situation wants to serve the client as best as possible. Is there a way to check in with each client to identify their intake needs? Each situation is going to be different, and therefore, attempting to focus on whom a particular action intends to support may be a useful guide.

Most of the advice antiracists receive is important and not actually contradictory when we look at specific contexts. Consider what kind of support you need to continue honing your ability to read the situation and know what to do. Both Janet and the Latinx supervisor offer important insights for Madison. Madison will need to prepare herself to engage important conversations with both women. There may be Black, Asian, and Latinx clients who would benefit from engaging with someone other than Madison. So how can they adapt the intake process to be most beneficial for the client and tailored to client needs?

Educate Yourself about Different Models of Accountability

Familiarize yourself with accountability models that prevent imbalanced relationships through mutual accountability and the expectation that all do their own healing work. This kind of model focuses on cultivating a healthy identity (rather than relying on shame or guilt) and supports the inclusion of multiple perspectives to get to the best innovative thinking.[110] If we practice articulating the model we follow, we will be in a better position to navigate sticky situations when the directives we receive run counter to our integrity and commitments.

Educate Yourself about Racial Identity

Studying and learning about White racial identity helps us understand others and ourselves. We also should read and learn about People of Color's different racial/ethnic/cultural identity development processes.[111] Much insight comes when we understand that People of Color are also moving through their own identity journeys. When we understand that some directives from People of Color derive from unhealed pain and trauma, we can recognize where a person is in their identity development, and it helps us depersonalize issues more easily and stay focused on the overall needs of the moment.

A CASE STUDY MOMENT: TO WHOM ARE YOU MOST ACCOUNTABLE?

In a workshop about racial equity and racial justice, Christine encountered an African American man who asked her in front of the entire group to stop identifying as a White person and to identify as European American. He asked her to stop naming whiteness and to talk about racism. The pain it caused him resonated with her and others in the room. In her use of those words, he heard her committing to the racial hierarchy and her comfort at the top of that hierarchy.

While she acknowledged the pain she caused him, she shared that her integrity and accountability was to the Black man who had created the curriculum for Courageous Conversations, founder and CEO Glenn Singleton. She shared why naming the system of inequity is necessary before we can abolish the current construct of race in its entirety.

Christine's heart raced the entire time. Her voice shook at points. She named that she never wants to intentionally harm People of Color, so it was a struggle to continue to talk about White people and whiteness. And her accountability was to her mentor and teacher. If she had not developed a clear sense of who she is as a White person working to end racism as long as this current construct of race exists, she would not have been able to guide herself and the group into a deeper exploration of racism and what it means to be in a just relationship with one another across race.

- When have you had to offer a differing perspective in response to a request from a Person of Color?
- What did you draw on to offer that perspective with integrity and humility?

REFLECTION

Dear Reader: You've made it to the end of another chapter. Before you go, we ask you to consider at least two of these questions, in a journal or through another method of self-reflection.

Thinking of Yourself:
- What feels familiar about Ryan, Madison, and Alex's stories? If you have experienced *Immersion/Emersion* before, do you have new insights about prior experiences?
- What lessons from this chapter are new to you? What do you most want to remember?
- How can a both/and attitude help you avoid becoming unhelpfully rigid about the "rules" of antiracism or overly deferential to People of Color?
- What will it take for you to seek out and join an antiracist organization or community that can support you to articulate and live out your "personal stake" in racial justice?

Thinking of Others:
- What feels difficult about engaging with others using an *Immersion/Emersion* frame of mind? How will you need to stretch yourself?
- Who are the people in your life or community with whom you might partner as you learn and take action?

- How can learning more about empowering models for engaging in antiracism help you deliver life-giving messages about antiracism to others? Is there room for you to share your journey with people in your workplace or faith community?

SUMMARY FOR TRANSFORMATION: IMMERSION/EMERSION

In *Immersion/Emersion*, we engage in a cycle of learning and engaging in action as we develop our antiracist practice; we recognize the value of building community with other White antiracist people.

Far-right messages we are susceptible to in this position:	Antiracist messages that are harmful in this position:	Suggested approaches:
• Stop Making Everyone Victims • You're a Hypocrite • Antiracists Traffic in Cancel Culture	• You're Either Oppressed or Oppressive • White Culture Is Whiteness • Everything We Do Is White Supremacy Culture • Antiracism Has Rules • Always Defer To People of Color	• Use both/and thinking to balance the need to learn, take action, be accountable, and cultivate our antiracist voice • Name and explain the false equivalences that exploit complexities and seemingly conflicting antiracist messages • Study models that provide inclusive, empowering, and life-affirming approaches to justice work

11

Positive Antiracist White Identity

Autonomy

"The way you two White women started this meeting, asking if I'm comfortable while sitting on either side of me, takes me to a bad place. It reminds me of how White women at my old job would smile at me right before they'd stick the dagger in."

I breathe deeply as I take in the experience of my Black co-facilitator.

In that breath, I release the distancing thoughts ("That's not me"), the defensive thoughts ("That's not fair to compare me"), and the dismissive thoughts ("Was it really that bad?") to remain present. I believe his history with untrustworthy White women and can see how my actions tap into it.

"Would you like to tell us more about that?" I, Christine, am in Autonomy *for the conversation.*

In *Autonomy*, our foundation is solid and we hold the both/and of antiracism with more ease. Our earlier work results in us having positive White role models as well as positive role models of color. We can both appreciate our individuality and feel connected to a larger White collective. Happily, our commitment to antiracist action comes from a sense of responsibility and accountability that is not destabilizing or overwhelming. We feel positive about ourselves and our place in the world.

The word *Autonomy* does not suggest that we do our antiracism alone, nor does the term imply a lingering value of individualism. Having become conscious of our socialization and gained sufficient insight and skill, we collaborate with people of any racial background to work

 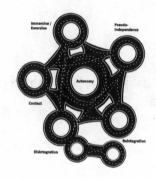

Figure 11.1 Autonomy. ARTIST: LIZ WILTSIE

for a just society; our focus is on our collective struggle toward liberation for all.

All of this is possible because we are psychologically healthier in *Autonomy*. We no longer carry the fear, guilt, or shame we felt earlier. Our moral definition of what it means to be White is now a stable and central component of who we are, leading us to feel more secure in who we are. We find joy in our antiracism and in the sense of belonging that it brings; we even appreciate philosophical and creative humor about race that pushes against racism.

Our stronger grounding allows us to enter interracial relationships and multiracial spaces with a combination of humility, curiosity, and integrity. When we do encounter rejection or criticism, we have the skills and clarity that interrupt impulses to fight, flee, freeze, or fawn.[112] We have the emotional resilience to move into mindfulness about what is happening for ourselves and for the larger collective. We are flexible and responsive, and our understanding shifts and changes over time as circumstances change. Operating from *Autonomy* is dynamic, enriching, and fulfilling.

In *Autonomy*, we recognize the harm racism causes for People of Color *and* White people and the complex differences of its scope and severity on different racial groups. Working toward the healing of all racial groups supports a more resilient form of antiracism. We are more sure-footed as ongoing learning and action is our way of life.

Part of our practice involves taking what we know about individual racial development and applying it to collective events or situations. For example, on the *Teaching While White* podcast, Dr. Helms applied her racial identity framework to understanding the January 6th insurrection on the US Capitol.[113] While this type of application and analysis can happen in both *Immersion/Emersion* and *Autonomy*, in *Autonomy* we can more instinctively use our knowledge to understand the psychological patterns at play. We're able to *both* meet individuals where they are *and* explore the workings of a White community (like a school, church, or workplace) through the lens of racial identity.

While *Autonomy* brings more certainty and joy, it does not mean perfection. We still make mistakes and learn new things. We bump into others, veer off track, and correct our course. In *Autonomy*, we have the emotional capacity to repair the harms and get back into good relationship with our partners. Correcting course is not as painful or all-consuming as it was earlier. We've internalized it as part of the process.

It bears repeating that these frames of mind are not fixed. We do not enter *Autonomy* as though we have arrived forevermore. Just because we can operate from this position sometimes does not mean we do so all the time. Operating from *Autonomy* on a consistent basis remains a goal.

Dear Reader: We understand that you may feel disappointed about still having issues to navigate even in *Autonomy*. What is the point of all this striving if we continue facing confusion and making mistakes? This concern highlights a beautiful paradox: the more we develop our antiracism, the more we accept imperfection in ourselves, others, and the world. This is part of leaving behind the demands of white supremacy culture and appreciating the fundamental complexity of life. The release that comes with a deep appreciation for nuance is a source of joy and liberation, even when we face the conundrums described in this chapter. In other words, take heart. This journey is worth it, and *Autonomy* is worth striving to achieve.

As you read, take note of how the messages Alex, Madison, and Ryan encounter push and pull you. Be gentle with yourself as you read the various stories, allowing yourself to feel whatever it is that you feel. If it all feels unfamiliar and overwhelming, that is okay. If it makes you angry and defensive, that is okay. Noticing our thoughts and feelings and then reflecting on what is driving them is an important part of developing the capacity to operate from this position.

FAR-RIGHT MESSAGES

The two far-right messages discussed in this section raise complicated questions for antiracists, and this is part of their power.

Message: Stop These Racists

As the anti–critical race theory movement gained momentum, the far right cast a wide net at antiracist efforts and declared them racist. Included are programs focused on diversity, equity, and inclusion, social justice, and socio-emotional learning. To the far right, anything addressing structural racism is discriminatory and suggests White people are racist. Their goal is to eliminate all antiracist programming across all industries, although they have found the most fertile ground in schools. Because White parents are understandably concerned about their children being shamed, they are susceptible to the claim that antiracist curriculum teaches children to judge White people based on the color of their skin.

As we wrote this, at least 7 states passed laws against teaching critical race theory and other antiracist frameworks and over 20 states had legislation in the works. Schools and districts across the country have fired teachers for violating some of the policies and laws. Organized mobilization efforts have effectively recruited parents to raise objections to anything they believe fits under the broad net they call critical race theory.

In an earlier chapter, we saw how people in the earlier positions are susceptible to this claim under the guise of "protecting the innocent" and "antiracism shames White kids." Here, in *Autonomy*, the effort to "stop these racists" destabilizes us in three different ways. First, the vitriol and constant critique can exhaust us and lead to defensiveness and reactivity.

Second, our exhaustion can prevent us from using our skills to generate effective responses. Third, the self-assuredness we now have to combat disingenuous criticism can prevent us from recognizing genuine critiques of how we have contributed to conflict.

Consider Alex, who lands in hot water after making a last-minute choice at the end of a lesson. The day's class focuses on how many White people's reactions to desegregation efforts during the civil rights era mirror current-day reactions to economic and legislative policies. Students read excerpts from Heather McGhee's book, *The Sum of Us*, highlighting how we would all prosper together if we reduced White racism. Right before the bell rings, a White student asks, "if we really were all going to prosper, why didn't we end racism already?" Alex sees several of her students nod their heads in agreement.

Alex makes the snap decision to share a link to a one-page handout that draws on Jonathan Metzl's book, *Dying of Whiteness*. She offers it to the students saying, "Unfortunately, a lot of White people would rather die than give up their whiteness." The class has no prior exposure to the term "whiteness" and so they do not understand it as referring to systemic dominance and advantage.

A few days later, the principal tells Alex she received calls from a few parents complaining that Alex told students that if they're White, they're racist. They assert that Alex is the one being racist toward White students. Alex knows this is not what she said or did. She describes the lesson to the principal and acknowledges that she should have prepared her students before giving them the handout.

She also explains her experience with the anti-CRT movement and her belief that the movement's disingenuous work is inspiring these calls. She tells her principal that she feels confident in her lesson and her ability to repair the moment with her students. She also offers to talk to any of the parents directly. And indeed, her follow-up work with her students goes well. No parent calls her, although Alex hears about a community member complaining about her on social media.

The following week, about 10 people from a local anti-CRT group, including a parent, attend the school board meeting and demand that the district fire Alex. After the meeting, Alex meets with three other colleagues, one White, one Black, and one Indian American. They all express concern that the heat will spill over onto them. The White teacher suggests that Alex write an apology letter and make it public. Alex shares the follow-up work she did with the students and her concern that an apology will undermine the validity of her work with them. She is very clear that her approach is not racist to White people. Her colleagues agree on that point.

Although outwardly projecting confidence, Alex is unsettled. So, she focuses on her students, not wanting to give the situation more energy. She does not reach out to her White antiracist network, her colleagues, or her administration for further processing.

Over the next two weeks, the criticism continues as the district declines to fire Alex. However, they do publicly share that they will be implementing a new approval process with the superintendent of Curriculum and Instruction for all resources dealing with race and racism. Teachers across the district are upset at the administration and at Alex for the new restriction.

- From your perspective, who is blameworthy in this situation? For what?
- What lessons can we learn from Alex's experience with the "stop these racists" attacks?

Build Relationship

What do we do when we feel overwhelmed, unfairly attacked, or misunderstood? Alex chose to isolate, keep her head down, and work through it. A different outcome might have been possible had she kept engaging with her antiracist network, colleagues, and administration. Hiding her vulnerable feelings and putting on a brave face is not the most helpful choice. Alex will now need to spend time repairing the relationship with colleagues affected by the district's decision.

While in the heat of our own challenge, it is hard to stay attentive to what others are experiencing. Yet, doing so is part of what can help us work through a complicated situation. What were the concerns of Alex's close colleagues? What were the concerns of the administration? How could they have collaborated on a response to the situation that avoided an either/or dynamic—either you apologize or stay silent? What other possibilities could they imagine?

Working through the range of concerns could bring them to a solution that addresses the emotions of the parents and supports the validity of the lesson. This was a missed opportunity to help the entire community understand what teachers teach and why. It was a missed opportunity to clarify how antiracist work is not racist to White people. It was a missed opportunity to show how the attack on Alex was a coordinated effort to take down the whole program.

Embrace Both/And Thinking

A key to getting through sticky situations is staying humble enough to recognize our own imperfections and missteps, even when we have a strong, guiding foundation. The attacks were unfair, mischaracterizing the work Alex has a right to be proud of. She can hold that as true *and* still self-reflect to realize where she could (or should) have done things differently. Alex's last-minute decision to share a document that her students were not prepared to receive was an error. Without careful framing, she left her students to process complex and provocative information on their own. This kind of error provides fuel for the fires set by the far right. Even amid the flames, Alex needs to think about which criticisms are valid and which are not.

Alex's lack of public engagement also contributed to the increased oversight of their program. She, her department, and the administration can all reflect on lessons from the situation and determine what repair will be needed. In the end, there is much for them to learn collectively so they can evolve to better support student education rich in critical inquiry and resist disingenuous attempts to end that education.

Message: Stop the Antiracist Industrial Complex

Many people on the far right disingenuously push the idea that it is the "far left" that keeps racism alive. They often use the phrase "the antiracist industrial complex" to argue their point. Antiracists often join this bandwagon and miss the far right's primary motive—to stop antiracism. The result is that we contribute to the tearing down of antiracists who make a living doing the work. Part of the reason this far-right strategy is effective is because there are significant philosophical differences within and between antiracism's educational, organizing, and activist circles. These issues include:

1. *Seeking Change from the Inside versus the Outside:* When working within systems, antiracists push organizations to demonstrate their commitment by allocating funds in a way that values the time and expertise of people implementing antiracist efforts. This butts up against the perspective of antiracists working outside systems who are critical of capitalism, reject reforming systems, and call for direct action to construct new systems from the ground up.

2. *Interactions between People in Different Identity Positions:* The far right claims that long-time practitioners, whose careers are dedicated to antiracism, are the ones keeping racism alive in order to profit from it. People in the earlier positions often hear that claim and then attack those practitioners, not realizing they are extending a far-right talking point that seeks to sow division, demoralize efforts, and undermine racial justice. This can have serious consequences for people who have dedicated their lives to fighting racism.

3. *Unprepared Practitioners:* Sometimes people in *Disintegration, Reintegration,* and/or *Pseudo-Independence* put themselves forward as professional facilitators too soon. They do not yet have the skills, insight, expertise, and resolved emotion to do the work effectively and with care for everyone in their sessions. This leads to valid criticism.

These factors complicate our ability to navigate the far-right attacks regarding antiracists making money. Antiracists, even those operating in *Autonomy,* can feel thrown off. Because we care about individual and collective accountability to People of Color and our White community, we work hard to engage, whether paid or unpaid, with integrity. We take genuine critiques of capitalism and antiracism seriously; we consider how we give to the larger collective in our thought, time, energy, and finances.

However, we lose stability when we unwittingly help push (or allow for) far-right narratives. Keep in mind that the far right *loves* capitalism and free markets; it is a red flag when they attack people for making a living. The key problem here is that we undermine our own efforts when we use a far-right critique to tear down and ostracize antiracists. The result is the draining of time, energy, and capacity to organize and fight racism itself.

Antiracist people attacking one another is also off-putting to those witnessing this dynamic. They worry that if experienced antiracists are subject to such attacks, anything they do may draw criticism and vitriol as well. This causes many who otherwise might raise their voice and use their creativity to work against racism to silence themselves, undercutting the movement's reach.

To capture the breadth of this challenge, consider that Alex, Madison, and Ryan all attend a social justice conference where well-known paid speakers will present. Two weeks before the conference, the far right exposes financial information related to one of the speakers' contracts with a public university. The reporting begins in *Campus Reform*, a far-right online media outlet that criticizes the school's spending. By the next week, a Fox News opinion personality attacks the university's use of public funds as well as the speaker, saying that the "antiracist industrial complex" is at it again. Provocative media personalities like Ben Shapiro blast the "hypocrisy" of antiracists, claiming that it goes against antiracism's radical, Marxist dedication to anti-capitalism.

By the start of the conference, critical opinion pieces run in mainstream media across the political spectrum. Attendees representing a large cross-section of antiracists (organizers, activists, educators, social workers, etc.) are abuzz with discussion. Ryan is there as part of a small cadre from his high school. The last few months with the Social Justice Club brought him into contact with local activists, and he is fascinated with the way they discuss social change theory. Ryan finds one older White man, Alan, particularly interesting. Alan's analysis of how capitalism and racism combine to keep most of the society suffering makes a lot of sense. He listens intently to Alan's critiques of the corrupt system. Madison is there with Janet, a Black co-worker, to bring resources back to the center to support their staff development program. They are friends now, and Madison trusts her judgment. Alex is present as both a workshop presenter and attendee.

Over the course of three days, conversations about the speaker take over, with people debating whether it is okay to make money from antiracism. Without realizing it, Ryan mixes together the far-right critique with the anti-capitalist ideas he learned from Alan. As a result, he spends most of his time arguing with other conference attendees that making money from antiracism allows a corrupted, racist system to stay in place. He feels frustrated by those who tell him he is playing into far-right manipulation.

Madison finds herself unsteadily searching for a solid position. She understands the need for people to do the work professionally, and yet she feels torn. She listens intently to Janet, who insists that White people should never receive money for antiracist actions. She also hears from other People of Color who believe their White antiracist colleagues who work alongside them should be paid. Some facilitators of color argue that White people who do antiracism work for free undermine their ability to earn a living. Madison strives to find her own stance.

Alex feels thrown off balance as well. Although she is not receiving money for her presentation at this conference, she is starting to accept paid invitations to work with other schools. She has done so with the encouragement of some People of Color in her life who no longer want to help transform White people. They specifically recommend her. She wants to align with the People of Color with whom she has relationship, but she hears the critiques of White people making money and is conflicted.

The challenge here is that we cannot wholeheartedly dismiss all the critiques because they do raise important questions about integrity and accountability. White people do need to think about the quality of the work they offer, the substance of their accountability relationships, and their own relationship to capitalism. Yet, if we descend into viewing antiracists as the main problem, then we allow the claims to undermine the effectiveness of our work and the strength of our relationships with one another.

- What messages have you heard regarding people making money from antiracist work?
- How can we remain open to critical self-reflection without allowing far-right attacks to turn us against one another?

Educate Yourself

We need to tease out what is a genuine or not genuine critique by looking at where it starts. Who has launched the critique? How is their effort designed to redirect antiracist energy and undermine the overall goal of dismantling systemic racism? We need to know enough about how the far right operates to avoid falling into their trap and mixing up legitimate antiracist concerns with far-right narratives. Always investigate the source of critique and their commitment to antiracism.

Offer Perspective

Once we've distinguished between disingenuous far-right critiques and valid antiracist critiques, we need to be strategic about how we offer perspective. We need to defend those on the forefront when they are being deluged by far-right attacks. Simply claiming someone is falling for a far-right trap is not sufficient. We need to specifically name the attack, its source, and its intention, which is to undermine antiracism and disrupt the movement.

When offering critiques of antiracists, we need to make sure we are not providing fodder to the far right to take down our efforts. And we should intentionally adopt the abolitionist value that no one is disposable. How do we hold each other in loving accountability?

Engage Critical Thinking

While we point a finger directly at the far right when they are the source, we also need to self-reflect. What is the substance that allows this critique to have energy? Do we hold people working for racial justice to the same standard as people who work in other careers? Is someone who works as a teacher, doctor, or lawyer less obligated to donate their time or resources to antiracism? Why or why not? How might we invite everyone into a just accountability when it comes to dedicating time and resources to antiracism? And strategically plan that invitation based on where they are in their racial identity process?

How do we define our personal accountability and our collective accountability? Is our position grounded in justice? How do we navigate our personal finances, whether this includes donations, paid work related to social justice, consultant/speaker fees, or book royalties? If we make money working for justice, do we also amplify, support, or contribute to the efforts of those who organize for justice for no money? Is there a way our practice can and should improve?

Embrace Both/And Thinking

Autonomy allows us to stand in what we know with all the complexity it entails, holding a both/and position. We resist the urge to fall into the "only one right way" characteristic of white supremacy culture as discussed by Okun.[114] This can allow us to acknowledge fair critiques while also valuing people for their contributions to antiracism. We need to resist either/or narratives that result in more people deciding to leave antiracism than joining us.

ANTIRACIST MESSAGES

The messages explored in this section are complex and they confuse White people observing the dynamics, whether they are operating from *Autonomy* or an earlier position. This can make antiracism appear unattractive, unhealthy, and even anti-White, while making the simplicity of far right critiques seductive.

Although we try to present the messages discussed below in clear terms, we could spend days discussing their nuances and implications. At this apex of identity development, we can focus so narrowly that we fail to realize the impact of these messages on people in other positions on the roundabout, the very people we need to actively recruit into antiracism.

Dear Reader: Please note that although these complexities exist, they do not represent the daily experience of antiracism within *Autonomy.* These are the bumps in an otherwise clear and life-affirming road. Take note of the feelings that arise. Use your own both/and mindful self-talk to put these messages into context and not allow them to overtake you and shut you down. Remember that the point of naming and illustrating these dynamics is to help us better navigate them when they arise.

Message: Demands for Accountability Mask Jealousy and Competitiveness

Within antiracism, there are individual White people and White groups who have successfully shifted culture, policies, procedures, and laws toward antiracism. These successes happen nationally and locally in schools, businesses, houses of religion, and other organizations. Unfortunately, these successes can prompt our unresolved emotions to rise to the surface, causing us to feel a sense of jealousy and competition. Perhaps deep down we feel that we are not good enough, while we wish we could get the same recognition. We may envy people's ability to enjoy vibrant cross-race relationships with solidarity partners, wishing we had that too.

Jealousy and competitiveness can lead us to criticize those who receive accolades. We focus on what they did wrong, what they did not do, or how their actions reflect their privilege. We may even criticize them for feeling good after receiving praise. The unmistakable pattern is that we prop ourselves up as we tear them down. We often say we want to "hold someone accountable" for a perceived infraction, while unacknowledged jealousy is our true motivation.

This pattern is destructive in a number of ways. It hinders our ability to see ourselves accurately, damages our relationships with other White people (who won't trust us) as well as People of Color (who see our instability), and diverts our energy away from the collective effort to end racism.

A small-scale version of this pattern results in Madison's co-worker, a White woman named Susan, facing criticism for a resource she created to serve clients at the community center. Susan has been at the center for

several years and has close working relationships with the staff of color.
Madison has noticed that Susan does not show the same level of deference to People of Color that Madison expects from an antiracist. One
of Madison's close White colleagues, Angie, is also jealous of Susan's
confidence and comfort. Angie and Madison do not know Susan well,
although Susan sometimes comes to the center's White antiracist group,
which Madison and Angie now attend religiously.

One day at a staff meeting, Susan shares a resource she created to
help their clients navigate their programming more easily. As Susan
presents the guide, fellow staff members express gratitude for the work.
She receives even more praise because she used the small amount of
remaining funds left in her budget for translation and web services to
ensure that more versions are accessible to the center's large Spanish-
speaking population.

At the next White antiracist meeting, Angie and others note that
Susan's Spanish translation fails to meet the needs of their Korean
American population. They discuss how Susan fell into a well-trod pattern of racism where White people ignore the needs of Asian Americans. They also wonder about the negative impact on Korean American
staff members.

Although Madison would not say she feels jealous of Susan, she joins
the group as they reinforce the idea that Susan's behavior is not in line with
antiracist principles. At one point, Angie says, "She thinks she's above this
work. That's why she doesn't come to our meetings every month." They
decide that the antiracist thing to do is to hold Susan accountable for the
harm they believe she has caused.

This subgroup of White co-workers invites Susan and the full White
antiracist group to have a special session to discuss an accountability
process. Susan balks, both confused and put off by this group's sense of
authority. Susan goes to the center's director to ask if attending this "special session" is required. The director calls a meeting of this subgroup to
discuss the situation. She says she appreciates their concern about the
need to translate the document into Korean, but says they overstepped by
calling this meeting.

By this time, Angie, Madison, and their co-workers already have shared their plans and word has spread throughout the agency. The issue now blows back on the director, as though she circumvented an important process, angering some staff of color who also recognize the need for a Korean translation. The director spends the next staff meeting addressing the issue, with several White people and People of Color stating that the agency needs to define a process to hold people accountable for errors that reinforce white supremacy. It takes several additional meetings to resolve the situation and refocus on the primary issue: the need to locate funding for a Korean translation and make it happen.

- What experience do you have with underlying jealousy or competitiveness motivating calls for accountability? If none, how does this story make you feel?
- What could have prevented the turmoil?

Take Care of Self

Before sharing criticism of someone receiving accolades for their action for justice, take a pause. Ask yourself: Why do you want to offer the critique right now? Is it in service of the larger goal of fixing an inequity or ending racism? If it is, how can you offer the critique in a way that acknowledges the effort made and enhances the relationship? If it is not, what is coming up for you that makes you want to go after the person? Is it possible that a past trauma or personal pain underlies your reaction? What or who can help you identify your tendencies so that you default to supporting fellow antiracists rather than joining a bandwagon that undermines relationship building?

Build Relationship

Accept that a mistake or oversight does not necessarily require an accountability process. This does not mean that a correction is not necessary. The center needs a Korean translation. Imagine the difference in bridge-building between Susan and the Korean American staff members. Speaking directly to the people involved to repair the situation is more productive than turning the issue into an abstract version of accountability, publicly shaming someone who otherwise did something very good.

Offer Perspective

A feature of the individualism characteristic of white supremacy culture is "valuing competition more highly than cooperation." Consider reviewing the "White Supremacy Culture—Still Here" article by Tema Okun for antidotes we can use within organizations to help avoid falling victim to this pattern.[115] Collaborative processes could have alerted Susan to the need for the Korean translation earlier. This can be done in a productive, generative, supportive way. We can help people improve their practice without making it a heightened issue of accountability.

Message: Our Language Is the Top Priority

The language of antiracism and social justice constantly evolves. Our language changes when terms become too limiting or fail to meet the needs of the moment. Sometimes, we learn that our language causes harm to particular groups and maintains systemic racism. We adjust our language to reflect the new learning. These efforts are meaningful. Our words matter.

Keeping up with new insights about language is important; however, linguistic choices are complex. For example, we have witnessed shifts in the definition of racism, what it means to be nonracist versus antiracist, and the addition of "Latinx" and "BIPOC" to the discussion. Because of its evolving nature, the adoption of new language does not occur all at once. Sometimes new terms receive pushback and dismissal as we struggle to find better ways of expressing complicated ideas. In other words, when paying attention to language matters, the updates contain moments of debate.

Two unhelpful patterns can trip us up. First, we can focus so much on the choice and meaning of our words that it takes us away from action. In some cases, we can even revert to the *Reintegration/Pseudo-Independence* tactic of attacking people who use outdated language to show we're "good White people." Second, our heady analysis can be confusing and/or off-putting to people new to antiracism. If our goal is to build a larger, healthy collective, we need to adjust our approach. The key is to not allow language-policing to become our primary work.

Ryan becomes part of this dynamic when the Social Justice Club participates in the school's Diversity Day. The club plans to divide into small groups to present a different activity. Because the school is 85 percent White while the club is 70 percent students of color, some club members want to influence more White people. As they brainstorm, several of the White students reflect on why they joined the club. Each agrees that seeing how racism exists today made a huge difference. In the end, four White students, including Ryan, settle on creating a workshop to recruit more peers.

At their next meeting, the recruiting team is joined by a newer, White club member without much experience. She joined this group as a way to learn more. Of the five students, Ryan and Jess went to the social justice conference the month before. Jess offers a handout she received as a resource. The group likes the handout, but one member is concerned that the phrase "white supremacy system" will turn students off.

As they discuss alternatives, suggestions include institutional racism, systemic racism, or just plain racism. As they debate, Jess stands firm that "it is important to speak the truth even if it makes people feel uncomfortable." Others agree that, "we have to call it what it is" and "people need to hear the reality." Another offers that the language will turn people off, but also worries that changing the words demonstrates their fear. She is torn. Do they even have the right to change the words on the handout? Also of concern is whether their peers of color will be mad if they use less provocative language. While the debate goes on, they never ask the newest member what she thinks.

The group spends the entire planning time on language. At the end of meeting, their faculty sponsor stops to check on them and affirms that their wrestling over the language is just as important as the workshop itself. He encourages them to keep struggling to find clarity. Ryan leaves the meeting feeling energized and conflicted at the same time. The newest member of the club leaves unmotivated to return, feeling disconnected during this extended argument.

- What do you hope the group will do next? Why?
- If you were part of this effort, how might you help the group navigate?

Stay Strategic and Meet Your Audience Where They Are

We can *make a decision* without *making a rule* to give us flexibility as problem-solvers. The concern over what language the team should use to be "good" antiracists and avoid critique diverts them from what will be most effective for their purpose. Trying to use certain language to please people who are not the intended audience can leave them satisfied with their performance without having achieved their goal of reaching more White students.

The students are correct that the different terms they consider have different and distinct meanings and, as the faculty sponsor noted, it is a useful learning experience to practice articulating those distinctions. That said, their process so far has done little to help them plan for the actual workshop or to meet their primary goal. Staying strategic will help balance the learning and the planning.

Stay Strategic and Focus on Your Goal

To stay true to purpose, decisions should be grounded in goals. Ryan's team wants to entice more White people to join their club. Choosing specific terms that will engage their peers is not evidence of a lack of courage or a too-soft approach to antiracism. Instead, it reflects an appreciation for the racial identity process and an effort to meet people where they are. And clarity about the goal of meeting people where they are will also help the group to respond to critiques if they come. Unfortunately, Ryan's team got lost in their own debate and lost a new team member—the opposite of their goal.

An important issue many antiracists fail to consider is that we are likely to be more successful enticing people to join antiracism if we hone our tactics to match people's psychological process. This means we may need to lead people bit by bit toward our perspective without alienating or giving up on them.

The faculty sponsor could help the group balance their learning process with the strategic decision to change the language, even if it does not perfectly capture all of racism's reality. Making decisions with people's stages of development in mind can help us steady ourselves and not falter in the face of criticism; these choices do not make us a good or a bad antiracist.

For example, some readers may notice that we do not use the phrase "Black, Indigenous, and People of Color" (BIPOC) terminology regularly in this book. Although increasingly popular during the two years leading up to this writing, we made our choice to use "People of Color" based on a number of factors. These include our investment in connecting with the broad range of our anticipated audience and the mixed messages we received from our solidarity partners of color about this term. Some may disagree with our choice. That is okay.

REFLECTION

Dear Reader: You've made it to the end of the first chapter describing the challenges that can send us off course when in *Autonomy*. Before you move on, we ask you to consider a few of these questions by journaling or through another method of self-reflection.

Thinking of Yourself:
- How does it feel to imagine yourself in *Autonomy*, to have a healthy antiracist White identity?
- What can help you move closer to a life where you consistently act from *Autonomy*?
- Who are your role models that operate out of *Autonomy*? What can you learn from them and their experience?

Thinking of Others:
- How can we be there for one another when we make mistakes or are struggling?
- What support can you give to other White people so they might experience a healthy racial identity?

CHAPTER 11

SUMMARY FOR POSITIVE ANTIRACIST WHITE IDENTITY: AUTONOMY

In *Autonomy*, we experience a positive, antiracist White identity that draws more people toward antiracism; we work effectively with people of all races to counter racism and advance justice.		
Far-right messages we are susceptible to in this position: • Stop These Racists • Stop the Antiracist Industrial Complex	Antiracist messages that are harmful in this position: • Demands for Accountability Mask Jealousy and Competitiveness • Our Language Is the Top Priority	Suggested approaches: • Use self-reflection and both/and thinking to identify far-right tactics, engage people where they are, and focus on shared goals • Center on integrity to navigate how to be accountable to People of Color • Build relationships with White antiracists and People of Color for ongoing support and accountability

12

It's Okay to Be White

Autonomy

The phone rings, and I pick it up. Tracey says "Tabitha wants me to speak at the board meeting tonight as a White parent. I don't want to take the focus from the kids' plan to speak. What do I do?" We talk. Tracey writes a two-minute speech.

The phone rings after the meeting finishes. "The school is going to dedicate more resources to equity work! They're speeding it up because of what I said to support the kids. I'm so grateful."

I feel her excitement, along with a deep sense of pride and satisfaction that our White antiracist community has supported her to move from a disintegrated position toward consistent, effective advocacy in less than two years. Tracey and I, Shelly, are both in Autonomy *this evening as we relish the moment.*

This second chapter on *Autonomy* highlights that the racial identity journey, by necessity, leads to a place where we love ourselves authentically, not defensively, and we have the capacity to more fully love others. We know that everyone deserves to heal from the harm racism has wrought and no one is disposable. We stand strong in this belief, even when challenged.

From this position, we assert: It is okay to be white. It is okay to love ourselves. It is important that we love each other.

It must be okay. If it is not, we leave the door open for white nationalists to exploit people's confusion and concern while in earlier positions on the roundabout. Thankfully, many antiracist people recognize the truth

Figure 12.1 Autonomy. ARTIST: LIZ WILTSIE

of this and are dedicated to working collectively in the spirit of "Let's all get free!"

However, our ability to embrace ourselves and generate empathy for other White people depends on us making a distinction between White people and whiteness. Recall from chapter 2 that White people (humans born into the White category) and whiteness (a system of oppression) are not the same. White people, particularly those who reach *Autonomy*, consistently attempt to disrupt whiteness. In other words, being a White person is okay, but reinforcing and benefiting from whiteness is not.

Unfortunately, many antiracists equate White people with whiteness and deliver a set of messages that we need to examine.

MESSAGES CONFLATING WHITENESS WITH WHITE PEOPLE

Conflating whiteness and White people is widespread within antiracism, and it leads to three unhelpful messages that create problems in all positions on the roundabout:

1. White people cannot be valuable leaders in the fight for justice.
2. Racism does not damage White people; only People of Color need and deserve healing and wholeness.
3. It is not okay to be White; as long as we are White, we will be a problem.

Collectively, these messages can result in the following:

- The idea that White people need to disrupt internalized racism in themselves, but do not need healing as part of the disruption.
- Unhealthy relationships with White people, People of Color, and ourselves.
- Limited possibilities and roles for White people in ending racism.
- Fewer White people joining antiracism.

In the end, all of these reduce our ability to work toward collective liberation.

Madison, Alex, and Ryan each run into forms of this conflation on their journey. As you read, consider how you would respond to what they face. How might you appreciate the concerns expressed while not falling into an unhelpful conflation?

Message: White People Cannot Be Valuable Leaders in the Fight for Racial Justice

In *Autonomy*, we dedicate ourselves to combating the system of oppressive whiteness that results in racial inequities. Part of this includes White people learning to follow the leadership of People of Color and ensuring that racially conscious People of Color attain positions of power and influence. Each of these is important. Where we run into trouble is when White people become equivalent to whiteness in people's minds. This limits our vision for how White people can be useful and necessary partners/leaders in ending racism and undermining white supremacy.

Madison experiences this after completing her graduate program and accepting a new supervisor position at the community center, with encouragement from the Latinx executive director. After years working at the center, interrogating her whiteness, attending to cross-race partnerships, and engaging in ongoing learning inside and outside of school, Madison is ready for this next step. Her excitement turns to dread as she inadvertently overhears some co-workers responding to the announcement of her promotion by saying, "Whiteness is really taking over this place. How could they do this?"

Although confident in her abilities, Madison wonders if the fact that she is White means that she should not be in a leadership position at the center.

- What do you think and feel about White people holding leadership positions?
- How can Madison become a good leader and ensure that she does not replicate dominating whiteness?

Engage Critical Thinking

Madison needs to remember that there is an important distinction between who she is as a White person and how she shows up to do her work. What racial consciousness does she bring to her role? What do people need from her? She must remain attentive to her tendencies, ensuring that she does not fall into patterns of whiteness that betray a history of entitlement and privilege. How she shows up will make a huge difference.

A difficult truth we can wrestle with is that people of all racial identities can enact whiteness and white supremacy culture. People of Color have their own identity journeys and there are those who assimilate into the norms of white supremacy successfully and impose them on others as well. In *Autonomy,* we have more skills to navigate the differences in how White people and People of Color support whiteness. For Madison, this means an honest reckoning of her skills as a White person and as a leader and not avoiding conversations about whiteness with the people in the community center.

Embrace Both/And Thinking

In most situations, the leadership of People of Color is important. And the leadership of racially conscious People of Color is *very* important. It is also true that White people who have done deep personal growth can play important antiracist leadership roles. All of this is true.

Build Relationship: With White People

Examples like Madison's emphasize the importance of intentionally engaging a collective of White antiracist people. Madison needs help to stay balanced and process the criticism. A group can help her identify the valid critiques that might require change as well as moments when the critiques are not really about her. Without support, the claim that White people are not needed in leadership can prompt Madison to return to the individualistic feelings of *Pseudo-Independence* and *Immersion/Emersion*. However, a committed White antiracist community can help her consider how other White people have learned to lead, guided by antiracist principles.

Build Relationship: With People of Color

A person in *Autonomy* has had many discussions with People of Color about how accountability and solidarity function in their relationships and in their shared cross-racial work. There is open and honest dialogue about power dynamics and not overly burdening People of Color. When there is genuine reciprocity in a cross-racial relationship, where everyone has done their internal racial identity and consciousness work, healthy models of interracial work can emerge.

In these relationships, Madison can offer some self-assessment *and* ask for direct feedback about ways whiteness is and is not showing up in her leadership. There is a shared sense of commitment and an ongoing understanding of racialized and racist power differentials. These relationships depend on intentionality, integrity, and fidelity to ending racism.

Message: White People Do Not Need Healing

Whiteness is a system of dominance that prioritizes White norms and advantages White people. White people express our whiteness when we act out of a sense of entitlement, privilege, and internalized superiority. When some people talk about "decentering whiteness," they mean we need to stop allowing White norms, entitlement, and privilege to dominate. Decentering whiteness is essential.

Unfortunately, when people conflate whiteness with White people, they believe that wherever White people are, the dominance of whiteness is reinforced. Within this belief, White accountability groups serve to reinforce whiteness. While it is true that vigilance against whiteness is necessary, we firmly believe in the importance of intentionally antiracist

White groups. If all group members are doing is reaffirming whiteness, they need to overhaul their group.

In addition, some believe that White people spending time learning about ourselves reinforces and recenters whiteness. In this view, reading White authors about White identity issues (i.e., reading this book) and the entire *Immersion* process re-centers whiteness. Instead of recognizing these activities as necessary on the road to undoing whiteness, they perceive them as problems to avoid. Again, we firmly believe that White people need time to learn about how whiteness infects us, recognize the harm it does to ourselves and People of Color, and heal from our socialization.

As James Baldwin writes in *The Fire Next Time*, "White people in this country will have quite enough to do in learning how to accept and love themselves and each other, and when they have achieved this—which will not be tomorrow and may very well be never—the Negro problem will no longer exist for it will no longer be needed."[116] Without the space to shed our tendencies to enact whiteness, to learn to love ourselves and each other, White people will not become healthy partners in the fight for collective liberation.

Alex runs into this issue when she's asked to start a White affinity group at Ryan's high school, which already has affinity groups for students of color. Ryan's friend wants a place for White students to work on their identity as well. As part of the initial outreach, Alex meets with the school's Social Justice Club. In the discussion, a student of color asks, "Why do White people need a group? Why do they get everything? The entire school is for them."

The White sponsor hesitates. "We have been trying to decenter whiteness. This may be going in the wrong direction." Jess, who has been vocal about not coddling White people before, states they would not tell people to attend because, "Why would I want to sink myself into more whiteness? That's what I'm trying to get rid of."

Ryan listens intently and is not sure what to think. He would not be where he is today without someone like Alex helping him process all the new things he has learned. It sounds like Alex is advocating for a group to work together to do that for each other.

- What thoughts and feelings do you have about groups of antiracist White people meeting together?
- What do you hope Alex might say to those who are skeptical?

Offer Perspective about Needed Support

When White people attempt to step out of the norms of whiteness, there is often a lot of confusion and pushback. Yet, we need a place where we can learn about our own racial identity journey and get support in becoming an antiracist White person. We need help to stay strong in the face of messages telling us we should not participate in accountability/affinity spaces. Otherwise, we risk unsupported White people defending and retreating into whiteness. For example, when a racial slur is used on campus, those who have participated in affinity are more likely to know how to take leadership from the harmed individual and recognize whether responses focus on minimizing and dismissing the event.

Offer Perspective about Accountability

When White people interrogate our whiteness, we can notice, name, and disrupt our tendencies toward entitlement and privilege, making us better partners across race in the fight against racism. With clarity and conviction, Alex can talk about how effective affinity works, how it maintains integrity to antiracist principles, and how it can operate in accountability to—and in solidarity with—People of Color affinity groups.

Take Care of Self

Do you feel unsteady arguing that White people deserve time and space for healing? Why? What is the emotion that comes up for you? What underlies the belief that we do not deserve to be healthy? How can we trust ourselves to do this work with each other? How can we support one another to stand strong in what we know? Make sure the affinity groups that you participate in balance learning, action, and healing.

Message: It Is Not Okay to Be White

Antiracist people who deliver the message "It is not okay to be White" do not hate White people. They do believe, however, that identifying with being White is part of whiteness. People who hold this philosophical position want us to dismantle and abolish whiteness (the system of oppression). They want us to uncover and eliminate our sense of entitlement, our White privilege, and our internalized superiority. They want us to restore our humanity by dedicating ourselves to all of humanity, not just the White group. These are all important goals.

Part of what underlies the conflation between "being White" and "whiteness" is our history. The political elite in the colonial era invented the category "White" to institute the systemic privileging of White people (whiteness) to keep European- and African-descended free and enslaved people from banding together to overthrow the still-growing capitalist system.[117] In other words, we cannot separate the creation of whiteness from the creation of the category White. For some this means working for a future where racial categories cease to exist, where no one will be White any longer.

As people in *Autonomy* work to dismantle whiteness, many speak as though systemic whiteness and White identity are the same. The problem is that most White people do not understand the nuance. Most who hear "be less White" or "abolish whiteness" interpret it as meaning that it is not okay to be a person born with light skin or part of the White group.

However, many antiracists believe developing a positive, White antiracist identity supports White people's ability to dismantle and abolish whiteness. We take on the challenge to maintain a healthy racial sense of self so that we can be more effective in ending racism. This entire book is a rallying cry for this position.

The goals of these two orientations are ultimately the same: to end racism's grip on all of us. Both offer essential insights. The problem is that if we approach them with an either/or attitude, we leave ourselves open to 1) being misunderstood, 2) allowing the far right to entice White people, and 3) remaining less healthy than we need to be to achieve our goals.

Ryan wrestles with this tension at a local activist meeting. Recall that Ryan has been enjoying listening to the political analysis of Alan, a White abolitionist. At this meeting, two activists debate how to organize to support unhoused people living on the streets. On one side is Michael, who is a member of Showing Up for Racial Justice (SURJ), which follows the lead of People of Color groups. Following their lead, he advocates a racially conscious approach to the campaign, having White people organize in White neighborhoods and People of Color organize in the neighborhoods with higher populations of People of Color.

As a decades-long community organizer, Alan argues that inserting race into the campaign will be divisive. He refuses to identify as White and says, "Any campaign that tells people they should identify with their whiteness reinforces its power." Ryan recognizes the value in SURJ's adoption of the People of Color plan *and* respects Alan. He feels torn.

- What messages have you encountered about what it means to identify as White?
- What can help us stand solid when encountering differing perspectives?

Educate Yourself

Knowledge is power. The more we know, the more we can interpret the messages we receive and help support others and ourselves from being turned off from antiracism. Understanding the history and philosophy underlying antiracism's core principles and philosophies will keep Ryan from faltering when he encounters philosophical differences. Honing our analysis is how we know that dismantling whiteness is not an assault on White people.

Embrace Both/And Thinking

There is no need to choose between the idea of abolishing whiteness and developing a positive, antiracist White identity. Both goals can live side by side when we do not conflate whiteness with White people.

We can enjoy the intellectual struggle related to the long-term future of White identity and whiteness when we use a both/and mindset. Wrestling with these ideas is invigorating and leaves us wanting more. This is a completely different experience than in earlier positions because we no longer feel riddled with anxiety. Ryan's steadier sense of self will allow him to experience the debate as complex, enriching, and generative, helping him to know the world and himself more deeply. This will be true as long as the group focuses on the goal of a healthy multiracial future grounded in equity, inclusion, and liberation.

REFLECTION

Dear Reader: You've made it to the end of our exploration of the positions on the roundabout and the challenges we face within them. As we imagine how Alex, Madison, Ryan, and others will continue to navigate the complexities of antiracism, we anticipate they will travel back and forth between positions, honing their skills along the way. We also remain hopeful that something or someone in Tyler's life will spark him to return to *Disintegration* and that he will find the support he needs to shift toward an antiracist perspective.

We ask you to consider once more a few questions through writing or another method of self-reflection.

Thinking of Yourself:
- When have you encountered messages or language that conflates whiteness with White people? What have been the results?
- How are you able to distinguish yourself as a White person from your socialization into whiteness?

Thinking of Others
- What actions can you take to build intentional White antiracist groups or gatherings that work toward *Autonomy*?
- How do you explain the idea that it's okay to be White?

A FINAL *DEAR READER*

We wrote this book because today's changing society requires White people to grapple with questions of racial identity. White nationalists actively organize around the idea that White people are under assault; they offer messages of empowerment and pride. Antiracist messaging must counter this with an empowering message of its own:

We can be proud antiracist White people who work with people of all racial identities toward an inclusive democracy that benefits everyone. We can be strong and powerful in our commitment when we understand that each of us has a purpose-filled role to play.

And because the journey toward this positive antiracist life requires enhancing our skills and careful navigation, we are profoundly grateful for the White people and People of Color who act as role models and mentors for us, paving our way forward. We hope each of you will find people to play these roles in your life. We need all of us on this journey, supporting one another. We both reach forward, following the lead of others, and reach back, pulling others along with us, as we strive toward the inclusive society we envision.

And the journey continues, and we invite you to join us. Visit Being WhiteToday.com for more. And, once again, thank you.

Summary for It's Okay to Be White: Autonomy

In *Autonomy*, we grapple with the widespread pattern of antiracists conflating White people with whiteness and attempt to model how these are different.	
Antiracist messages conflating whiteness and White People: • White People Cannot Be Valuable Leaders in the Fight for Racial Justice • White People Do Not Need Healing • It Is Not Okay to Be White	Suggested approaches: • Reframe conflating messages • Persist in the face of complexity by valuing the both/and aspects of the challenges we face

Appendix

Summary of Messages, Approaches, and Dilemmas

Chapter 3: *Contact*		
In *Contact*, we feel neutral, colorblind, like race does not affect us in any way. We may feel curious or fearful about People of Color, but do not give it much thought.		
Far-right messages we are susceptible to in this position: <ul><li>Being Colorblind Is American</li><li>Join the Fight to Protect the Innocent</li></ul>	Antiracist messages that are harmful in this position: <ul><li>Being Colorblind Is Racist</li><li>Of Course, You Are White and Racist</li><li>You're Ignorant</li></ul>	Suggested approaches: <ul><li>Ask three to five questions before offering your own ideas</li><li>Share personal stories that offer different perspectives</li><li>Share stories of People of Color to expand awareness</li></ul>

Chapter 4: *Disintegration* (Moral Dilemmas)

When we encounter racism, we confront moral dilemmas that move us into DISINTEGRATION. We question the accuracy of our vision of the world and how it works.

Key Dilemmas:

- *Colorblindness*—Does race make a difference in people's lives?
- *Love and Compassion for All*—Why is care not extended to people equally?
- *Inaction in the Face of Racism*—Does not acting against racism cause it to continue?
- *Moral and Equal Treatment for All*—Are some people treated badly because of their race?
- *Freedom and Democracy for All within an Equitable Democracy*—Are US policies really designed to support everyone?
- *Individualism*—Are all people actually treated based on their individual merit?

Chapter 5: *Disintegration* (Defending Whiteness)

In *Disintegration*: Defending Whiteness, we dismiss the racism we encounter, telling ourselves the status quo is fair.

• White Privilege Isn't Real, but It Is Real Racist	• Stop Being "Fragile!" That Is Your White Privilege	• Ask questions to understand why people think and believe as they do
• The Real Issue Is People of Color	• Get Systemic	• Use both/and thinking to talk about the complexity of the moral dilemmas
• Racism Is in the Past, Get over It		• Normalize the emotions we feel when facing moral dilemmas
• "I'm Not Racist, but . . ."		• Share personal stories to help people recognize that stereotypes and bias are the source of racial fears

Chapter 6: *Disintegration* (Toward Antiracism)		
In *Disintegration*: Toward Antiracism, we feel conflicted by what we learn about race and its effects; we realize the world does not operate like we thought it did.		
• Why Bother to Help If They Hate You Anyway • No One Can Take a Joke Anymore	• Stop Being a White Savior • You Need to Be Accountable • Yes, All White People (Are Racist)	• Pose questions about people's experience with the moral dilemmas • Try to understand why people think as they do; what underlies their beliefs? • Build people's capacity to see themselves as associated with racism through personal stories
Chapter 7: *Reintegration* (Retreating into Whiteness)		
In *Reintegration*: Retreat into Whiteness, we recognize being White as a meaningful part of our identity and seek to defend it; we believe discrimination is more widespread against White people than People of Color.		
• Antiracism Is Anti-White • Equity Is Un-American • Cancel Culture Threatens Free Speech and America's Foundation • Defend True Patriots	• The US Is Founded on White Supremacy • Equity Is Much More Important than Equality • I Can Prove You Wrong (with Data) • You Aren't Worth It	• Be curious and learn how the person's beliefs developed • Use both/and thinking to acknowledge how White people have contributed positively to our nation's history while sharing ideas that complicate that history • Offer stories that question if prejudicial ideas are really true • Seek to remain connected by avoiding direct critique of the person's heroes

Chapter 8: *Reintegration* (Emerging Antiracism)		
In *Reintegration*: Emerging Racism, we recognize that we are associated with a long history of racism and often experience complex, upsetting emotions as a result; we feel for People of Color and want racism to end.		
• You Are Damned If You Do, Damned If You Don't; It Will Never Be Enough • Antiracism Shames White Kids and Teaches Them to Feel Guilty	• You're Not Doing Enough • White People's Feelings Don't Matter • Don't Coddle White People • Your Intent Doesn't Matter	• Acknowledge the difference between guilt and shame and the need to reduce shame to engage in effective antiracist action • Use both/and thinking to understand our role as individuals within a system and how to embrace loving accountability • Offer support and encouragement, anticipating challenging emotions
Chapter 9: *Pseudo-Independence*		
In *Pseudo-Independence*, we feel a false sense of confidence in our antiracist stance; we believe we skillfully do what we can to help People of Color, and we do not perceive ourselves as enacting racism.		
• You Should Be Able to Appreciate Your Ancestors Too • People of Color Want Power over You	• All White People Are Racist • You Are Not Ready! You Need More Work! • It's Okay to Make Fun of White People • Stop Worrying about Whether You Are a Good Person	• Use both/and messages to support self-reflection that unearths the role guilt, shame, and cultural values may play in attitudes toward ourselves and other white people, other White people, and People of Color • Join an antiracist community for encouragement, support, and inspiration

Chapter 10: *Immersion/Emersion*

In *Immersion/Emersion*, we engage in a cycle of learning and engaging in action as we develop our antiracist practice; we recognize the value of building community with other White antiracist people.

• Stop Making Everyone Victims • You're a Hypocrite • Antiracists Traffic in Cancel Culture	• You're Either Oppressed or Oppressive • White Culture Is Whiteness • Everything We Do Is White Supremacy Culture • Antiracism Has Rules • Always Defer To People of Color	• Use both/and thinking to balance our need to learn, take action, be accountable, and cultivate our antiracist voice • Name and explain the false equivalences that exploit complexities and seemingly conflicting antiracist messages • Study models that provide inclusive, empowering, and life-affirming approaches to justice work

Chapter 11: *Autonomy* (Positive Antiracist White Identity)

In *Autonomy*, we experience a positive, antiracist White identity that draws more people toward antiracism; we work effectively with people of any racial background to counter racism and advance justice.

• Stop These Racists • Stop the Antiracist Industrial Complex	• Demands for Accountability Mask Jealousy and Competitiveness • Our Language Is the Top Priority	• Slow down to self-reflect and use the both/and thinking to identify and name far-right tactics, engage people where they are, and focus on shared goals • Center in personal integrity to navigate how to be accountable to People of Color • Build relationships with White antiracists and People of Color for ongoing support and accountability

Chapter 12: *Autonomy* (It's Okay to Be White)	
In *Autonomy*, we grapple with the widespread pattern of antiracists conflating White people with whiteness and attempt to model how they are different.	
• White People Cannot Be Valuable Leaders in the Fight for Racial Justice • White People Do Not Need Healing • It Is Not Okay to Be White	• Reframe conflating messages • Persist in the face of complexity by valuing the both/and aspects of the challenges we face

ENDNOTES

Introduction

1 Kendi, Ibram. "The Mantra of White Supremacy: The Idea That Anti-Racist Is the Code for Anti-White Is the Claim of Avowed Extremists." *The Atlantic*, November 30, 2021. https://www.theatlantic.com/ideas/archive/2021/11/white-supremacy-mantra-anti-racism/620832.

2 Barnes, Jack, and Barry Sheppard. "Interview with Malcolm X." *Young Socialist 8*, no. 3 (1965): 63. https://www.marxists.org/history/etol/newspape/youngsocialist/1964-1965/v08n03-w63-[2nd-w63]-mar-apr-1965-young-socialist-ysa.pdf. Thompson, Becky. A Promise and a Way of Life: White Antiracist Activism. Minneapolis: University of Minnesota Press, 2021.

3 Our decision to capitalize White comes from listening to a larger discussion among Black scholars like Nell Irvin Painter to challenge "the choice" of White Americans to be "something vague, something unraced and separate from race." In Painter's view, the capitalization helps to support the idea of a White racial identity—that, in fact White people are not separate from race. This aligns with our focus on moving White people to a positive racial identity. In addition, we push back against the Associated Press' argument that "capitalizing the term white, as is done by white supremacists, risks subtly conveying legitimacy to such beliefs." Our approach is to capitalize it when it refers to identity and not to capitalize it when it refers to nationalism and supremacy. See: Painter, Nell Irvin. "Why White Should Be Capitalized Too." *Washington Post*, July 2, 2020. https://www.washingtonpost.com/opinions/2020/07/22/why-white-should-be-capitalized/. Associated Press. "Examining AP style on Black and white." AP News, July 20, 2020. https://apnews.com/article/archive-race-and-ethnicity-9105661462.

Chapter 1

4 Neither author of this book are political scientists or experts in conservative politics. Delineating the differences in right-wing ideologies can be confusing. There is useful analysis in the *Pod Save America* episode, "Cold War, Hot Mic" (Jon Favreau, Jon Lovett, and Tommy Vietor, *Pod Save America*, podcast, January 25, 2022, https://podcasts.apple.com/us/podcast/cold-war-hot-mic/id1192761536?i=1000548915440, at approximately minute 24). Although conservatives share some particular White, Christian norms and values, there are three disparate groups within the right wing: 1) neo-conservatives, who want to defend democracy in a bellicose way; 2) paleo-conservatives, who are isolationist and promote America first policies; and 3) fascistic conservatives, who admire White, religious, authoritarian leaders who push traditional gender roles and an anti-LGBTQ agenda. While dominant White values may thread throughout all of them, it is in the second and third groups where we are likely to find the most overt racism and orientation toward white power. Also see Kathleen Belew and Ramón Gutiérrez, *A Field Guide to White Supremacy* (Oakland: University of California Press, 2021).

5 Lesbian, gay, bisexual, transgender, queer/questioning, intersex, asexual, and more.

6 Janet Helms, *A Race Is a Nice Thing to Have: A Guide to Being a White Person or Understanding the White Persons in Your Life* (San Diego, CA: Cognella Academic Publishing, 2020).

7 AWARE-LA, "Theory of Personal Transformation"; AWARE-LA, "Toward A Radical White Identity," both accessed September 29, 2022, https://www.awarela.org/toolkit.

8 Beverly Daniel Tatum, "Teaching White Students about Racism: The Search for White Allies and the Restoration of Hope," *Teachers College Record* 95, no. 4 (2021): 462–77; Tatum, *Why Are All the Black Kids Sitting Together in the Cafeteria? And Other Conversations about Race* (New York: Basic Books, 2017).

9 For important perspective on the value that "no one is disposable," see adrienne maree brown, *We Will Not Cancel Us and Other Dreams of Transformative Justice* (Chico, CA: AK Press, 2020).

10 Steven Gardiner and Tarso Luis Ramos, "Capitol Offenses: January 6th 2021 and the Ongoing Insurrection: PRA State of the Right Report," *Political Research Associates*, January 12, 2022, https://politicalresearch.org/2022/01/12/capitol-offenses-january-6th-2021-ongoing-insurrection.

11 For more on their presence in the military, see Leo Shane, "Is the Military Doing Enough to Look for Signs of White Nationalism in its Ranks?" *Military Times*, February 11, 2020, https://www.military times.com/news/pentagon-congress/2020/02/11/is-the-military-doing -enough-to-look-for-signs-of-white-nationalism-in-the-ranks/.

12 DEO, "The Rhetoric Tricks, Traps, and Tactics of White Nationalists," *Medium*, June 14, 2018, https://medium.com/@ DeoTasDevil/the-rhetoric-tricks-traps-and-tactics-of-white -nationalism-b0bca3caeb84.

13 Nicolas Jones, Rachel Marks, Roberto Ramirez, and Merarys Ríos-Vargas, "2020 Census Illuminates Racial and Ethnic Composition of the Country," US Census Bureau, August 12, 2021, https://www .census.gov/library/stories/2021/08/improved-race-ethnicity-measures -reveal-united-states-population-much-more-multiracial.html; William Frey, "The US Will Become 'Minority White' in 2045, Census Projects: Youthful Minorities Are the Engine of Future Growth," Brookings Institute, March 18, 2018, https://www.brookings.edu/blog/the -avenue/2018/03/14/the-us-will-become-minority-white-in-2045 -census-projects/.

14 Gene Denby, Jess Kung, and Leah Donnella, "The Folk Devil Made Me Do It," *Code Switch*, podcast, September 1, 2021, MP3 audio, 37:00, https://www.npr.org/2021/08/20/1029775224/ the-folk-devil-made-me-do-it.

15 Marisa Lati, "What Is Critical Race Theory, and Why Do Republicans Want to Ban It in Schools?" *Washington Post*, May 29, 2021, https://www.washingtonpost.com/education/2021/05/29/ critical-race-theory-bans-schools/.

16 Andrew Daniller, "Majorities of Americans See at Least Some Discrimination against Black, Hispanic and Asian People in the U.S." Pew Research Center, March 18, 2021, https://www.pewresearch.org/ fact-tank/2021/03/18/majorities-of-americans-see-at-least-some -discrimination-against-black-hispanic-and-asian-people-in-the-u-s/.

17 Ben Lorber, "'America First Is Inevitable': Nick Fuentes, the Groyper Army, and the Mainstreaming of White Nationalism," *Political Research Associates*, January 15, 2021. https://politicalresearch.org/2021/01/15/america-first-inevitable.

18 Marc Fisher, "From Memes to Race War: How Extremists Use Popular Culture to Lure Recruits." *Washington Post*, April 30, 2021, https://www.washingtonpost.com/nation/2021/04/30/extremists-recruiting-culture-community/; Kevin Roose, "The Making of a YouTube Radical." *New York Times*, June 8, 2019, https://www.nytimes.com/interactive/2019/06/08/technology/youtube-radical.html.

19 Shelly Tochluk, "Onramps and Lanes on the Racial Justice Freeway," *Medium*, December 3, 2017, https://shellytochluk.medium.com/on-ramps-and-lanes-on-the-racial-justice-freeway-9ff2ee051042.

Chapter 2

20 Glenn Singleton, *Courageous Conversations about Race: A Field Guide for Achieving Equity in Schools* (Thousand Oaks, CA: Corwin Press, 2015).

21 American Medical Association, "New AMA Policies Recognize Race as a Social, Not Biological, Construct," November 16, 2020, https://www.ama-assn.org/press-center/press-releases/new-ama-policies-recognize-race-social-not-biological-construct; American Anthropological Association, "AAA Statement on Race," May 17, 1998, https://www.americananthro.org/ConnectWithAAA/Content.aspx?ItemNumber=2583.

22 Jacqueline Battalora, *Birth of a White Nation: The Invention of White People and Its Relevance Today*, 2nd edition (New York: Routledge, 2021).

23 Neda Maghbouleh, *The Limits of Whiteness: Iranian Americans and the Everyday Politics of Race* (Stanford, CA: Stanford University Press, 2017).

24 For further learning, see Karen Brodkin, *How Jews Became White Folks and What That Says about Race in America* (Piscataway, NJ: Rutgers University Press, 1998); Thomas Guglielmo, *White on Arrival: Italians, Race, Color, and Power in Chicago, 1890–1945* (New York: Oxford University Press, 2003); Ian Haney López, *White by Law: The Legal Construction of Race* (New York: New York University Press, 1996); Noel

Ignatiev, *How the Irish Became White* (New York: Routledge, 1995); Matthew Jacobson, *Whiteness of a Different Color: European Immigrants and the Alchemy of Race* (Cambridge, MA: Harvard University Press, 1998); Nell Painter, *The History of White People* (New York: W.W. Norton & Company, 2010); and David Roediger, *Working toward Whiteness: How America's Immigrants Became White* (New York: Basic Books, 2005).

25 Judith Katz, "White Culture and Racism: Working for Organizational Change in the *United States*," Whiteness Paper No. 3 (2009), 44. Katz on our struggle to see culture: "Part of our cultural blindness comes in the form of seeing only similarities among [People of Color] and seeing only differences among [White people]. It is often easy for white people to notice the ways in which we differ from each other—along lines of nationality, style, dress, economic class, etc. But when we view [People of Color] they all seem alike—that is, not us."

26 Merriam-Webster.com, s.v. "whiteness," accessed September 29, 2022, https://www.merriam-webster.com/dictionary/whiteness.

27 For more historical perspective, see Michelle Alexander, *The New Jim Crow: Mass Incarceration in the Age of Colorblindness* (New York: The New Press, 2012); Battalora, *Birth of a White Nation*; Ibram Kendi, *Stamped from the Beginning: The Definitive History of Racist Ideas in America* (New York: Nation Books, 2017); Painter, *The History of White People*; and Shelly Tochluk, *Witnessing Whiteness*, 3rd edition (Lanham, MD: Rowman & Littlefield, 2022).

28 Carol Anderson, *White Rage: The Unspoken Truth of our Racial Divide* (New York: Bloomsbury USA, 2017).

29 Jonathan Metzl, *Dying of Whiteness: How the Politics of Racial Resentment Is Killing America's Heartland* (New York: Basic Books, 2019); Heather McGhee, *The Sum of Us: What Racism Costs Everyone and How We Can Prosper Together* (New York: One World, 2021).

30 AWARE-LA, "White Supremacy System Model," accessed September 29, 2022, https://www.awarela.org/toolkit.

31 Llewellyn Smith, "The House We Live In," episode 3 of *Race: The Power of an Illusion* (California Newsreels, 2003), DVD.

32 Richard Rothstein, *The Color of Law: A Forgotten History of How Our Government Segregated America* (New York: Liveright Publishing, 2017).

33 American Bar Association, "CROWN Act, More: Untangling Implicit Bias, One Strand at a Time," February 17, 2020, https://www.americanbar.org/news/abanews/aba-news-archives/2020/02/crown-act--more--untangling-implicit-bias--one-strand-at-a-time/.

34 HipLATINA, "Alexandria Ocasio-Cortez Wears a Braid to Honor Her Afro-Latina Roots," November 26, 2018, https://hiplatina.com/alexandria-ocasio-cortez-wears-braid-honor-afro-latina-roots/.

35 Tema Okun, "White Supremacy Culture: Still Here," accessed Sept 29, 2022, http://www.Whitesupremacyculture.info/uploads/4/3/5/7/43579015/White_supremacy_culture_-_still_here.pdf.

36 Andrew Whitehead and Samuel Perry, *Taking America Back for God: Christian Nationalism in the United States* (New York: Oxford University Press, 2020), pp. 10 and 86.

37 For more on this experience at a far-right Christian conference, see Shelly Tochluk, "My Day with the Far Right, Where I Live and Breathe," *Medium*, May 29, 2018, https://shellytochluk.medium.com/my-day-with-the-far-right-where-i-live-and-breathe-b93429b25129.

38 For examples of how pundits promote colorblindness, see Ben Shapiro, "When Diversity Becomes a Problem," *Fox News Talk*, podcast, February 22, 2016, MP3 audio, 21:57, https://radio.foxnews.com/2016/02/22/ep-1-ben-shapiro-when-diversity-becomes-a-problem/; Brian Kilmeade, "Tucker Carlson on the Dangers of Race Obsession in the Pursuit of a Color Blind Meritocracy," *Fox News Talk*, podcast, April 8, 2018, https://radio.foxnews.com/2021/04/08/tucker-carlson-on-the-dangers-of-race-obsession-in-the-pursuit-of-a-color-blind-meritocracy.

39 For an example of an identitarian, see Southern Poverty Law Center, "Jared Taylor," accessed September 29, 2022, https://www.splcenter.org/fighting-hate/extremist-files/individual/jared-taylor.

40 For more on white abolition, see Noel Ignatiev and John Garvey, *Race Traitor* (New York: Routledge, 1996); Noel Ignatiev, "Abolish the White Race," *Harvard Magazine*, September–October 2002, https://www.harvardmagazine.com/2002/09/abolish-the-white-race.html.

41 Janet Helms, *A Race Is a Nice Thing to Have: A Guide to Being a White Person or Understanding the White Persons in Your Life*, 3rd edition (San Diego, CA: Cognella Academic Publishing, 2020).

42 Beverly Tatum, *Why Are All the Black Kids Sitting Together in the Cafeteria: And Other Conversations about Race* (New York: Basic Books, 2017).

43 Beverly Tatum, "Talking about Race, Learning about Racism: The Application of Racial Identity Development in the Classroom," *Harvard Educational Review* 62, no. 1 (1992): 12.

44 Tatum, *Why Are All the Black Kids Sitting Together in the Cafeteria*, 188.

45 Jenna Chandler-Ward and Elizabeth Denevi, "Racial Identity for White People with Dr. Janet Helms," episode 16 of *Teaching While White*, podcast, March 4, 2021.

46 Chandler-Ward and Denevi, "Racial Identity for White People."

Chapter 3

47 Ian Haney López, *Dog Whistle Politics: How Coded Racial Appeals Have Reinvented Racism and Wrecked the Middle Class* (New York: Oxford University Press, 2014), 181. The idea of "commonsense" racism "expresses the intuitive certainty that many things are just what they are, widely known, widely recognized, and not needing any further explanation. For many in our society, whites and nonwhites too, racial beliefs operate in this fashion. For many, it simply seems 'true,' an unquestioned matter of commonsense, that blacks prefer welfare to work, that undocumented immigrants breed crime, and that Islam spawns violence."

48 We acknowledge the request of disability justice activists to not use colorblind because of the ableism of using a disability as a metaphor for problematic behavior and/or limitations. We chose to use the language most often heard in far right and most mainstream discourse about race. We understand the hurt this may cause. We support a move to language such as "color-evasive"; however, we struggled to make it work with the messages and discourse people have in different racial identity positions.

We also recognize that the use of American to mean of the United States offends many throughout North, Central, and South America because of its colonizing view that the United States is the exclusive owner of the term. We've kept American when the far right uses it in order to be precise in our analysis of their messages. We've also kept it when referring to people's identity; for example, "Mexican American." However, we have worked to use the adjective "US" when speaking about citizenship from an antiracist perspective.

49 Nikole Hannah-Jones, *The 1619 Project: A New Origin Story* (New York: One World, 2021). Critical race theory (CRT) is a framework to examine race and racism first developed in legal studies by Black scholar Derrick Bell. Kimberlé Crenshaw added to this Black scholarship with her work on intersectionality. Gloria Ladson Billings brought the framework into education. Critical race theory scholarship is usually taught at the graduate level. However, opponents have disingenuously used the term to go after almost anything that mentions race, such as antiracism, culturally relevant teaching, and social-emotional learning. For a primer on CRT, see Richard Delgado and Jean Stefancic, *Critical Race Theory: An Introduction*, 3rd edition (New York: New York University Press, 2017).

50 Eduardo Bonilla-Silva, *Racism without Racists: Colorblind Ideology and the Persistence of Racial Inequality in America* (Lanham, MD: Rowman & Littlefield, 2018).

51 Wes Moore, *The Other Wes Moore: One Name, Two Fates* (New York: Spiegel and Grau, 2011).

52 Nell Painter, *The History of White People* (New York: W.W. Norton & Company, 2010).

53 Rebecca Hershey, " What Happened When Dylann Roof Asked Google for Information about Race?" *NPR*, January 10, 2017, https://www.npr.org/sections/thetwo-way/2017/01/10/508363607/what-happened-when-dylann-roof-asked-google-for-information-about-race.

54 Bryan Stevenson, *Just Mercy: A Story of Justice and Redemption* (New York: One World, 2018).

Chapter 5

55 Peggy McIntosh, "White Privilege: Unpacking the Invisible Knapsack," in *On Privilege, Fraudulence, and Teaching as Learning: Selected Essays 1981–2019* (New York: Routledge, 2020).

56 Terri Gross, "How a Rising Star of White Nationalism Broke Free from the Movement," *Fresh Air*, podcast, September 24, 2018, https://www.npr.org/2018/09/24/651052970/how-a-rising-star-of-White-nationalism-broke-free-from-the-movement.

57 Robin DiAngelo, *White Fragility: Why It's So Hard for White People to Talk about Racism* (Boston: Beacon Press, 2018).

58 Richard Herrnstein and Charles Murray, *The Bell Curve: Intelligence and Class Structure in American Life* (New York: Free Press Paperbacks, 1994).

59 Heather McGhee, *The Sum of Us: What Racism Costs Everyone and How We Can Prosper Together* (New York: One World, 2021).

Chapter 6

60 For more on White people and solidarity, see Clayborne Carson, *In Struggle: SNCC and the Black Awakening of the 1960s*, 2nd edition (Cambridge, MA: Harvard University Press, 1995); Martin Luther King Jr., *Where Do We Go from Here: Chaos or Community?* (Boston, MA: Beacon Press, 2010); Doug McAdam, *Freedom Summer* (New York: Oxford University Press, 1988); and Kwame Ture and Charles Hamilton, *Black Power: The Politics of Liberation* (New York: Vintage Books, 1992).

61 For racial White affinity/accountability/caucus resources, see Robin DiAngelo and Amy Burtaine, *The Facilitator's Guide for White Affinity Groups: Strategies for Leading White People in an Anti-Racist Practice* (Boston, MA: Beacon Press, 2022); Pippi Kessler, "How to Plan a White Caucus Agenda," *Medium*, January 10, 2019, https://medium.com/@PippiKessler/how-to-plan-a-white-caucus-agenda-9049847e9bd5.

62 For more detail on how white nationalists use strategic recruitment tactics, see DEO, "The Rhetoric, Trips, Traps, and Tactics of White Nationalists," *Medium*, June 14, 2018, https://medium.com/@DeoTasDevil/the-rhetoric-tricks-traps-and-tactics-of-white-nationalism-b0bca3caeb84.

63 Bryan Stevenson, *Just Mercy: A Story of Justice and Redemption* (New York: One World, 2018), 17–18.

Chapter 7

64 Dog whistles, when used for political purposes, are "coded racial appeals that carefully manipulate hostility toward nonwhites." See Ian Haney López, *Dog Whistle Politics: How Coded Racial Appeals Have Reinvented Racism and Wrecked the Middle Class* (New York: Oxford University Press, 2014), ix.

65 To learn more about the author of the phrase, "Antiracist is a code word for anti-white," which has inspired white nationalist recruiting campaigns and violence, see Lenz, "Bob Whitaker, Author of the Racist 'Mantra' on White Genocide, Has Died," Southern Poverty Law Center. June 7, 2017, https://www.splcenter.org/hatewatch/2017/06/07/bob-whitaker-author-racist-mantra-white-genocide-has-died.

66 To explore some of these questions, consider Oluo, *So You Want To Talk about Race* (Seattle, WA: Seal Press, 2019) and/or other resources in the bibliography.

67 Karl Giberson, *Saving the Original Sinner: How Christians Have Used the Bible's First Man to Oppress, Inspire, and Make Sense of the World* (Boston: Beacon Press, 2015).

68 For an example of the rhetoric that argues equity is the problem, see: Carson, "Moving Our Focus from Equality to Equity Won't Defeat Racism. It's Another Type of Racism."

69 Heather McGhee, *The Sum of Us: What Racism Costs Everyone and How We Can Prosper Together* (New York: One World, 2021).

70 Dan Romero, "Trump Denounces Statue Toppling during July Fourth Celebration at Mount Rushmore," *NBC News,* July 3, 2020, https://www.nbcnews.com/politics/donald-trump/trump-denounces-statue-toppling-during-july-fourth-celebration-mount-rushmore-n1232893.

71 Dennis Mihalopoulos, "Kenosha Shooting Suspect Fervently Supported 'Blues Lives,' Joined Local Militia," *NPR,* August 27, 2020, https://www.npr.org/sections/live-updates-protests-for-racial-justice/2020/08/27/906566596/alleged-kenosha-shooter-fervently-supported-blue-lives-joined-local-militia.

72 Bernard Condon, "Kenosha Shooter's Defense Portray Him as 'American Patriot,'" *US News and World Report,* September 24, 2020, https://www.usnews.com/news/us/articles/2020-09-24/kenosha-shooters-defense-portrays-him-as-american-patriot.

73 Condon, "Kenosha Shooter's Defense."

74 David Campt, *White Ally Toolkit: Using Active Listening, Empathy, and Personal Storytelling to Promote Racial Equity* (Las Vegas, NV: I AM Publications, 2018).

75 Paul Kivel, *Living in the Shadow of the Cross: Understanding and Resisting the Power and Privilege of Christian Hegemony* (Gabriola Island, BC: New Society Publishers, 2013).

76 AWARE-LA, "White Supremacy System Model," accessed September 29, 2022, https://www.awarela.org/toolkit.

77 Jonathan Metzl, *Dying of Whiteness: How the Politics of Racial Resentment Is Killing America's Heartland* (New York: Basic Books, 2019).

78 Andrew Whitehead and Samuel Perry, *Taking American Back for God: Christian Nationalism in the United States* (New York: Oxford University Press, 2020). After identifying the profile of Christian nationalists and how they are distinct from both Christians and conservatives in general, this text explains that Christian nationalism trades moral standards for power, idealizes a mythic society featuring white, native-born, Protestant control, and perceives threats to traditional, patriarchal, heterosexual, nuclear families as undermining the fabric of society.

79 Christine Saxman, Shelly Tochluk, and Joanna Schroeder, and Western States Center Staff, "Confronting Organized Bigotry and Conspiracy Theories at Home: A Guide for Parents and Caregivers, Western States Center," Western States Center, accessed September 29, 2022, https://www.westernstatescenter.org/caregivers.

Chapter 8

80 Shakti Butler and Rick Butler (dir.), *Mirrors of Privilege: Making White Visible* (World Trust Educational Services, 2008, DVD); Shakti Butler, *Cracking the Codes: The System of Racial Inequity* (World Trust Educational Services, 2014, DVD).

81 Jennifer Harvey, *Raising White Kids: Bringing Up Children in a Racially Unjust America* (Nashville, TN: Abingdon Press, 2019).

82 Jamie Utt and Shelly Tochluk, "White Teacher, Know Thyself: Improving Anti-Racist Praxis through Racial Identity Development," *Urban Education* 55, no. 1 (2016), https://journals.sagepub.com/doi/pdf/10.1177/0042085916648741.

83 Bettina Love, "White Teachers Need Anti-Racist Therapy," *Education Week*, February 6, 2020, https://www.edweek.org/teaching-learning/opinion-White-teachers-need-anti-racist-therapy/2020/02.

84 AWARE-LA, "White Supremacy System Model," accessed September 29, 2022, https://www.awarela.org/toolkit.

85 Resmaa Menakem, *My Grandmother's Hands: Racialized Trauma and the Pathway to Mending Our Hearts and Bodies* (Las Vegas, NV: Central Recovery Press, 2017).

86 Annaliese Singh, *The Racial Healing Handbook: Practical Activities to Help You Challenge Privilege, Confront Systemic Racism, and Engage in Collective Healing* (Oakland, CA: New Harbinger Publications, 2019).

87 Yolanda Sealey-Ruiz, "Healing through the Archaeology of Self™." Arch of Self, LLC, accessed September 29, 2022, https://www.yolandasealeyruiz.com/archaeology-of-self.

88 Shelly Tochluk, *Witnessing Whiteness: The Journey into Racial Awareness and Antiracist Action*, 3rd edition (Lanham, MD: Rowman & Littlefield, 2022).

89 Lee Mun Wah, *The Art of Mindful Facilitation* (Berkeley, CA: Stirfry Seminars and Consulting, 2004).

90 AWARE-LA, "Saturday Dialogues," accessed September 29, 2022, https://www.awarela.org/saturday-dialogue.

91 AWARE-LA, "White Antiracist Culture Building Toolkit," accessed September 29, 2022, https://www.awarela.org/toolkit.

Chapter 9

92 Paul Kivel, *Living in the Shadow of the Cross: Understanding and Resisting the Power and Privilege of Christian Hegemony* (Gabriola Island, BC: New Society Publishers, 2013).

93 To learn how our level of racial consciousness impacts People of Color, see Paul Gorski and Noura Erakat, "Racism, Whiteness, and Burnout in Antiracism Movements: How White Racial Justice Activists Elevate Burnout in Racial Justice Activists of Color in the United States," *Ethnicities* 19, no. 5 (March 21, 2019), https://journals.sagepub.com/doi/full/10.1177/1468796819833871.

94 Donald Grinde, "The Iroquois and the Development of American Government," *Historical Reflections / Réflexions Historiques* 21, no. 2 (1995): 301–18.

95 To explore White antiracist role models, see Cross Cultural Solidarity History Project, "Short Portraits of White Antiracists in U.S. History," accessed September 29, 2022, https://crossculturalsolidarity.com/wp-content/uploads/2021/05/White-Antiracists-in-U.S.-History.pdf; Elizabeth Denevi and Lori Cohen, "White Antiracist Activists," Teaching While White, accessed September 29, 2022, https://www.teachingwhite white.org/resources/white-antiracist-activists; W. E. B. Du Bois, *John Brown* (Overland Park, KS: Digireads.com Publishing, 2019); Virginia Durr, *Outside the Magic Circle: The Autobiography of Virginia Foster Durr* (Tuscaloosa: University of Alabama Press, 1985); Mab Segrest, *Memoir of a Race Traitor: Fighting Racism in the American South* (Cambridge, MA: South End Press, 1994).

96 Anne Braden, *The Wall Between* (Knoxville: University of Tennessee Press, 2009).

97 Jay Smooth, "How to Tell Someone They Sound Racist," YouTube video, https://www.youtube.com/watch?v=b0Ti-gkJiXc.

98 Karen Grigsby Bates, "What's in a 'Karen'?" *Code Switch*, podcast, July 15, 2020, https://www.wbur.org/npr/891177904/whats-in-a-karen.

99 Ruth King, *Healing Rage: Women Making Inner Peace Possible* (New York: Gotham Books, 2018).

Chapter 10

100 Steve Zalusky, "The State of America's Libraries 2022: A Report from the American Library Association," American Library Association, April 2022, https://www.ala.org/news/state-americas-libraries-report-2022.

101 adrienne maree brown, *We Will Not Cancel Us: And Other Dreams of Transformative Justice* (Chico, CA: AK Press, 2020).

102 adrienne maree brown, *Emergent Strategy: Shaping Change, Changing Worlds* Chico, CA: AK Press, 2017).

103 Jane Coaston, "The Intersectionality Wars," *Vox*, May 18, 2019, https://www.vox.com/the-highlight/2019/5/20/18542843/intersectionality-conservatism-law-race-gender-discrimination. Note that Crenshaw's work emphasizes that "the law seemed to forget that black women are

both black and female, and thus subject to discrimination on the basis of both race, gender, and often, a combination of the two."

104 AWARE-LA, "White Supremacy System Model," accessed September 29, 2022, https://www.awarela.org/toolkit.

105 Jondou Chase Chen, "On Nests and Cages: Facilitating toward Just Possibilities." National SEED Project, April 13, 2018, https://nationalseedproject.org/itemid-fix/entry/on-nests-and-cages-facilitating-toward-just-possibilities.

106 Judith Katz, "White Culture and Racism: Working for Organizational Change in the United States," Whiteness Paper No. 3 (2009): 44 (Crandall, Dosie, & Douglass Books).

107 This article elicits strong reaction. Many love it, and many are critical. We find it useful, and we recognize that what it names as characteristics of white supremacy culture can be interpreted from an international, global perspective as describing features inherent within capitalism and/or hierarchical organizational structures more generally. As capitalism and hierarchy in the US has been thoroughly intertwined with white supremacy for hundreds of years, referring to these characteristics as features of a white supremacy culture makes sense to us. Tema Okun, "White Supremacy Culture: Still Here," accessed Sept 29, 2022, http://www.Whitesupremacyculture.info/uploads/4/3/5/7/43579015/White_supremacy_culture_-_still_here.pdf.

108 Okun, "White Supremacy Culture," 30.

109 Okun, "White Supremacy Culture."

110 See AWARE-LA's model, *AWARE-LA and Accountability*, for an example of an accountability module focused on healthful, reciprocal relationships across race. AWARE-LA, "White Anti-Racist Culture Building Toolkit," accessed September 29, 2022, https://www.awarela.org/toolkit.

111 To learn more about racial identity development for People of Color, see Beverly Tatum, *Why Are All the Black Kids Sitting Together in the Cafeteria? And Other Conversations about Race* (New York: Basic Books, 2017); Charmaine Wijeyesinghe and Bailey W. Jackson (eds.), *New Perspectives on Racial Identity Development: A Theoretical and Practical Anthology*, 2nd edition (New York: New York University Press, 2012).

Chapter 11

112 Mia Frothingham, "The Beginner's Guide to Trauma Response," *Simply Psychology*, October 6, 2021, https://www.simply psychology.org/fight-flight-freeze-fawn.html. "Fawn" may be new to some. Fawning focuses on maintaining the comfort of the offender. Coddling and ingratiating oneself are both forms of fawning.

113 Jenna Chandler-Ward and Elizabeth Denevi, "Racial Identity for White People with Dr. Janet Helms (No 16)," *Teaching While White*, podcast, March 4, 2021, https://www.teachingwhileWhite.org/podcast/ywvyf5ocm5oleku1dzp10gxk666nqo.

114 Tema Okun, "White Supremacy Culture: Still Here," accessed September 29, 2022, http://www.Whitesupremacyculture.info/uploads/4/3/5/7/43579015/White_supremacy_culture_-_still_here.pdf.

115 Okun, "White Supremacy Culture."

Chapter 12

116 James Baldwin, *The Fire Next Time* (New York: Vintage, 1993), 12.

117 Jacqueline Battalora, *Birth of a White Nation: The Invention of White People and Its Relevance Today*, 2nd edition (New York: Routledge, 2021).

Bibliography

Alexander, Michelle. *The New Jim Crow: Mass Incarceration in the Age of Colorblindness.* New York: The New Press, 2012.

American Anthropological Association. "AAA Statement on Race." May 17, 1998. https://www.americananthro.org/ConnectWithAAA/Content.aspx?Item Number=2583.

American Bar Association. "CROWN Act, More: Untangling Implicit Bias, One Strand at a Time." February 17, 2020. https://www.americanbar.org/news/abanews/aba -news-archives/2020/02/crown-act--more--untangling-implicit-bias --one-strand-at-a-time/.

American Medical Association. "New AMA Policies Recognize Race as a Social, Not Biological, Construct." November 16, 2020. https://www.ama-assn.org/press-center/ press-releases/new-ama-policies-recognize-race-social-not-biological-construct.

Anderson, Carol. *White Rage: The Unspoken Truth of our Racial Divide.* New York: Bloomsbury USA, 2017.

Associated Press. "Examining AP style on Black and white." *AP News,* July 20, 2020. https://apnews.com/article/archive-race-and-ethnicity-9105661462.

AWARE-LA. "Saturday Dialogues." Accessed September 29, 2022. https://www .awarela.org/saturday-dialogue.

AWARE-LA. "Theory of Personal Transformation." Accessed September 29, 2022. https://www.awarela.org/toolkit.

AWARE-LA. "Toward a Radical White Identity." Accessed September 29, 2022. https://www.awarela.org/toolkit.

AWARE-LA. "White Antiracist Culture Building Toolkit." Accessed September 29, 2022. https://www.awarela.org/toolkit.

AWARE-LA. "White Supremacy System Model." Accessed September 29, 2022. https://www.awarela.org/toolkit.

Baldwin, James. *The Fire Next Time.* New York: Vintage, 1993.

Barnes, Jack, and Barry Sheppard. "Interview with Malcolm X." *Young Socialist* 8, no. 3 (1965): 63. https://www.marxists.org/history/etol/newspape/youngsocialist/ 1964-1965/v08n03-w63-[2nd-w63]-mar-apr-1965-young-socialist-ysa.pdf.

Battalora, Jacqueline. *Birth of a White Nation: The Invention of White People and Its Relevance Today.* 2nd ed. New York: Routledge, 2021.

Belew, Kathleen, and Ramón Gutiérrez. *A Field Guide to White Supremacy.* Oakland: University of California Press, 2021.

Bonilla-Silva, Eduardo. *Racism without Racists: Colorblind Ideology and the Persistence of Racial Inequality in America.* Lanham, MD: Rowman & Littlefield, 2018.

Braden, Anne. *The Wall Between.* Knoxville: University of Tennessee Press, 2009. First published 1999.

Brodkin, Karen. *How Jews Became White Folks and What That Says about Race in America.* Piscataway, NJ: Rutgers University Press, 1998.

brown, adrienne maree. *Emergent Strategy: Shaping Change, Changing Worlds.* Chico, CA: AK Press, 2017.

brown, adrienne maree. *We Will Not Cancel Us: And Other Dreams of Transformative Justice.* Chico, CA: AK Press, 2020.

Butler, Shakti, dir. *Cracking the Codes: The System of Racial Inequity.* World Trust Educational Services, 2014. DVD.

Butler, Shakti, and Rick Butler, dir. *Mirrors of Privilege: Making White Visible .* World Trust Educational Services, 2008. DVD.

Campt, David. *White Ally Toolkit: Using Active Listening, Empathy, and Personal Storytelling to Promote Racial Equity.* Las Vegas, NV: I AM Publications, 2018.

Carson, Ben. "Moving Our Focus from Equality to Equity Won't Defeat Racism. It's Another Type of Racism." *Washington Post*, April 18, 2021.

Carson, Clayborne. *In Struggle: SNCC and the Black Awakening of the 1960s.* 2nd ed. Cambridge, MA: Harvard University Press, 1995.

Chandler-Ward, Jenna, and Denevi, Elizabeth. "Racial Identity for White People with Dr. Janet Helms (No 16)." *Teaching While White*, podcast, March 4, 2021. MP3 audio, 31:42. https://www.teachingwhileWhite.org/podcast/ywvyf5ocm5oleku1dzp10gxk666nqo.

Chase Chen, Jondou. "On Nests and Cages: Facilitating toward Just Possibilities." National SEED Project, April 13, 2018. https://nationalseedproject.org/itemid-fix/entry/on-nests-and-cages-facilitating-toward-just-possibilities.

Coaston, Jane. "The Intersectionality Wars." *Vox*, May 18, 2019. https://www.vox.com/the-highlight/2019/5/20/18542843/intersectionality-conservatism-law-race-gender-discrimination.

Condon, Bernard. "Kenosha Shooter's Defense Portray Him as 'American Patriot.'" *US News and World Report,* September 24, 2020. https://www.usnews.com/news/us/articles/2020-09-24/kenosha-shooters-defense-portrays-him-as-american-patriot.

Cross Cultural Solidarity History Project. "Short Portraits of White Antiracists in U.S. History." Accessed September 29, 2022. https://crossculturalsolidarity.com/wp-content/uploads/2021/05/White-Antiracists-in-U.S.-History.pdf.

Daniller, Andrew. "Majorities of Americans See at Least Some Discrimination against Black, Hispanic and Asian people in the U.S." Pew Research Center, March 18, 2021. https://www.pewresearch.org/fact-tank/2021/03/18/majorities-of-americans-see-at-least-some-discrimination-against-black-hispanic-and-asian-people-in-the-u-s/.

Delgado, Richard, and Jean Stefancic. *Critical Race Theory: An Introduction.* 3rd ed. New York: New York University Press, 2017.

Denby, Gene, Jess Kung, and Leah Donnella. "The Folk Devil Made Me Do It." *Code Switch,* podcast, September 1, 2021. MP3 audio, 37:00. https://www.npr.org/2021/08/20/1029775224/the-folk-devil-made-me-do-it.

Denevi, Elizabeth, and Lori Cohen. "White Antiracist Activists." *Teaching While White.* Accessed September 29, 2022. https://www.teachingwhilewhite.org/resources/white-antiracist-activists.

DEO. "The Rhetoric, Trips, Traps, and Tactics of White Nationalists." *Medium.* June 14, 2018. https://medium.com/@DeoTasDevil/the-rhetoric-tricks-traps-and-tactics-of-white-nationalism-b0bca3caeb84.

Derman-Sparks, Louis, and Carol Brunson Phillips, Carol. *Teaching/Learning Anti-Racism: A Developmental Approach.* New York: Teacher College Press, 1997.

DiAngelo, Robin. *White Fragility: Why It's So Hard for White People to Talk about Racism.* Boston: Beacon Press, 2018.

DiAngelo, Robin, and Amy Burtaine. *The Facilitator's Guide for White Affinity Groups: Strategies for Leading White People in an Anti-Racist Practice.* Boston: Beacon Press, 2022.

Du Bois, W. E. B. *John Brown.* Overland Park, KS: Digireads.com Publishing, 2019.

Durr, Virginia Foster. *Outside the Magic Circle: The Autobiography of Virginia Foster Durr.* Tuscaloosa: University of Alabama Press, 1985.

Favreau, Jon, Jon Lovett, and Tommy Vietor. "Cold War, Hot Mic." *Pod Save America,* podcast, January 25, 2022. 01:12:00. https://podcasts.apple.com/us/podcast/cold-war-hot-mic/id1192761536?i=1000548915440.

Fisher, Marc. "From Memes to Race War: How Extremists Use Popular Culture to Lure Recruits." *Washington Post,* April 30, 2021. https://www.washingtonpost.com/nation/2021/04/30/extremists-recruiting-culture-community/.

Frey, William. "The US Will Become 'Minority White' in 2045, Census Projects: Youthful Minorities Are the Engine of Future Growth." Brookings Institute, March 18, 2018. https://www.brookings.edu/blog/the-avenue/2018/03/14/the-us-will-become-minority-white-in-2045-census-projects/.

Frothingham, Mia. "The Beginner's Guide to Trauma Response." Simply Psychology, October 6, 2021. https://www.simplypsychology.org/fight-flight-freeze-fawn.html.

Gardiner, Steven, and Tarso Luís Ramos. "Capitol Offenses: January 6th 2021 and the Ongoing Insurrection: PRA State of the Right Report." Political Research Associates, January 12, 2022. https://politicalresearch.org/2022/01/12/capitol-offenses-january-6th-2021-ongoing-insurrection.

Giberson, Karl. *Saving the Original Sinner: How Christians Have Used the Bible's First Man to Oppress, Inspire, and Make Sense of the World.* Boston: Beacon Press, 2015.

Gorski, Paul, and Noura Erakat. "Racism, Whiteness, and Burnout in Antiracism Movements: How White Racial Justice Activists Elevate Burnout in Racial Justice Activists of Color in the United States." *Ethnicities* 19, no. 5 (March 21, 2019). https://journals.sagepub.com/doi/full/10.1177/1468796819833871.

Grigsby Bates, Karen. "What's in a 'Karen'?" *Code Switch,* podcast, July 15, 2020. MP3, 23:28. https://www.wbur.org/npr/891177904/whats-in-a-karen.

Grinde, Donald. "The Iroquois and the Development of American Government." *Historical Reflections / Réflexions Historiques* 21, no. 2 (1995): 301–18. http://www.jstor.org/stable/41299029.

Gross, Terri. "How a Rising Star of White Nationalism Broke Free from the Movement." *Fresh Air,* podcast, September 24, 2018. MP3 audio, 41:00. https://www.npr

.org/2018/09/24/651052970/how-a-rising-star-of-White-nationalism-broke-free
-from-the-movement.

Guglielmo, Thomas. *White on Arrival: Italians, Race, Color, and Power in Chicago, 1890–1945*. New York: Oxford University Press, 2003.

Haney López, Ian. *Dog Whistle Politics: How Coded Racial Appeals Have Reinvented Racism and Wrecked the Middle Class.*.

Haney López, Ian. *White by Law: The Legal Construction of Race*. New York: New York University Press, 1996.

Hannah-Jones, Nikole. *The 1619 Project: A New Origin Story*. New York: One World, 2021.

Harvey, Jennifer. *Raising White Kids: Bringing Up Children in a Racially Unjust America*. Nashville, TN: Abingdon Press, 2019.

Helms, Janet. *A Race Is a Nice Thing to Have: A Guide to Being a White Person or Understanding the White Persons in Your Life*. 3rd ed. San Diego, CA: Cognella Academic Publishing, 2020.

Herrnstein, Richard, and Charles Murray. *The Bell Curve: Intelligence and Class Structure in American Life*. New York: Free Press Paperbacks, 1994.

Hershey, Rebecca. "What Happened When Dylann Roof Asked Google for Information about Race?" *NPR,* January 10, 2017. https://www.npr.org/sections/thetwo-way/2017/01/10/508363607/what-happened-when-dylann-roof-asked-google-for-information-about-race.

HipLATINA. "Alexandria Ocasio-Cortez Wears a Braid to Honor Her Afro-Latina Roots." November 26, 2018. https://hiplatina.com/alexandria-ocasio-cortez-wears-braid-honor-afro-latina-roots/.

Ignatiev, Noel. "Abolish the White Race." *Harvard Magazine*, September–October 2002. https://www.harvardmagazine.com/2002/09/abolish-the-white-race.html.

Ignatiev, Noel. *How the Irish Became White*. New York: Routledge, 1995.

Ignatiev, Noel, and John Garvey. *Race Traitor*. New York: Routledge, 1996.

Irving, Debby. *Waking Up White and Finding Myself in the Story of Race*. Cambridge, MA: Elephant Room Press, 2014.

Jacobson, Matthew. *Whiteness of a Different Color: European Immigrants and the Alchemy of Race*. Cambridge, MA: Harvard University Press, 1998.

Jones, Nicolas, Rachel Marks, Roberto Ramirez, and Merarys Ríos-Vargas. "2020 Census Illuminates Racial and Ethnic Composition of the Country." US Census Bureau, August 12, 2021. https://www.census.gov/library/stories/2021/08/improved-race-ethnicity-measures-reveal-united-states-population-much-more-multiracial.html.

Katz, Judith. "White Culture and Racism: Working for Organizational Change in the United States." Whiteness Paper No. 3, (2009): 44. Crandall, Dosie, & Douglass Books.

Kendi, Ibram. "The Mantra of White Supremacy: The Idea That Anti-Racist Is the Code for Anti-White Is the Claim of Avowed Extremists." *The Atlantic*, November 30, 2021. https://www.theatlantic.com/ideas/archive/2021/11/white-supremacy-mantra-anti-racism/620832.

Kendi, Ibram. *Stamped from the Beginning: The Definitive History of Racist Ideas in America*. New York: Nation Books, 2017.

Kessler, Pippi. "How to Plan a White Caucus Agenda." *Medium*, January 10, 2019. https://medium.com/@PippiKessler/how-to-plan-a-white-caucus-agenda-9049847e9bd5.

Kilmeade, Brian. "Tucker Carlson on the Dangers of Race Obsession in the Pursuit of a Color Blind Meritocracy." *Fox News Talk*, podcast, April 8, 2018. MP3 audio, 56:24. https://radio.foxnews.com/2021/04/08/tucker-carlson-on-the-dangers-of-race-obsession-in-the-pursuit-of-a-color-blind-meritocracy.

King, Martin Luther, Jr. *Where Do We Go from Here: Chaos or Community?* Boston: Beacon Press, 2010.

King, Ruth. *Healing Rage: Women Making Inner Peace Possible*. New York: Gotham Books, 2018.

Kivel, Paul. *Living in the Shadow of the Cross: Understanding and Resisting the Power and Privilege of Christian Hegemony*. Gabriola Island, BC: New Society Publishers, 2013.

Lati, Marisa. "What Is Critical Race Theory, and Why Do Republicans Want to Ban It in Schools?" *Washington Post*, May 29, 2021. https://www.washingtonpost.com/education/2021/05/29/critical-race-theory-bans-schools/.

Lee, Mun Wah. *The Art of Mindful Facilitation*. Berkeley, CA: Stirfry Seminars and Consulting, 2004.

Lenz, Ryan. "Bob Whitaker, Author of the Racist "Mantra" on White Genocide, Has Died." Southern Poverty Law Center, June 7, 2017. https://www.splcenter.org/hatewatch/2017/06/07/bob-whitaker-author-racist-mantra-white-genocide-has-died.

Lorber, Ben. "'America First Is Inevitable': Nick Fuentes, the Groyper Army, and the Mainstreaming of White Nationalism." Political Research Associates, January 15, 2021. https://politicalresearch.org/2021/01/15/america-first-inevitable.

Love, Bettina. "White Teachers Need Anti-Racist Therapy." *Education Week*, February 6, 2020. https://www.edweek.org/teaching-learning/opinion-White-teachers-need-anti-racist-therapy/2020/02.

Maghbouleh, Neda. *The Limits of Whiteness: Iranian Americans and the Everyday Politics of Race*. Stanford, CA: Stanford University Press, 2017.

McAdam, Doug. *Freedom Summer*. New York: Oxford University Press, 1988.

McGhee, Heather. *The Sum of Us: What Racism Costs Everyone and How We Can Prosper Together*. New York: One World, 2021.

McIntosh, Peggy. "White Privilege: Unpacking the Invisible Knapsack." In *On Privilege, Fraudulence, and Teaching as Learning: Selected Essays 1981–2019*. New York: Routledge, 2020.

Menakem, Resmaa. *My Grandmother's Hands: Racialized Trauma and the Pathway to Mending our Hearts and Bodies*. Las Vegas, NV: Central Recovery Press, 2017.

Menakem, Resmaa. *The Quaking of America: An Embodied Guide to Navigating Our Nation's Upheaval and Racial Reckoning*. Las Vegas, NV. Central Recovery Press, 2022.

Metzl, Jonathan. *Dying of Whiteness: How the Politics of Racial Resentment is Killing America's Heartland*. New York: Basic Books, 2019.

Mihalopoulos, Dan. "Kenosha Shooting Suspect Fervently Supported 'Blues Lives,' Joined Local Militia." *NPR*, August 27, 2020. https://www.npr.org/

sections/live-updates-protests-for-racial-justice/2020/08/27/906566596/
alleged-kenosha-shooter-fervently-supported-blue-lives-joined-local-militia.

Moore, Wes. *The Other Wes Moore: One Name, Two Fates*. New York: Spiegel and Grau, 2011.

Oluo, Ijeoma. *So You Want to Talk about Race*. Seattle, WA: Seal Press, 2019.

Okun, Tema. "White Supremacy Culture: Still Here." Accessed Sept 29, 2022. http://www.Whitesupremacyculture.info/uploads/4/3/5/7/43579015/White_supremacy_culture_-_still_here.pdf.

Painter, Nell Irvin. *The History of White People*. New York: W.W. Norton & Company, 2010.

Painter, Nell Irvin. "Why White Should Be Capitalized Too." *Washington Post*, July 2, 2020. https://www.washingtonpost.com/opinions/2020/07/22/why-white-should-be-capitalized/.

Roediger, David. *Working toward Whiteness: How America's Immigrants Became White: The Strange Journey from Ellis Island to the Suburbs*. New York: Basic Books, 2005.

Romero, Dennis. "Trump Denounces Statue Toppling during July Fourth Celebration at Mount Rushmore." *NBC News*, July 3, 2020. https://www.nbcnews.com/politics/donald-trump/trump-denounces-statue-toppling-during-july-fourth-celebration-mount-rushmore-n1232893.

Roose, Kevin. "The Making of a YouTube Radical." *New York Times*, June 8, 2019. https://www.nytimes.com/interactive/2019/06/08/technology/youtube-radical.html.

Rothstein, Richard. *The Color of Law: A Forgotten History of How Our Government Segregated America*. New York: Liveright Publishing, 2017.

Rufo, C. (@realchrisrufo). "The Goal Is to Have People Read Something Crazy in the Newspaper and Think Critical Race Theory." Twitter, March 15, 2021, 2:17 pm, https://twitter.com/realchrisrufo/status/1371541044592996352.

Saxman, Christine, Shelly Tochluk, Joanna Schroeder, and Western States Center Staff. "Confronting Organized Bigotry and Conspiracy Theories at Home: A Guide for Parents and Caregivers, Western States Center." Western States Center. Accessed September 29, 2022. https://www.westernstatescenter.org/caregivers.

Sealey-Ruiz, Yolanda. "Healing through the Archaeology of Self™." Arch of Self, LLC. Accessed September 29, 2022. https://www.yolandasealeyruiz.com/archaeology-of-self.

Segrest, Mab. *Memoir of a Race Traitor: Fighting Racism in the American South*. Cambridge, MA: South End Press, 1994.

Shane, Leo. "Is the Military Doing Enough to Look for Signs of White Nationalism in its Ranks?" *Military Times*, February 11, 2020. https://www.militarytimes.com/news/pentagon-congress/2020/02/11/is-the-military-doing-enough-to-look-for-signs-of-white-nationalism-in-the-ranks/.

Shapiro, Ben. "When Diversity Becomes a Problem." *Fox News Talk*, podcast, February 22, 2016. MP3 audio, 21:57. https://radio.foxnews.com/2016/02/22/ep-1-ben-shapiro-when-diversity-becomes-a-problem/.

Singh, Anneliese. *The Racial Healing Handbook: Practical Activities to Help You Challenge Privilege, Confront Systemic Racism, and Engage in Collective Healing*. Oakland, CA: New Harbinger Publications, 2019.

Singleton, Glenn. *Courageous Conversations about Race: A Field Guide for Achieving Equity in Schools.* Thousand Oaks, CA: Corwin Press, 2015.

Smith, Llewellyn, dir. "The House We Live In." Episode 3 of *Race: The Power of an Illusion* California Newsreels, 2003. DVD.

Smooth, Jay. "How to Tell Someone They Sound Racist." YouTube video, 2:59. https://www.youtube.com/watch?v=b0Ti-gkJiXc.

Southern Poverty Law Center. "Jared Taylor." Accessed September 29, 2022. https://www.splcenter.org/fighting-hate/extremist-files/individual/jared-taylor.

Stevenson, Bryan. *Just Mercy: A Story of Justice and Redemption.* New York: One World, 2018.

Tatum, B. D. "Talking about Race, Learning about Racism: The Application of Racial Identity Development in the Classroom." *Harvard Educational Review* 62, no. 1 (1992): 12.

Tatum, Beverly Daniel. "Teaching White Students about Racism: The Search for White Allies and the Restoration of Hope." *Teachers College Record 95*, no. 4 (2021): 462–77.

Tatum, Beverly Daniel. *Why Are All the Black Kids Sitting Together in the Cafeteria? And Other Conversations about Race.* New York: Basic Books, 2017.

Thompson, Becky. *A Promise and a Way of Life: White Antiracist Activism.* Minneapolis: University of Minnesota Press, 2021.

Tochluk, Shelly. "My Day with the Far Right, Where I Live and Breathe." *Medium*, May 29, 2018. https://shellytochluk.medium.com/my-day-with-the-far-right-where-i-live-and-breathe-b93429b25129.

Tochluk, Shelly. "Onramps and Lanes on the Racial Justice Freeway. *Medium*, December 3, 2017. https://shellytochluk.medium.com/on-ramps-and-lanes-on-the-racial-justice-freeway-9ff2ee051042

Tochluk, Shelly. *Witnessing Whiteness: The Journey into Racial Awareness and Antiracist Action.* 3rd ed. Lanham, MD: Rowman & Littlefield, 2022.

Ture, Kwame, and Charles Hamilton. *Black Power: The Politics of Liberation.* 2nd ed. New York: Vintage Books, 1992.

Utt, Jamie, and Shelly Tochluk. "White Teacher, Know Thyself: Improving Anti-Racist Praxis through Racial Identity Development." *Urban Education* 55, no. 1 (2016). https://journals.sagepub.com/doi/pdf/10.1177/0042085916648741

Whitehead, Andrew, and Samuel Perry. *Taking America Back for God: Christian Nationalism in the United State*s. New York: Oxford University Press, 2020.

Wijeyesinghe, Charmaine, and Bailey W. Jackson (Eds.). *New Perspectives on Racial Identity Development: A Theoretical and Practical Anthology.* 2nd ed. New York: New York University Press, 2012.

Zalusky, Steve. "The State of America's Libraries 2022: A Report from the American Library Association." American Library Association, April 2022. https://www.ala.org/news/state-americas-libraries-report-2022.

Index

About the Authors

Shelly Tochluk is a professor of education at Mount Saint Mary's University –Los Angeles. She is the author of *Witnessing Whiteness: The Journey into Racial Awareness and Antiracist Action* and *Living in the Tension: The Quest for a Spiritualized Racial Justice*. She is the co-author of Western State Center's toolkit, *Confronting Conspiracy Theories and Organized Bigotry at Home: A Guide for Parents and Caregivers*. Shelly also volunteers with AWARE-LA (Alliance of White Anti-Racists Everywhere-Los Angeles) to co-produce *Unmasking Whiteness*, a four-day institute that leads White people into a deeper understanding of their personal relationship to race and systemic racism. She can be found at shellytochluk.com

<hr/>

Christine Saxman is a racial and social justice facilitator with 20 years of experience providing training and coaching for educational, corporate, not-for-profit, and government organizations. She works on staff for the National SEED Project (Seeking Education Equity and Diversity). She is also a co-author of Western State Center's toolkit, *Confronting Conspiracy Theories and Organized Bigotry at Home: A Guide for Parents and Caregivers*. She can be found at christinesaxman.com.

CPSIA information can be obtained
at www.ICGtesting.com
Printed in the USA
BVHW080741020623
665208BV00001B/1